GPS

{GOALS & PROVEN STRATEGIES}

SUCCESS for

...from the Industry's Leading Experts

GPS for Success
Copyright © 2010

Published in the United States by
INSIGHT PUBLISHING
Sevierville, Tennessee
www.insightpublishing.com
Cover Design: Emmy Shubert
Interior Format & Design: Chris Ott

ISBN: 978-1-60013-568-2

10 9 8 7 6 5 4 3 2 1

Disclaimer: This book is a compilation of ideas from numerous experts who have each contributed a chapter. As such, the views expressed in each chapter are of those who were interviewed and not necessarily of the interviewer, Insight Publishing, or the other contributing authors.

Table of Contents

A Message from the Publisher

THE INTERVIEWS

A Message from the Publisher

Our ancestors had to go to some rather extreme measures to keep from getting lost. They used landmarks, maps, and the sky to help them find their way. Navigation is much easier today. For less than one hundred dollars, you can get a pocket-sized gadget that will tell you exactly where you are on Earth at any moment. As long as you have a Global Positioning System (GPS) receiver and a clear view of the sky, you'll never be lost again.

So exactly what is the Global Positioning System? It is actually a constellation of twenty-seven Earth-orbiting satellites (twenty-four in operation and three extras in case one fails). The orbits are arranged so that at anytime, anywhere on Earth, there are at least four satellites "visible" in the sky. A GPS receiver's job is to locate four or more of these satellites, figure out the distance to each, and use this information to deduce its own location.

We thought that this system is a great word picture to illustrate the concept of navigating your way to success in business and in life. We've changed the acronym—GPS—and for the purposes of this book, it stands for Goals and Proven Strategies. These elements are vital for success.

The search was on. We wanted to find interesting speakers/authors who believed they had valuable information to contribute regarding this important topic—and we succeeded. Each chapter provides a unique insight into this concept.

I think you will find this book to be extremely helpful and an excellent addition to your library. *GPS for Success* belongs in the home of everyone who wants to know how to navigate the sometimes bewildering path along the road to success.

A rewarding experience awaits you. And it begins with this book.

David Wright is President and Founder
of ISN Works and Insight Publishing

CHAPTER ONE

Great Things Happen When Companies Speak in One Voice in the Marketplace

An interview with...
GEORGE THORNE

DAVID E. WRIGHT (WRIGHT)

Today we are talking with George Thorne, president and founder of One Voice Research, Planning and Development. Mr. Thorne is a dynamic, motivational speaker, writer, and an inspiring team-builder. He specializes in taking leadership teams through the One Voice Excellence Through Leadership Program℠ to unite their companies and synchronize all key factors that impact sales. These key factors that drive sales and profits in every company are its 7 Points of Power℠.

Mr. Thorne was president of his own advertising agency for many years and has won numerous national and regional awards for marketing, advertising, and direct marketing programs. He was a columnist for the international marketing publication, Ad Age's *Business Marketing,* and has worked with hundreds of large and small companies across America. He brings twenty-five years of experience to his corporate and entrepreneurial clients.

George Thorne, welcome to *GPS for Success: Goals and Proven Strategies.*

GEORGE THORNE (THORNE)

Thank you very much.

WRIGHT

What do you believe is the single, biggest reason why most companies, large and small, don't reach their sales and profit potential?

THORNE

After working with hundreds of businesses across America, I continue to see the same phenomenon occur time and time again. Companies do not recognize and coordinate all of the key factors that determine the customer's ability to buy and buy again—and it costs them dearly in sales and profits. *It has been my experience that the vast majority of companies leave 20 percent to 50 percent or more lost sales on the table every year for this very reason.* The responsibility for growth falls on the shoulders of a handful of departments in larger organizations and on just a few areas in smaller ones. Given the intense competition that exists, plus the extraordinary challenges facing our economy, this approach is no longer effective. It is just not enough anymore to get the job done.

There is a new mindset today, however, that opens the door for companies that seriously want to generate greater sales and profits and reach their potential. It is a fundamental approach operators of large and small businesses alike will hopefully consider and embrace: namely, it takes the whole company to get and keep a customer.

The future will be about companies facing intense competition while chasing highly selective customers with fewer dollars to spend who demand greater value in everything that they buy. Only the future is here—now! It literally takes everyone working together in this environment for the organization to grow!

We know that there are eleven players on a football team. Imagine how hard it would be to win if some were playing the game and the rest were doing something else. What would be the result if a few players had a game plan while the others were going in different directions? The answer would be underachievement and chaos. This is the condition I have found most businesses in, with few exceptions, for twenty-five years. Too often, the individual players—the various departments within the organization—are marching to the beat of different drummers. Because companies are so compartmentalized, often there is no unifying focus and course of action that puts everyone on the same page to gain and keep more customers. All of the necessary forces that are available are not brought to bear within the organization to rein in potential customers and capitalize on existing ones. Going back to the football analogy, it's like leaving the running back and full back on the sidelines during the game. It is impossible under these conditions for companies to optimize sales and profits.

WRIGHT

Does the name of your firm, One Voice, directly relate to the results that you are helping companies to achieve?

THORNE

Yes, absolutely. The short answer is for companies to speak in One Voice to their customers in all aspects of their business. The reason for doing so is fundamental: to close the gap between what companies do versus what customers want and need to buy and buy again. It takes the coordinated effort of several factors within the organization to optimize sales. Overlook even one and your company will lose revenues and profits every day.

Managers use The One Voice Excellence Through Leadership Program, developed and refined over the last dozen years, to synchronize all of the critical factors that affect sales. The company sets the stage for success by first creating a cross-functional leadership team, which represents the key departments that impact the customer's decision to buy and buy again. The leadership team works together to create focus, consensus, and a strategic game plan to bring the company into alignment with all of the customer's key buying needs.

The program is a powerful, team-building, customer-driven (through focused market research) planning and action process that brings the entire organization together to speak in One Voice in its marketplace. The One Voice Excellence Through Leadership Program is formatted from start to finish and is readily adaptable for any company. One Voice is a systematic process to synchronize all key areas in the company that affect gaining and keeping customers—profitably.

The business, as a result, develops the right mix of products and services, pricing, points of sale, people—both sales and customer service—positioning, and promotion. These dynamic factors are the 7 Points of Power. These are the key elements that drive customer growth, sales, and profits. Coincidentally, one of America's premier global corporations, McDonald's, uses a similar approach that has been the cornerstone of its unprecedented growth for over five years now.

Businesses that take control of their future in such a way become customer-centered, as the customer becomes central to the company's culture. Think of the customer as being on your board of directors and as an integral part of the group that shapes your company's future growth. Think of the customer, at a minimum, as having a good seat inside every department that impacts the purchase and repeat purchase decisions.

Companies that become customer-centered experience substantial growth and often see remarkable results. We have had companies double and triple sales within a few years' time. Managers also recognize that when sales increase 20 percent to 25 percent, these incremental revenues often turn into profits because overhead costs have already been covered. The customer is the company's North Star for it to become better organized and achieve its sales potential!

WRIGHT

How do the 7 Points of Power determine whether or not the customer buys and buys again?

THORNE

The 7 Points of Power are functions that virtually every company performs to some degree or another in order to grow and become profitable. They are the same functions that represent the customer's key buying needs. Curiously, some of these factors are often overlooked inside of organizations, because: 1) they are so obvious that they are taken for granted; 2) few recognize how much each one can contribute to greater sales; 3) the process of getting and keeping customers is not widely perceived as a holistic, company-wide effort; and 4) managers are confronted with so much so often that it is difficult to know what and where to focus. This is the most important point of all. Every day they are deluged with endless streams of data, challenging situations, and changing economic and societal events.

Constant focus on improving the 7 Points of Power is an empowering and unifying way for managers to bring their companies together and keep the spotlight on what is truly important in order to grow. Let me outline the 7 Points of Power in their broadest terms, and explain how each one affects the purchase and repeat buying decisions.

1. **Products**—Did you know that perceived product quality is the single biggest factor that contributes to profitability for large and small businesses alike? This was a key finding of the landmark research study, *Profit Impact of Marketing Strategy* (PIMS), which has been conducted across the United States since 1970. PIMS emphasizes that perceived product quality can also be enhanced through at least two other Points of Power: one is better customer service (People Service) and, two, a better image (Promotion).

   Companies with products or services similar to their competitors can generate greater sales if they focus on improving their customer service or image. The trend toward mass customization of products is a great example of customer service above and beyond the norm. Companies create automobiles, insurance policies, hamburgers, computers and the like, which are all semi-customizable, in order to better meet the customer's individual needs. To fully comprehend what it means to improve a business through a better image, look no further than soft drink brands like Coca-Cola and Pepsi. These products, which are largely flavored sugar water with added coloring, are two of the strongest brands in the world.

Customers buy products and services to meet their wants and needs. The central function of business is product innovation to fulfill these needs or to offer products with greater quality and value than competitors. Think about these questions in your business: To what extent do customers want and need your products? Do they perceive quality in your products? Is your business in a continuous state of innovation to improve and enhance its products for its customers? Can you "customize" your products to better serve your customers' individual needs?

2. **Price/Value**—I had the privilege of working with a very prestigious company that produces high quality boats for leisure and recreation. The company spares no expense creating the finest leisure craft in their class year after year. Because of this level of quality, these boats at one time came equipped with a very expensive price tag. As the company grew, management was not convinced, however, that it was anywhere close to reaching its potential. New pricing was established that set the highest price point at no more than 15 percent above the competition. This was difficult to achieve because of the extraordinary emphasis on quality. The company remained steadfast, however, in its quest. The new price/value ratio was immediately perceived by the marketplace. The company doubled its sales in short order.

    Businesses generally set prices so that customers will buy and so they can make a profit. The right price, of course, certainly doesn't mean being the cheapest. When prices are too low, often the consumer cannot envision the potential for product quality. The answer concerning price is that the customer is always looking for maximum value, no matter how expensive the product or service in question. The cumulative effect of the 7 Points of Power translates into greater value for the customer and greater sales for the company. An important question is: do customers see the value in the pricing of your business' products and services?

3. **Points of Sale**—Several years ago, a leading domestic automobile manufacturer moved two of its luxury car dealerships closer to a freeway

so that they would have greater visibility. Sales went up 42 percent after making this change and no other. Products, pricing, salespeople, service, and advertising all remained the same.

The customer needs to be able to see the products he or she is thinking about buying at the Point of Sale. The company needs some visible place where the customer can buy the products it has to offer. It is imperative that the Points of Sale are convenient, accessible, visible, and appropriate for the products being presented. The right Points of Sale can substantially increase sales, yet businesses don't always give them full recognition. Packaged goods companies readily acknowledge the points of sale or shelf space as critical to their success. The Internet is also an increasingly important Point of Sale.

Pizza Hut and Domino's recently reported, for example, that their online sales now account for over 20 percent of total revenues, with aggressive projections set for the future. Questions: How many locations are there where your company's products and services can be purchased? Is your company effectively managing them all? Are there enough? Are they visible? Are they appropriate?

4. **People-Sales**—The Nielsen Company conducted an important study on sales with significant implications for every industry. It focused on the salesperson's relationship with the customer regarding the sale of new automobiles. The study revealed that the salesperson, once he or she developed the customer's trust, has the capability to switch prospective customers from one automobile brand to another. The salesperson's relationship with the customer, in one sense, is more valued than the automobile or the brand itself. This is what a Point of Power really means! The customer needs to buy products and services from a representative of the company, unless it's online, or it is in a packaged goods category and occupies a place on the store shelf. Even in these circumstances, there are more exceptions than not. Online inquiries often lead to one-on-one conversations between the prospective customer and the sales representative. Salespeople as well are to be found in many departments of the bare bones warehouse stores. It is now more important than ever that salespeople have the necessary training and product knowledge to make them more effective and of greater service to the customer.

Questions: Do you have sufficient salespeople to address the needs of your potential customers? Are they well trained and do they have sufficient product knowledge and motivation? Do they effectively cross-sell to make existing customers aware of other products and make your business more profitable once the initial sale has been completed?

5. **People-Service**—Taco Bell, in the 1990s, conducted an eye-opening analysis that proves real profits are definitely made on the front lines. The fast-food giant examined the differences among servers with high and low turnover rates. The findings were astonishing! Sales were double and profits 55 percent greater in the stores where employee turnover was the lowest, compared with those units where employee turnover was the highest. The study revealed that the longer the server worked at Taco Bell, the greater the level of customer satisfaction and productivity per employee.

Think of the implications. One of the world's dominant marketers spends hundreds of millions of dollars a year advertising to consumers. Yet, even though the advertising, products, pricing and points of sale were virtually the same throughout the chain, profits varied tremendously, based on the length of time employees have been with the organization. This is not what many companies normally associate with the marketing effort. Customers, regardless of the business, demand service before, during, or after the sale, or in some combination, especially as competition heats up more than ever today.

Questions: Are your customers' service needs adequately taken care of after the sale? What is your company's percentage of repeat customers? Does your company's customer service have the influence it should on sales?

6. **Positioning**—Positioning, it has been said, is the cheapest way to rebuild a company without having to rebuild the company. It is the overall perception the consumer has of the product and/or company in his or her mind and it is that which differentiates the product from the competition. Consumers must be able to differentiate the product they are going to buy from all of the other purchase options they have available. This is true now more than ever because of extreme product parity, meaning products are essentially the same due to so much competition.

Companies, on the other hand, must differentiate their products to stand out in the marketplace. Unfortunately, most are not doing a very good job at this. Only about one out of five—21 percent—of 1,847 products studied in 75 different categories had any meaningful points of differentiation to consumers in a national study.

Strategic positioning is mandatory for success. Many smart companies have relied on effective positioning through advertising to reach their growth goals. Here are just a few legendary examples:

Considering how many brands of toothpaste there are on store shelves, nothing did more to launch one of the category's leaders, Crest Toothpaste, than when it received the endorsement of the American Dental Association. Note how the Apple brand stands out among the parade of computer manufacturers for its humanizing approach to technology. If you're in the market for a luxury car, you might want to look at Mercedes Benz, "Engineered Like No Other Car in the World" or BMW, "The Ultimate Driving Machine." If you want to customize your fast food, you might want to dig in at Burger King, where you can "Have it Your Way." Athletes and semi-athletes know they can turn to Nike where they hear their battle cry, which extends far beyond selling the product, to "Just Do It."

So many companies align themselves with the customer's other buying needs, but fail to differentiate their products and company from their competitors. If they don't do it, how is the customer supposed to know the difference? The right positioning can catapult a company's products to the top of the sales chart.

Questions: Can consumers tell the difference between your company and its products and services next to your competition? Is it the right difference?

7. **Promotion**—Customers need to be aware of the products and services and the benefits they provide before they make any purchase. Companies need to let customers know that they have products and services to sell and identify their benefits to them. Experts spar over the value of advertising and what its role is in selling products and services. The dialogue is taking on added impetus because of the advent of the Internet and social media.

If two companies produce essentially the same product and one advertises its product and the other does not, the company that advertises, generally speaking, will sell more product. What becomes confusing is the endless debate as to whether or not advertising itself *sells*. The need for promotion is fundamental in that it creates awareness, communicates information, bolsters demand, and helps to build and reinforce the brand. It is certainly not going to "sell" if no one knows about it and unless the other Points of Power are in alignment with the customers' needs.

It should be noted that there are so many different forms of promotion. We are only speaking of it here in the broadest sense. Direct marketing, for example, either via mail, the Internet, or television, now accounts for 25 percent of all marketing communications expenditures.

Public Relations is a powerful communications vehicle that can bring credibility and awareness to a company, product, or service. The key is for promotion efforts to be strategically integrated through the various messages to the intended audience—just like the 7 Points of Power.

Questions: What percentage of consumers knows about your company's products and services? How can they buy if they aren't aware of them? Since each of the 7 Points of Power conveys an image to the potential customer, are they all making the same impression? Is each one of the Points of Power, in other words, reinforcing the others?

WRIGHT

What is the financial effect of each of the 7 Points of Power on sales?

THORNE

Here's how each of the 7 Points of Power contributes to sales growth.

Potential Sales Growth - 7 Points of Power

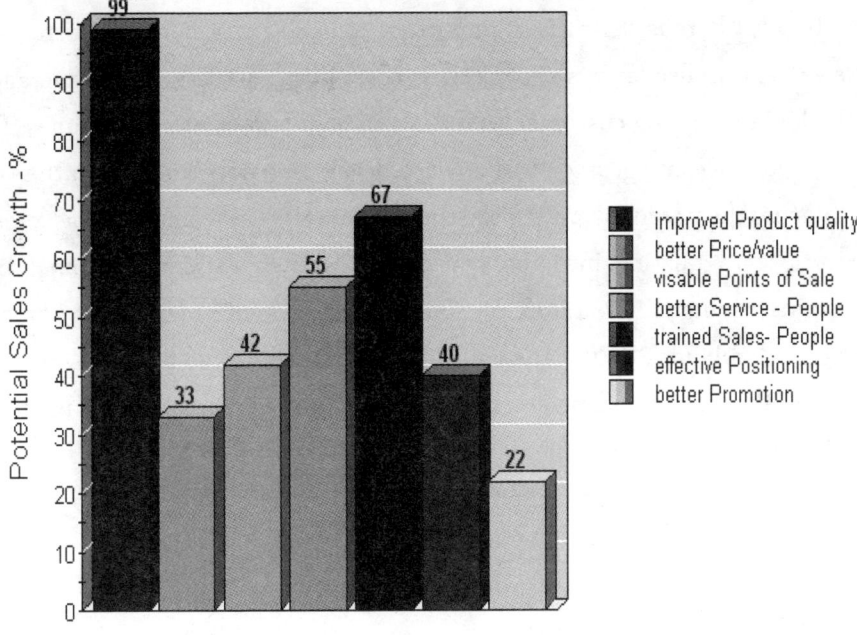

The 7 Points of Power

Legend:
- improved Product quality
- better Price/value
- visable Points of Sale
- better Service - People
- trained Sales- People
- effective Positioning
- better Promotion

Note: There are a number of different studies that track the effectiveness of each of these vital factors. While the results sometimes vary, one constant remains. Each of them, when correctly executed, will make a substantial contribution to the company's revenue and profit picture.

WRIGHT

Is this why One Voice consistently emphasizes that "it takes the whole company to get and keep a customer?"

THORNE

Yes. One of the premier management experts and teachers of our time, Peter Drucker, emphasized that the fundamental purpose of business is "to get and keep a customer." It is vital for managers to consider how successful their companies would be if all of their key departments were synchronized and aligned with the customer's buying needs. This is more important than ever today.

Implicit here is that it is as important to keep a customer as it is to gain a new one. It is also far less expensive. It costs five times less, on the average, to develop an existing customer as it does to gain a new one. Companies, from my experience, are geared more toward developing new business, rather than achieving the potential among existing customers. Few companies, as a result, are close to tapping into the real worth of their existing customer base. Imagine having a 100, 1,000, or 100,000 trees in your own private orchard. Still, you only pick half of the fruit, leaving the rest to go to waste, or worse, leaving them for someone else to come along and harvest. If you want to talk about marketing effectiveness, which advertising is more beneficial: when the customer stays with the company for a year, or if he or she is a good-paying customer for five years?

Two quick examples highlight the worth of a long-term customer. A lifetime pizza customer will spend over $8,000 on pizza. A luxury automobile owner will spend $320,000 on the purchase of luxury automobiles.

Questions: Are you tapping into the potential of your existing customers? What is the value of a good customer over the course of a year? Three years? Five years? What percentage of your customers returns to buy again? What percentage are satisfied customers? Are they buying the different products your company has to offer?

WRIGHT

What happens to sales if even one of the 7 Points of Power isn't meeting customers' critical buying needs?

THORNE

If one of the 7 Points of Power in your organization isn't meeting a key buying need, it is costing your company customers and sales, and these losses are often significant. The following scenario illustrates what I mean. The reasons for lost sales and customers broadly outlined here happen every day in large and small companies across America.

- Let's assume customers like your company's products and services.
- What if, however, they don't see the value in its pricing?
- What if customers like your products and pricing, but the points of sale are hidden from view, inconvenient, unattractive, unclean, or the shelf space in stores is too limited?
- What if customers like all of the points above, but the customer service (People-Service) is slow or there are too few people to provide good service, or the company demands too great a price for service?
- What if customers like the products and services, pricing, points of sale, and customer service, but the sales staff (People-Sales) doesn't have the product knowledge, isn't adequately trained, attentive to customer needs, or is too small to accommodate demand?
- What if the customer likes the above, but can't differentiate your company's products and services from that of your competitors (Positioning)?
- What if customers would like the company's products, pricing, points of sale, and people, both sales and service, only they aren't aware of any of it because there hasn't been any advertising, direct marketing, public relations efforts, or social media (Promotion)?

The 7 Points of Power constitute the majority of your company's resources, including the majority of people in your company. The viability of each one directly depends on the effectiveness of the others. When managers begin to see their company in this light, they will know that each of these factors has an immediate as well as a lasting effect on customer growth, retention, and profits. The sum is greater than the whole of the parts and all of the parts must be considered when adding up what they all look like to the customer. When your team begins to see and manage these critical factors collectively, as well as individually, they will appreciate that this is a practical way for them to grasp what is most important every day for their company to succeed.

WRIGHT

Will you tell us about the success companies have when they speak in One Voice?

THORNE

We are proud of the successes clients have achieved using the One Voice Excellence Through Leadership Program. Here are a few case histories. I don't talk about client companies by name to ensure confidentiality. Hopefully, what stands out is what is possible when companies move into alignment with their customers and synchronize everything that affects sales. Often this means answering the following question: "Who is the real customer?"

- A nationally recognized cruise line discovered through One Voice that its Point of Sale was quite different than what management for years had thought. The company annually spent millions of dollars advertising to potential passengers to call its 800 number. As a result, a color brochure was sent to them by mail. The goal was for the prospective customer to call the company and discuss with the sales agent when and what cruise the potential passenger would like to take. The Point of Sale was at the company itself, where passenger prospects would talk one-on-one over the telephone. The research revealed, however, that 86 percent of its existing but limited passenger base booked their cruises through travel agents, not through the company, even though the company hardly had any sales and marketing programs in place to encourage and support these agents. Total sales, as a result, were markedly less than what was possible because this was not the company's focus.

  The leadership team embraced the findings wholeheartedly, shifted their attention to the agents, and sales increased 20 percent the first year. Sales tripled within a few years and the company eventually went public.

- A national seafood processing company that faced bankruptcy used One Voice to review and revamp its entire mode of operations. The company was initially selling to local restaurants. Research revealed that the real market was among major national distributors who, in turn, sold to large restaurant chains, hotels, and similar entities throughout the country. Management then had the vision to temporarily halt all sales and promotion activities, during which time the plant operations were transformed into a major point of pride.

Proprietary technology ensuring food safety and quality was the driving force behind the company's success, but identifying the real customer was critical to penetrating the market. The sales efforts also turned from local to national, and premier industry trade shows soon became strategic Points of Sale. The company, with the guidance of One Voice, was also positioned as the leader in its category across America.

Today, it has lived up to its name and is a nationally recognized company, with an ever-growing list of premier customers from across the nation. Perceived product quality is the foundation of its success. Revenues increased 35 percent while cost of goods and labor dropped 20 percent within one year of the program's inception. Most of the company's clientele have been satisfied customers for years and continue to buy on a regular basis.

- A chain of pizza restaurants situated in several southwestern states began by only selling a medium-size pizza at a low price. A seven-figure promotion budget allowed for extensive television advertising to reinforce the value proposition. The owners of the pizza chain were experienced restaurant and fast-food operators who always emphasized delivering value to their customers. They had added a few video games in their various locations as an attraction for the kids.

While the restaurants were profitable, management felt the chain could do better. Once again, market research, focused on uncovering the status of the 7 Points of Power, held the kernel of truth. The findings were startling. The primary reason customers frequented the restaurants wasn't for the pizza—it was for the video games. It turned out that more than 80 percent of the customers were families, a higher percentage than even McDonald's customers.

The owner/operators quickly made use of the findings. Soon, there were actual merry-go-rounds in some of the stores. Additional managers were trained to oversee the growing number of video games that were placed in each of the restaurants.

It also didn't take long for these Points of Sale to take on a heightened family atmosphere. A new, larger pizza was added with more pizza toppings at a more profitable, higher price. Birthday parties held on Saturday mornings became another profit item, along with the second pizza product and new video games. Collectively, the company was positioned as a place for good food, fun, and games—all a great value. The company enjoyed increased profits because sales per unit increased and costs were largely covered. A new, more customer-focused business model ensured that new stores opened to immediate success.

The company, in other words, added real value for customers across the 7 Points of Power, definitely meeting all of their key buying needs.

- A premier insurance agency, located in one of San Diego's upper-scale beachside communities, decided after going through the One Voice process, to overhaul its customer service efforts and move to a fully automated system.

The agency dramatically improved its customer service program and now has more than a 95 percent retention rate among its customers. The new system created time for staff to focus on building the agency's business. Incentive programs were put in place to focus on cross-selling different products to existing customers. Annual sales growth is averaging 20 percent.

The agency has also become a leader in southern California in home and automobile coverage for The Hartford, long acknowledged as one of America's premier insurance companies.

WRIGHT

Is it possible to get an idea of how effective any company is at getting and keeping customers?

THORNE

Yes. We offer companies a simple, self-administered survey so that managers can see for themselves exactly where their company stands. The results, at this initial stage are quite subjective, but it is amazing how quickly everyone gets an idea of how effective their company is at getting and keeping customers. You can take the test yourself and see how you believe your company stacks up. It is equally important to know if your colleagues and customers agree with you.

How effective is your company at achieving real growth and profitability? Rate the following one to ten, with ten being excellent, beneath the heading of "You." How effective is each one when it comes to gaining and keeping customers?

	You	Managers	Customers
Products	_____	_____	_____
Pricing	_____	_____	_____
Points of Sale	_____	_____	_____
People-Service	_____	_____	_____
People-Sales	_____	_____	_____
Positioning	_____	_____	_____
Promotion	_____	_____	_____

Key questions: Would your other managers agree with you? What about (potential) customers? The One Voice Excellence Through Leadership Program engages the cross-functional leadership team to systematically move through a structured, highly focused process to bring all of these critical factors into alignment and synchronize everything in the company that affects sales. If one of these factors is not a ten, then the other Points of Power have to compensate. If the products are only a six or seven, then Customer Service and perhaps Promotion/Image and Pricing, for example, have to be more effective to overcome the lack of product quality and product differentiation.

WRIGHT

Why is it important to understand the difference between one- and two-customer companies?

THORNE

The driving force behind successful companies who speak in One Voice is knowing who the customer really is. This essentially means the customer is the person who writes the company a check for its goods and services. In this context, customers can be distributors, agents, retail stores, franchisees, dealers, as well as end-users.

Rather than debate which is most important, the end-user or the distributor, One Voice categorizes these sales set-ups as two-customer companies. This encourages the company to treat its distributors as the groups that are largely going to determine success for the sale of its products and services. The business that looks at its dealers, retailers or distributors as being of lesser importance, runs the risk of losing sales and sales support at the street level.

One of the complaints for years among automobile dealers was that the major automakers did not accord them proper respect, or give them the full support they deserved. Travel agents certainly feel this way about the airlines. A recent public relations fiasco occurred when a major fast-food marketer ran a coast-to-coast introductory promotion, offering its new product free, but many of its franchisees across the country were not on board when the promotion ran. The free product quickly ran out, creating mayhem among thousands of disappointed customers!

Once the concept of the two-customer company is embraced, it is then easy to apply the 7 Points of Power to meet the needs of the "second" customer as well. Building a close-knit dealer and/or distribution network and responding to the needs of the retail stores, dealers, or franchisees will definitely make the difference when it comes to sales and profits.

WRIGHT

How does One Voice help companies build their brands with the 7 Points of Power?

THORNE

Contemporary brands were initially associated with building a logo and image that were constantly reinforced through media advertising. Consider Betty Crocker, Jolly Green Giant, and Coca Cola. Increasingly, psychological and emotional associations have been built into brands so that consumers can satisfy deeper wants and needs for more fun, greater satisfaction in life, better health, or adventure. Today, because of the intense competitive environment where consumers have a myriad of choices no matter what they purchase, the brand literally represents the company's entire relationship with the customer

The brand, as a result, can now be divided into two parts: The brand promise and the brand experience. Once more, the 7 Points of Power bring structure to what is too often an esoteric exercise—building and reinforcing the brand. The brand promise is what we traditionally think of when it comes to branding. The brand promise embraces Positioning and Promotion, including image and packaging, and People-Sales. The brand experience embraces the company's Products, Pricing, Points of Sale, and People-Service—what the customer actually encounters in the process of making the purchase.

Increasingly, countless purchase options for the consumer makes it impossible for "Madison Avenue" to create a sexy image that will sell products without equivalent substance in the brand experience, especially in this economic climate. Here are two extremes to make the point: Look at General Motors and COSTCO.

General Motors, its very existence threatened today, spent $10 billion in advertising over the past ten years, without equivalent product quality and too many similar products, each with just a different logo and price point.

COSTCO, with nearly six hundred stores around the world, $71 billion in annual sales and ranked twenty-ninth among the Fortune 500, does virtually no advertising, except for direct mail and the Internet. Still, COSTCO has a powerful brand, built on the spectacular brand experience enjoyed by its millions of customers. COSTCO is recognized for its great quality and low prices, which translate into real value.

At One Voice, today's brand constitutes the collective experience encountered by the customer as he or she comes into contact with the all of the 7 Points of Power. It is imperative for the leadership team to drive both the brand promise and brand experience throughout the organization to achieve ultimate success.

WRIGHT

How would you summarize the greatest benefits of your One Voice program?

THORNE

One Voice supports the leadership team to synchronize all key factors in the company that affect sales—the 7 Points of Power—to improve its organizational and financial health and create a better future. When a company speaks in One Voice it is:

1.   Customer-centered—the leadership team closes the gap between what the company is doing and what more customers need to buy and buy again;
2.   United and focused in achieving its mission—the leadership team has the whole organization on the same page, going in the right direction;
3.   Effective in setting its most important priorities as it develops the right Products, Pricing, Points of Sale, People-Sales and Service, Positioning, and Promotion—the 7 Points of Power;
4.   Stronger in its leadership abilities, as the leadership team harnesses the power of its entire organization to bring it into focus with its customers and their needs;
5.   Efficient in its allocation of resources;
6.   Holistic and synchronistic because departments and the people in them work better together as a team;
7.   More competitive, by any measure, in its marketplace;
8.   Powerful and focused in its internal and external (marketing) communications;
9.   Successful in building a stronger, more powerful brand—both the brand promise and the brand experience; and
10.   Better equipped to increase revenues and build profits.

Everybody wins in the final analysis. Customers benefit from a seamless, compelling buying experience and find greater value in the products and services that they purchase and return to buy more often. This benefits the customer-centered company as it takes advantage of all opportunities to create a more profitable future. The entire company is synchronized for greater sales and profits. The company is synchronized for success.

ABOUT THE AUTHOR

GEORGE THORNE, president and founder of One Voice Research, Planning & Development, works with leadership teams to synchronize all key factors that affect sales. These key factors that drive sales and profits in every company are its 7 Points of Power^{SM}.

Mr. Thorne was president of his own 4A's (American Association of Advertising Agencies) agency for many years, and has won numerous national and regional awards for marketing, advertising, and direct marketing programs. He was a columnist for the international marketing publication, Ad Age's *Business Marketing*, and has worked with hundreds of large and small companies across America. He brings twenty-five years of experience to his corporate and entrepreneurial clients. He is a dynamic, motivational speaker and an inspiring team-builder, taking leadership teams through the One Voice Excellence Through Leadership Program^{SM} to help their companies reach their sales and profit potential.

GEORGE THORNE

545 B Avenue

Coronado, CA 92118

619-866-8023

www.onevoiceforgrowth.com

CHAPTER TWO
When I Grow Up

An interview with...
SCOTT SCHWEFEL

DAVID E. WRIGHT (WRIGHT)

Today we're talking with Scott Schwefel. In 1995 he founded what became Minnesota's largest technology training company, Benchmark Computer Learning, and then sold his stake in that company for more than a million dollars in 2003. His company was named one of the fifty fastest-growing private companies in Minnesota in 1997 and 1998, and he was named to *Minnesota Business Journal's* "40 under 40" list, the publication's annual compilation of "the region's most talented and successful young leaders." Scott has been speaking professionally for over twenty years and has spoken to thousands. In addition to being a great keynote speaker, he is also Managing Partner of Scotland-based Insights Learning and Development's Twin Cities' office. Scott currently trains and coaches CEOs, presidents, and senior executives. As a professional speaker, he brings the magic of Insights Discovery to thousands around the world.

Scott has lived remotely with the Hadza and Massai tribes in Tanzania. He founded SelfConfidence.com to give away over 20,000 copies of his first book, *I Think I'll Stand Up*. Scott also travels throughout the United States and Canada as a featured speaker for Vistage, the largest organization of CEOs in the world. He lives in Excelsior, Minnesota, with his wife, Linda, and his three children McKenzie, Connor, and Scottie Nicole.

Scott, welcome to *GPS for Success*.

SCOTT SCHWEFEL (SCHWEFEL)

Thank you David, it's great to be here.

WRIGHT

Sounds like you're at an airport.

SCHWEFEL

I am, and I hope that's not too bothersome. I'm tucked away in what I think might be a quiet corner here in George Bush Intercontinental in Houston.

WRIGHT

Not at all, you're a busy man; we're just glad we caught up with you.

So what role does passion play in an individual's success?

SCHWEFEL

I'm smiling David—what a great first question. I really believe that it's paramount to sustained success. For most people, the level to which they choose to be engaged passionately will determine their resulting level of success. When people are able to apply passion to what they do, it brings into being different actions and forces that they simply cannot access when they are not engaged fully and emotionally. It's no surprise that people know what passion looks like and feels like to them, but the vast majority only know their passion from sports, their hobbies, or their social circles.

How many people can really say that they experience passion in the daily work they do? When passion can be applied to the work you do, where most of us spend forty or fifty hours a week, the results are significantly different. A lot of us have passion in areas other than our work because we don't realize that we can align the two—our passion and our work. If we do it on purpose—if we consciously align the thing that we truly love and care about with our career choice—the results will be significant and life-fulfilling every time.

WRIGHT

So what is the one question everyone needs to answer?

SCHWEFEL

David, it is a question that we were all able to answer when we were children, and that's what's so unique and powerful about it. It's a question that at age four, five, six, or seven, everybody in the world had a pretty good answer to. The question was, and still is, "what do I want to be when I grow up?"

What happens, as we age and as we grow and as we do the work that we choose to do as adults, is that we fall prey to the demands of life. We tend to forget both the question and the answer we once had. The passion we felt about becoming a fireman, a doctor, or even a superhero subsided and was replaced with what we felt we should do rather than what we really and truly wanted to do.

We all know people who have stayed true to the passions of their youth or found a new truth that drives them today, but they are rare indeed. Those are the folks who are truly passionate in their work. They are doing what they really love to do and in my experience, in most cases it is the same passion they felt in the fourth grade. They have taken a desire to be a superhero and translated it into an occupation that delivers the same passion today that they felt way back then.

If I translated the question, "what do I want to be when I grow up?" to one that I would have people answer today, it would be, "if you had all the money in the world right now, and you were going to live forever, what would you do?" It's just a more qualified version of what do you want to be when you grow up, what do you love, and what are you passionate about? I've asked these questions of hundreds, and maybe thousands of people. I do this at various times like today when I'm sitting next to someone on a plane. You would be both amazed and saddened that rarely can anyone give me an answer. And yet, isn't that why we are all here? Isn't it why we have God-given talents? How could we forget why we are on this Earth, and how we should spend the precious minutes, hours, and days that we have? It's a big question, and everyone needs to be able to answer it.

WRIGHT

I've asked these questions to literally thousands of people, so I'll ask it one more time because I get some great answers—how do you define success?

SCHWEFEL

I have two answers for you. One is my definition, which I have borrowed from Richard Leider, a very successful author and speaker. Richard asked me the question while we were in Tanzania, Africa, together. His question to me was, "If you were to define success by doing what you love, with people you love, in the place you're meant to be, might that make you truly happy?" My answer was yes, and then I began to look at my life through a new lens. I realized that to be able to answer his question I had to make some changes. That trip to Africa with Richard is what led me to sell my business and do exactly what I am doing now, which is the work that I love, with people I love, in the place I am meant to be.

The second definition of success I will give is yours, whatever that may be, provided it is a worthy definition of success. Back in 1956, Earl Nightingale defined success as "the ongoing progression towards a worthy goal." It really is different for everybody. To know what this answer is in detail requires that I ask it of everyone I meet because it is yours and yours alone. Ask yourself right now, "What are you passionate about, what do you love to do, and does it make you truly happy?"

WRIGHT

An intelligent man told me many years ago that if I were walking down the road and saw a turtle sitting on top of a fencepost I could bet he didn't get up there by himself. Who are the people who helped you along the way—who are your role models?

SCHWEFEL

Well you know, having just mentioned Earl Nightingale to you, he is certainly a role model for me. When I was twenty-five years old, a roommate and friend of mine, Tom Schaff, gave me my first motivational tape. Until then, I didn't even know what a motivational tape or book even was. Tom had hundreds at the time, and has thousands now. I had never even read or listened to a motivational tape of a book before then.

The tape cassette Tom gave me was Earl Nightingale's recording from 1956 called *The Strangest Secret*. It's the first thing that cracked open the idea in my head that I could determine my own destiny, and do it on purpose. I began to learn that I could make choices and act on those choices and change the course of my life. So that was a big change from the way I viewed the world, others, and my own circumstances up until that time. I had been reacting my way through life up until that point. Listening to Earl's message hundreds and hundreds of times made it become real for me. It prompted me to establish written goals, something I still do today.

Others who have helped me along the way are the top motivational speakers and writers of the last thirty years, especially Richard Leider and Richard Rohr. Richard Leider took me on one of his Inventure Expedition walking safaris into Tanzania (and into myself), which helped me live my life more fully on purpose. He helped me first by writing the global bestseller *Repacking Your Bags,* and secondly by bringing a group of us on an Inventure, literally an adventure within ourselves, enabling us all to release our intentions and our purpose into the world.

Richard Rohr is a Catholic priest who runs the Center for Action and Contemplation in New Mexico (see www.cacradicalgrace.com). The Center helps mainly men understand and deal with the second half of their lives also with a focus, albeit it more spiritual, on purpose.

The last and most important influence on me has been my wife, Linda. Linda has achieved everything she has ever set her mind to, and rather than tell me how determination, commitment, and focus on what we want can bring all our heart's desires into our lives, she did it. And she still does after twenty years.

WRIGHT

Two days ago I listened to *The Strangest Secret* by Earl Nightingale in my car. I hadn't heard it or read it in probably twenty or twenty-five years and someone mailed it to me.

SCHWEFEL

Well, I believe everything happens for a reason and that there are *no coincidences.*

WRIGHT

Well said. Is there a role that personality plays in shaping a person's destiny?

SCHWEFEL

Yes, personality always plays a role, but what I found is that the "secret sauce" for each of us is the degree to which you (or anyone) as an individual truly understand the unique gifts of your personality and, at the same time, understand some of the flaws that may come from overusing or over extending the natural gifts of your personality. People's level of awareness of their own strengths and weaknesses determines their level of success. Therefore, it's not enough to say, "My personality is this way, therefore I'll probably show up this way." It becomes really valuable to say instead, "If I tend to be very determined and competitive in life, it's not the opposite traits that tend to bring me down, it's actually doing too much of what I naturally do well." This is because a strength overused becomes a weakness, and nowhere is that more apparent than in personality. If I'm energetic and enthusiastic, which I tend to be, I show up well within my natural personality, but if I'm too energetic and too enthusiastic, it comes off as a weakness rather than as a strength. If people are cautious and reserved, great, but if they show up too cautious, and too reserved, their natural personality gifts work against them.

My company, Insights, helps people understand their own personalities in great detail, with a short online survey. (Visit www.experienceinsights.com to learn more.)

Yes, personality plays a role; it can be our biggest asset and a moment later, it can bring us down. Awareness is the key.

WRIGHT

Would you tell our readers a little bit about goals and goal-setting for effectiveness?

SCHWEFEL

Oh, absolutely, courtesy again of Earl Nightingale. We become what we think about. It's really that simple. If we understand the concept that what we believe and what we think is who we become, then set a goal each day and *think about that goal,* we will achieve it.

However, here's what really happens to the majority of us on any given day. We get up, grumble about how early it is, and think about the fact that we have to go to work. Then we read the paper and turn on the morning news. We hear about crime, recession, bad politics, and so on. We don't even realize that we are actually programming ourselves for the entire day. We have accidently programmed our brains to seek out evidence of crime, recession, bad politics, and so forth. What a shame. Grab anyone as he or she is walking through daily routine and ask, "Hey, what are you thinking about right now?" Nine out of ten people won't have any idea how to answer this question, and the truth is that they didn't know how to answer it when they started their day either. The whole concept of goal-setting is predetermining what you're going to be thinking about when you don't know what you're thinking about.

Once I realized this (when I was twenty-five years old), I became a fanatic of writing down my goals for the year, defining where I was headed, taping that printout on my bathroom mirror, and reading it every morning and every night. And you know what? I still do it today. What I've chosen to do is predetermine what my ideal thoughts would be rather than leave to chance what I think about all day long. I find opportunities to bring my goals into reality and they do—they really do.

Try it yourself. Write down just one thing you want to make real this coming year. Read it out loud every morning and every night, and you too will realize that this is the first step in making it happen. Find your own opportunities and make them real. I encourage everyone to do this, absolutely everyone—write down your goals and read them out loud every day.

WRIGHT

So how do people move from their heart, their passion, into reality?

SCHWEFEL

Turning our passions into reality is what most people think is the hardest part, and surprisingly, it isn't. The reason most people do not achieve their stated goals is because they do not state their goals in the first place. Once you have done this, the next step is execution. That is how we translate passion into reality—through execution and making it happen. Most people believe they have not achieved all their personal goals because of how difficult it is to execute them and make them happen. I firmly believe that the reason is because for most people no goals are written down in the first place. Is execution difficult? Yes, at times it is; but when we know that our skills and our passions are aligned toward a worthy goal, nothing can get in our way.

If I set my goals and walk around thinking about them all day, what it's going to do is start to move me in that direction. But all it does is start me. The only thing that is going to take me through what I really want to accomplish and what I really want to achieve is if I truly have a plan of execution and a direction. I will also need clarity of purpose and a team around me to support me to get there.

A favorite question I like to ask myself (and I don't always like the answer by the way) is what would the person I want to become do right now?

Think about this in terms of exercising, for example. You wake up and you're tired. You just have to ask yourself, "What would the person I want to become do now?" If the person you want to be is in shape, that person would get up and work out. That's the driver. It will push you toward execution. After setting your goals, it is execution that will make your goals a reality. Write down your goals, and execute and you will succeed.

WRIGHT

So how would someone learn more to achieve more?

SCHWEFEL

As I said, I'm a pretty avid reader and I became a *books on tape* fan many, many years ago. I subscribe to services that used to send me information on the topics I wanted to learn about. I don't think we realize how much time we truly have to continue to teach ourselves, especially now in the digital age. With iPods, MP3 players, and those types of digital media, there is an unlimited amount of time we have to program what we're thinking about. We can influence ourselves daily about what we're learning about, and how we can move forward. If you're on a long drive for instance, or you're on a flight, which I am weekly, and you don't have some content there that moves you toward your goal, you're missing an opportunity to grow and improve and learn more.

This is why I've always been in the training and learning industry—it makes the difference between winning and losing over time, never immediate, but over time. Learning is one of the key differences between achievers and those who settle for the middle ground. Don't settle. What have you learned this week that will move you toward your goals?

WRIGHT

So what role does integrity play? Does it really matter for success?

SCHWEFEL

Regardless of how one might define it, integrity is absolutely critical. I remember when I was about eleven or twelve, my dad was an attorney (he's since passed on, God rest his soul). One of my jobs on the weekend was to clean his office. I came in one Friday after school and he had just hung up with a client. He wrote down 1.25 hours. I asked, "What's that for?"

"That's how long I talked to that man," he answered, "and so that's how I bill him."

I remember saying, "You could just write down 1.5 if you wanted to, and make more money."

He looked up at me and said, "Well, I could, and then I would charge him more, but that just wouldn't be right would it?"

It just stuck with me then and there. Each of us will have a thousand opportunities to either write down 1.25 hours, or 1.5. My point here is there are so many easy ways to jump ahead in the short-term with a lack of integrity, but when integrity is behind you and it drives you, and you do the right things all the time, you will get a much better long-term result. Success will be yours to keep because you earned it and not because you stole it in the moment. Do the right thing—every time.

WRIGHT

What do you think turns dreams into practical reality?

SCHWEFEL

Part of it is the need for execution that I mentioned earlier. If you focus on what we've been talking about, it really is the summation of all these things.

As an example, to dream that I want to play in the NBA does not mean it will happen if I'm five feet, four inches tall—it's probably a goal that I'm not going to achieve. But if I've created alignment of my passions with my skills and with my capabilities, and I've laid out a plan of execution, then there are an unlimited number of things I can do. So there has got to be a reality-based component to what we all decide to do.

A quick example is my daughter, McKenzie, who is a senior as of this interview. She applied to a couple of schools and has been waiting to be accepted to Indiana. I've said to her every morning, "Think about how you're going to make it happen; put it down as a goal. Let's keep thinking hard about it and let's make sure that we move it forward." After being deferred, I'm happy to say she was accepted yesterday. It was a great way to reinforce the idea that you've just got to stay focused on the goal; keep your eyes on the prize. Go Hoosiers!

WRIGHT

So how can one sustain growth and learning through prosperity?

SCHWEFEL

I love your question because every year I work with two to three hundred CEOs throughout the United States and Canada, and every year there is a fair number of them who are somewhat unhappy with where they are in life. It is usually because they've learned, as they've achieved a certain level of success and financial independence, that this is really all they have in their future. When they achieve that goal, they've asked themselves, "Now what?" This is often because they haven't asked themselves enough of these questions. Many of them are successful, but have no idea of what to do next as they seek to move from success to significance.

One of the keys of sustaining oneself through prosperity is to enjoy the journey, but realize it's a journey—it's not a destination. Prosperity just means that I've got a new platform on which to move forward and I'd better know where I'm going. Again, it goes back to the original questions of, "What do I want to be when I grow up, what do I want to do today, and what do I want to do with the rest of my life?" There are a surprising number of people—a vast majority of people—who live too much in the moment and are not aware that if they achieve their goal in the moment, they don't know where to go next. Throughout your entire life you must have that journey mapped out through every future moment your life. Never stop looking ahead.

WRIGHT

Can people really achieve all of their dreams?

SCHWEFEL

I have made it a career policy to say yes. It's hard to imagine that if the human mind can conceive it, then the human being cannot achieve it. If you think about the number of things that have been done by individuals that thousands, if not hundreds of thousands of people have said could never happen but others have turned around and made happen, I just don't see how I could say for sure that this is not going to be the case. And I know that it doesn't cost me anything to say yes and to believe yes. Saying yes also enables me to support anybody.

One of the things that came out of my first book is a personal note I wrote that said, "If you'd like me to support you in your goals, e-mail them to me." Although the book had been downloaded (this is a few years ago) twenty thousand times or more, I've probably only gotten a hundred e-mails from people giving me their goals.

Two or three years later I received a note back from one of those individuals—a man in Australia who wrote that he and I had shared a flight three years ago. He wrote that I had shared my goal-setting philosophy with him. He was overweight and unhappy with his job and his personal life. In his e-mail he shared that he had lost eighty-three pounds, he had quit his job, and has a much better one, that he now loved his job, and that he was enjoying his family again. This was all because I had gotten him thinking about where he wanted to be and how goal-setting and execution could get him there!

Another young man and I shared a flight from New York to Minneapolis. Three years later he sent me a card. It read, "Scott, you might not remember me, but we shared a flight a few years ago and you challenged me to write down my goals, which I did. I now own my own business, I have twenty-five employees, and I wouldn't have done it if it hadn't been for you."

I didn't change these people—I only shared the secret of success with them, just as Earl Nightingale shared it with me so many years ago.

The formula works, it's just that too many people do not take action. Take action now and you too can realize your goals.

WRIGHT

So my final question is the only personal one. What makes you truly happy?

SCHWEFEL

What makes me truly happy? Well, my first thought is that I *am* truly happy. Part of me has to look around and say it's got to be who I'm with and what I'm doing and, going back to my definition of success, am I doing work that I love? Yes. With people I love? Absolutely. My family and the folks I work with around the world from Insights are colleagues and a peer group that I love to be with and I get to do it in a place that I love, which is in

Minnesota. But I'm a frequent flyer, as you can imagine, and what I do takes me all over the world. I get to see the rest of the world as well. So I truly am doing work that I love with people I love and it does make me truly happy. Thank you, Richard Leider.

WRIGHT

Well, Scott, what a great conversation. I've really learned a lot here today and I'm sure our readers will have a lot to think about as well. I really appreciate all this time you've taken to answer these questions.

SCHWEFEL

I also appreciate being able to share my ideas with you and our readers. You've left me with plenty of time to still make my flight, so thanks for talking with me.

WRIGHT

Today we've been talking with Scott Schwefel. In addition to being a great Minnesota keynote speaker, he is also a Managing Partner of Scotland-based Insights and Learning and Development in the Twin Cities. He trains and coaches CEOs, presidents, and senior executives. As a professional speaker, he brings the magic of Insights Discovery to thousands of people all around the world.

Scott, thank you so much for being with us today on *GPS for Success: Goals and Proven Strategies*.

SCHWEFEL

Thank you so much David, nice talking with you too.

About the Author

In 1995 SCOTT SCHWEFEL founded what became Minnesota's largest technology training company, Benchmark Computer Learning, and then sold his stake in that company for more than a million dollars in 2003. His company was named one of the fifty fastest growing private companies in Minnesota in 1997 and 1998. He was named to Minnesota's "40 under 40" list of successful top executives in the year 2003.

Scott has been speaking professionally for over twenty years, and enjoys groups from 100 to 5000. His programs are both entertaining and provide simple tools for participants to better connect and adapt with each other immediately afterward. Keynoting at the start of a multi-day conference, where the tools can be used immediately afterward, is the best possible engagement, and delivers lasting impact.

In addition to being a great Minnesota keynote speaker, Scott Schwefel is also Managing Partner of Scotland Based Insights Learning & Development in the Twin Cities. www.Insights.com He trains and coaches CEOs, presidents and senior executives, and as a professional speaker, brings the magic of Insights Discovery to thousands around the world.

He is also a published author, has lived remotely with the Hadza and Masai tribes in Tanzania, and is a featured speaker for Vistage, the largest organization of CEOs in the world (www.vistage.com).

Take a look at Scott's preview videos at www.scottschwefel.com and contact Him to speak at your next company meeting, retreat, or sales convention. To schedule Scott to speak at your next event, call him at 952-223-1147 or visit www.insightstwincities.com.

SCOTT SCHWEFEL

www.scottschwefel.com

CHAPTER THREE

Sh*t HOT Sales:

The Driving Force of Business Success

An interview with...

CHRISTINE HAMILTON csp, cmp

DAVID WRIGHT (WRIGHT)

Today we are talking with Christine Hamilton. Christine is the past Division Vice President of Sales and Marketing for Beazer Homes (NYSE:BZH), a national top ten home-builder. During her tenure as vice president, she led the sales and marketing teams to consistently exceed sales and closing goals. Prior to executive management, she was the company's top-selling Certified Sales and Marketing Professional (CSP, CMP) and she also served as a Mortgage Loan Counselor. She is a three-time winner of Major Achievements in Marketing Excellence (MAME) Salesperson of the Year, and won Rookie of the Year during her first year in the home-building business.

Christine was also awarded the National Association of Home Builders (NAHB) Silver Award for National Salesperson of the Year for California and Nevada, as well as the NAHB Gold Award for the Best New Home Salesperson in the Nation.

Christine has twenty-seven years of sales and marketing experience spanning the home-building industry, resale Real Estate, automobiles, office equipment, skin care, and food products. She is the author of the book series *Sh*t HOTTT Sales™: A Guide to Exceptional Salesmanship*. As an international speaker, trainer, sales coach, and author, her mission is to empower individuals and companies to succeed through maximizing sales.

Christine, welcome to *GPS for Success*.

CHRISTINE HAMILTON (HAMILTON)

Great, David! Thank you for inviting me.

WRIGHT

Christine, how did you choose the title to your latest book, *Sh*t HOTTT Sales: A Guide to Exceptional Salesmanship*? That is a great title!

HAMILTON

I chose the title *Sh*t HOTTT Sales*, not because I advocate expletives, but because that is how I describe truly exceptional salespeople. Exceptional salespeople are individuals who are self-motivated. They are driven from within to pursue personal and professional excellence. They are master communicators highly skilled in listening and presenting. They are professionals at uncovering and overcoming customer objections. Exceptional salespeople also assume responsibility for generating customers for their company. They are diligent at follow-up and are outstanding at closing for the immediate sale. They sell consistently, and consistently meet or exceed sales expectations. They are sales dynamos who do not need to be micromanaged because they always deliver results. Sh*t hot salespeople are the front-line team players who bring exceptional sales success to any company.

WRIGHT

What do you think is the primary goal of businesses today?

HAMILTON

David, today and always the primary goal of every business is maximum profit. The way to achieve maximum profit is by maximizing sales. Sales are the driving force and backbone of every company. As the saying goes, "nothing happens until somebody sells something." Everything else, such as managing customer care issues, becomes an important source of future sales through repeat business and referrals. Therefore, since maximum profit is realized through sales, a business must employ and develop the best salespeople money can buy.

WRIGHT

What is the most optimal way to motivate salespeople to sell with urgency?

HAMILTON

I am a huge advocate of a 100 percent commission-based competitive floor for most businesses because necessity is a natural motivator. In a competitive floor environment for selling new homes for example, the governing rule is "whoever writes it gets it." This means that the sales representative who completes the purchase agreement with the customer and closes the sale is the one who gets paid the entire commission. There are no protected leads, no shared sales or split commissions, and no guaranteed salaries.

First, there are no protected leads. Protected leads are when a customer "belongs" to a particular salesperson if the salesperson obtains the customer's contact information. When leads are protected, a salesperson who assists a non-buying customer one day who returns another day and purchases from a different salesperson, is entitled to all or part of the commission. Conversely, when there are no protected leads, the customer lead does not belong to any particular salesperson. Should the customer return and purchase from a different salesperson, the salesperson who writes the purchase agreement earns the entire sales commission. The lead is not protected for the first salesperson because the customer is the *company's* customer.

When salespeople's leads are protected, they have less need to close for the immediate sale. They know that whether or not they close the sale that day, the customer is still theirs. Likewise, should they fail to follow up and the customer comes back and makes a purchase on another day, they are still paid all or part of the commission, which also reduces their motivation to follow up.

Additionally, in a competitive floor model, salespeople are not permitted to split commissions or alternate who gets the credit for the sale. I have seen salespeople agree to split every commission or alternate signing purchase agreements so that each is getting an equal number of commissions within a community. I disagree with this practice because it also reduces their need to close with urgency. Their motivation is reduced because they are getting paid on half of the sales whenever they occur and regardless of who is responsible for getting the customer to contract.

Finally, there are no guaranteed salaries. Salaries are a crutch that reduce a person's drive to sell and close continually by reducing the necessity to earn commissions consistently. Commission-only pay raises the bar on what a salesperson must produce in order to get paid consistently.

Some believe that customers are better served when salespeople are not competing for customer loyalty and sales. There is a concern that customers may sense competitive tension among the salespeople. I believe that how a customer is treated by salespeople bespeaks each person's character, not the company's compensation plan. Exceptional salespeople compete fairly, rather than display cutthroat behaviors. In fact, a competitive floor actually improves the caliber of the salespeople and results in increased profits for the businesses that employ them. Anything other than a competitive floor is counterproductive because it handicaps the best salespeople and supports the weaker salespeople to the detriment of the business's profit margin.

Business is not like the game of golf. There are no competitive handicaps in the real world where every business competes for customers. A business only gets paid if and when it sells its customer a product or service and closes the sale. It only stands to reason that a salesperson's compensation plan mirrors the way the company that employs him or her is compensated by its customers.

This sort of compensation plan also lessens the need to micromanage the sales force because it reduces the need to monitor how they meet their goals. New home salespeople need to greet, ask questions, demonstrate, site, overcome objections, close for the sale, and follow up in order to make sales. I suggest a sales force will work harder to develop customer relationships because they need to earn the customer's loyalty. The sales force will work harder to overcome objections and close for the immediate sale. If you want your salespeople to obtain customer contact information and do their follow-up, don't protect their leads. You can bet they will manage customer relations better than those who do not need to concern themselves with losing an entire commission. A competitive floor motivates each individual by increasing his or her personal responsibility for success.

I learned this the hard way by losing a sale to my partner. A couple had purchased a home from me. Their purchase was contingent upon the sale of their current home. Their home did not sell within the time allotted, so we cancelled the sale. A few months later, they came back on my day off and purchased a home from my partner. Like any salesperson, I hated losing sales. But I did not blame my partner for completing the purchase agreement. I did not complain about the "whoever writes it gets it" rule. I had to take a good look in the mirror and be honest about the diligence of my follow-up. The truth of the matter was that I did not follow up with those folks after they had cancelled. Even though I lost potential income, I learned a valuable lesson about the importance of follow-up, which made me a better salesperson and later significantly affected what I expected of my sales force.

For instance, when I returned to Beazer as management, the division cancellation rate was significantly higher than industry standards. We began a practice of following up on all cancelled sales and managed to recoup four sales in one year. These additional sales generated approximately $1,000,000 in additional revenue for the company, not small change by any standards, especially in a downward trending Real Estate market. These extra sales were one of the reasons we exceeded our budgeted closings for the fiscal year.

WRIGHT

How does a competitive floor attract the best salespeople?

HAMILTON

A competitive floor not only brings out the best in salespeople, it rewards them for their hard work and effectiveness. Let's say, for example, a company has budgeted to sell and close a certain number of homes in a year. And let's assume that two hundred thousand dollars will be paid in sales commissions. In an environment where sales and commissions are equally shared, each person would earn one hundred thousand dollars.

Now consider a competitive floor where Salesperson A is sh*t hot. She gets to the office early, is willing to stay open late, and is willing to come in on her days off to assist a buyer. Salesperson A also excels at needs assessment, demonstrating product knowledge, selling against the competition, overcoming customer objections, closing for the sale, and follow-up. Salesperson B is good, but not quite as effective as Salesperson A. In fact, Salesperson A is responsible for 60 percent of the sales in the community, whereas Salesperson B brings in 40 percent of the sales. In a commissioned competitive floor, Salesperson A would earn one hundred twenty thousand dollars and Salesperson B would earn eighty thousand dollars. Based on results, that is fair compensation.

The best salespeople prefer to work in a competitive environment where they are rewarded based on the results they produce instead of being subject to supplement the income of weaker salespeople. Understandably, the best salespeople prefer this type of compensation plan because they know they are more effective than most and want to be paid for it. When a company has a reputation for paying the best based on results, it inherently attracts the strongest sales professionals and deters those who are less competitive.

WRIGHT

Christine, how important is training to a company's bottom line?

HAMILTON

One of the keys to my success was my constant pursuit of training. As a young person out in the job market, one of the questions I asked of every employer was what kind of training the company offered. I received training from several companies that taught me different sales techniques. At Swiss Colony, I was taught a six-step selling process. It started with the greeting, offering a sample to entice the customer into the store, discussing product uses, asking for the sale, adding-on, and cashiering.

In vehicle sales, I learned Volkswagen product knowledge, how to demonstrate an automobile, and how to close for the immediate sale.

Canon trained me in SPIN selling, which is Situation, Problems, Implications, and Needs-based solutions.

Beazer provided training in BOLT (Bulls, Owls, Lambs, and Tigers) Selling, which addresses how to sell to different personality types.

Later in my career, I sought and paid for training on my own. For instance, I paid to become a designated Certified Sales Professional through the National Association of Home Builders and learned the Critical Path to New Home Sales. Through the NAHB's Institute of Residential Marketing, I became a Certified Marketing Professional by taking classes in Market Research, Consumers, Marketing, and Management. I also attended Franklin-Covey's seminars in The 7 Habits of Highly Effective People, How to Lead in Economic Downturn, and What Matters Most. I spent the last year in Personal Development and Leadership Training through Klemmer & Associates.

In every sales job, I have excelled because of consistent professional training. The bottom line is this: if you want to develop the best in your sales force, provide different types of sales training and support them in getting supplemental training and coaching on their own.

WRIGHT

What type of sales training do you feel is important to the success of a company?

HAMILTON

Companies need to provide training in the features and benefits of their products as well as their competitors' products. In my book, I share a story about a time early in my career when I lost a sale to a competitor because I did not thoroughly know the features and benefits of what I was selling. I was a Facsimile Representative working for a Canon distributor. The company provided one week of training. But after only one week, I did not fully understand all of the features of the L770, our best-selling plain paper fax machine. Specifically, I knew nothing about delayed transmission, a feature that gives the end user the ability to delay the transmission of faxes until the phone rates are lower.

After I had lost the sale to a competitor, the customer phoned me and asked if our machine offered delayed transmission. I looked into it and called the customer back to let him know that yes, it did indeed. But at that point, the deal was done. He had already purchased a lower priced fax machine from a competitor. Unfortunately, the majority of the faxes that they sent were to long distant numbers. Had I understood all of the features of our machine, I could have provided them a more suitable solution, which would have saved them a significant amount of money in long distance charges and thereby justified our higher price. In the end, this resulted in a lose-lose-lose situation. I lost a sale and a potential commission. The customer lost the opportunity to purchase a fax machine better suited to their needs and save money in the long run. And, my company lost potential revenue. Therefore, it is very important for companies to invest the time and money in product knowledge training.

Likewise, proactive companies will also provide training in their competitors' products. By knowing and understanding the competition, well-informed sales representatives better differentiate their company's products from their competitors'. You have to know about the competition before you can successfully sell against them.

Companies should also provide training in sales techniques and personality selling. Many salespeople sell the way they like to be sold. However, this approach is often ineffective with customers of a different personality type. A sales representative with an assertive personality may overpower someone who is friendly and supportive. Similarly, an analytical customer may not respect an enthusiastic salesperson who is less focused on facts, numbers, and details.

Learning personality selling empowers sales professionals to adjust their approach to reflect customers' mannerisms. As the sales professional adjusts to each customer's personality, the customer's trust in the salesperson increases. An assertive salesperson will soften his or her presentation and guide a friendly supporter into agreeing to purchase today. Likewise, an analytical salesperson may succeed in getting an excitable customer to ride the wave of excitement all the way to the closing table. The better the customer relates to the salesperson, the more sales the salesperson will successfully close with different personality types.

Additionally, businesses can disseminate information on outside training and coaching opportunities and encourage and support their salespeople in taking advantage of them. Exceptional salespeople often choose to invest in their own development because they know that as they become better people, they become better salespeople. The return on corporate and individual investment in sales training and personal development pays for itself repeatedly in increased sales and profits.

WRIGHT

How did you apply what you have learned about the importance of training when you were Vice President of Sales at Beazer Homes?

HAMILTON

Before I became management at Beazer, I "mystery-shopped" most of my salespeople. Many of them had been hired during the Real Estate boom when strong selling skills were not necessary to close sales. So I walked in their sales offices in my shorts and flip-flops and pretended to be a buyer.

At one new community, I noticed a panel in the garage that covered some plumbing equipment. When I returned to the sales office, I asked the representative what it was. His response revealed that he really had no idea what the equipment was. Not coincidentally, this salesperson was the lowest producer in the division. However, many of the other salespeople also did not know that the plumbing device was a Manibloc Plumbing Manifold. So, I learned all about it and taught it to my salespeople. In fact, it was one of the standard features that represented the value and quality of our homes. It was also one of our competitive advantages. They became experts at discussing its features and the benefits.

Mystery-shopping my sales force uncovered several other areas where we worked to improve product knowledge, which resulted in higher sales. Now, I mystery-shop other builders' salespeople and tailor my training sessions to target those areas that need improvement.

WRIGHT

Why is it important to train salespeople in the art of asking a customer questions?

HAMILTON

Asking questions demonstrates to customers that the salesperson wants to understand them and their situation. As the saying goes, "I don't care how much you know until I know how much you care." It demonstrates that they are not just out to make a sale. When customers feel the salesperson listens to them, they tend to be more receptive to what the salesperson has to say.

Training in product knowledge helps salespeople determine appropriate questions to ask a customer. Through asking questions, a salesperson discovers customers' situations—their wants, needs, and desires. As a salesperson digs deeper, he or she further uncovers the ensuing implications of a customer's situation.

A sharp salesperson further learns which companies and products he or she is competing against by asking, "What other companies are you considering seriously? What have you seen so far that you like or dislike and why? How do our products compare?" Every single facet of a customer's responses informs the salesperson how to proceed with the presentation. It clues the sales professional in on what features to demonstrate. It tells him or her what benefits to highlight in order to outsell the competition. Asking questions about the competition is one way top sales professionals assist customers in making comparisons in favor of their homes and products instead of needing to shop more.

Most importantly, people buy for their own reasons. Becoming a master at the art of asking questions enables a salesperson to understand a customer's reasons for buying. The salesperson uses the information to help customers do what they really want to do, which is to buy today. Exceptional salespeople are masters at asking questions in such a way that guides the customer's thinking to a "yes" buying decision. Teach your sales force the art of asking questions to improve the company's bottom line.

WRIGHT

What role does sales coaching play in a successful business?

HAMILTON

As important as a coach is to the championship of a professional sports team, a sales coach is to the success of a professional sales team. A sales coach helps individuals uncover their belief systems that prevent them from achieving the results they say they want. A sales coach assists people in detecting their mental and emotional roadblocks and overcoming them, even those extending as far back as what they learned in childhood about money and acquiring material things. Just as an exceptional salesperson uncovers and overcomes a customer's underlying objections, a sales coach guides salespeople to uncover and overcome underlying obstacles on their road to success. Additionally, the sales coach holds each salesperson accountable for his or her own results. A sales coach pushes team members to be their best, thereby helping them realize their potential. Realizing their potential helps align each salesperson's personal goals with the company's sales goals.

As a sales coach, I invest the time to understand the needs, wants, and desires of individual salespeople. To the extent I help people uncover their "why"—like their reasons for making money—I can support them in setting clear goals for how much they want to earn. If a salesperson wants to pay off his or her personal debt, I help him or her determine the number of sales needed to do so. I push salespeople to meet their goals, whether it is to prepare for retirement, to pay for their children's college tuition, to own a new car or boat, to travel, to support their favorite charity, or to earn the recognition they deserve. The result is a salesperson who is highly motivated from within. This level of inspiration is by far more effective than the carrot-and-stick approach that attempts to spur people through greed and fear.

WRIGHT

How does a sales professional know if a prospect is a qualified customer?

HAMILTON

Everyone is your customer. The question is do your salespeople qualify or disqualify prospects? How often do salespeople disqualify people because they don't "look right"? How often does a customer have to demonstrate that he or she is interested before the salesperson assists the customer? How often does the customer have to prove that he or she can qualify for a loan before a salesperson takes that person seriously? How often do salespeople disqualify customer because they are not comfortable greeting, approaching, asking questions, or being assertive? How many opportunities do salespeople allow to just pass customers by?

Let's say somebody walks into a new home sales office who has had a bankruptcy, a foreclosure, and has terrible credit—is that person a qualified customer? Should the salesperson greet him or her? Should the salesperson take the time to uncover the customer's needs and wants? Should the salesperson demonstrate the model homes? Should the salesperson go so far as to offer to show the customer home sites? Should the salesperson then ask if he or she wants to move forward today? How about asking if the customer knows anybody who may be interested in your homes? The answer to each question is absolutely *yes!*

I came to this realization one day when I was challenged to sell a button to a stranger on the street. I thought, "I can do this." The only guideline I was given was not to sell the button on the main street. As I walked along, it occurred to me to find a bookstore so I could tell the manager about the book I had just written (and possibly land a book deal), and while I was there, I would also ask if he or she wanted to buy my button.

I walked a couple of blocks and finally stopped a couple to ask them where I might find a bookstore. We started talking, and I asked them a bunch of questions to learn more about them, including where they were from and what they were doing in town. I explained that I was looking for a bookstore because I had this button to sell. I then asked them if they wanted to buy my button.

They replied, "How much do you want for it?"

I said, "What would you give me?"

They offered, "Five bucks."

I said, "Okay."

Mission accomplished. I had sold my button to the first customers I had talked to. However, I had failed to follow the rules because I was not supposed to sell the button on the main street.

The next day, I was challenged to sell a button again, this time within the guidelines. I had fifteen minutes to get out, walk beyond the main street, sell my button, and get back.

The first guy I saw was walking very fast, clearly in a big hurry. I decided, "I'm going to walk faster and catch up to him." I told him my story, including not following the rules the day before and having to resell my button right away. I cut to the close, "Are you interested in buying my button?"

He said, "Yes, I want to buy your button."

I said, "Great!"

Then he added, "But, I don't have any money on me. I am on my way to the ATM, which is on the main street. I will be back in a little bit."

I replied, "I only have ten minutes, so should I wait for you or go find another customer?"

He said, "You should go find another customer."

Literally, the next person I saw was a woman hurriedly unloading a van. I approached her and asked, "May I help you?"

She said, "Yes, you may. I am running late and I am supposed to have these things set up already."

I responded, "Great, let's go," and I helped her unload her van.

When we were finished unloading, I explained the reason I had stopped and helped her: "I have a button to sell and yesterday I sold it on the main street, which was against the rules. So, today I am selling it again. Would you like to buy it?"

She replied, "How much do you want for it?"

Instead of responding, "What would you pay for it?" as I had done the day before, I asked, "What's the maximum value you would give it?"

And she said, "Twenty bucks!"

Bam! I sold my button and returned on time.

From this experience, I learned two valuable lessons:

1. Help people the way they want to be helped and you will hit their "hot button" reason for buying today

2. When truly coming from a place of urgency, my customer is everyone who is in my path!

I asked if I could help her, and I did. More importantly, instead of buying my "story" as the couple did the day before, the woman "bought" the service she needed and was willing to pay four times as much for it.

To a business, every single person is a customer either now or in the future and a source of referrals unless and until the salesperson determines that he or she is not. Exceptional salespeople act with urgency by assuming that everyone is qualified, and remains qualified until they disqualify him or her. The only way to legitimately disqualify customers is by asking enough questions to truly know that they and everyone they know will never buy your product. Therefore, virtually everyone is qualified, one way or another. *Everyone* is your customer!

WRIGHT

Recently people have been talking about the importance of using social media in sales and marketing. Do you think it merits all the hype?

HAMILTON

Social media is today what magazine, newspaper, and yellow-page advertising were to yesterday. These days, it is not enough to just have a Web site. A company has to be on Facebook, Twitter, LinkedIn, and YouTube, etc. to successfully gain maximum market exposure.

Although social media can reach thousands of people, it is still one of the most passive forms of communication. I say it is a passive form of communication because it is only one way. Like an e-blast—even one with video—social media affords no real face-to-face interaction. It is easy for people to delete and ignore. Although many salespeople would like sales to magically come in through social media sites, that will not happen.

Social media is still an important form of advertising but it is too easy to rely on Internet marketing. It is an illusion when salespeople feel like they did something to advance the sale when they post a video on YouTube, send a tweet on Twitter, or a send video to a customer from their iPhone in lieu of networking and phone follow-up. No matter how catchy a social media site is, nothing outsells the personal impact that a well-trained sales professional can have on the heart, mind, and the buying decision of a customer. Hyundai says it best in one of its advertisements: "Step away from your hard drive and go for a real drive." The same thing goes for sales professionals. They must step away from their computers and talk to customers.

Exceptional sales professionals increase their value by generating leads. Remember the story about the plumbing manifold? I trained my salespeople to conduct presentations and network. We brought our Manibloc display unit with us and demonstrated its features and benefits at Real Estate offices, Rotary Clubs, and Chambers of Commerce. By educating others and leveraging contacts, sales professionals, attract customers and earn referrals.

A fifteen-minute office presentation will generate significantly more business than fifteen minutes of hiding behind a computer screen posting on the Internet. It is more effective to educate twenty people than to send twenty thousand tweets. Thirty minutes of phone follow-up will generate more return appointments than thirty of the cleverest e-mails. Therefore, the Internet and social media are marketing tools to magnify market presence, while presenting, networking, and phone follow-up are more effective strategies for increasing sales.

WRIGHT

So what type of marketing and advertising are the most effective?

HAMILTON

Because personal contact is so effective, advertisements that work the best are the ones where the call to action *is* to call. In my experience, whether advertising through a company Web site, Facebook, Twitter, magazine article, newspaper ad, or freeway billboard, the ads that work the best are ones where the 800 number is prominently displayed.

Additionally, it is important to have a well-trained, service-oriented sales representative available at all times, ideally 24/7. Customers call because they want assistance now, so representatives should avoid directing customers back to the company Web site. Deliver the assistance customers want and your company will create additional sales. Virtually everybody, regardless of age, has a cell phone with him or her at all times. The same cannot be said for Internet access, yet so many companies use their marketing to drive customers to a Web site where a phone number is difficult to find or non-existent.

To exemplify, in this challenging Real Estate market, I ran a full-page, full-color newspaper ad where the phone number was ten inches long by two inches high. That single newspaper ad generated seventy-three calls in one day! Our sales representative answered every one of the incoming calls and we sold thirty homes that day! Most companies would kill for those results. The key ingredients were the phone number and a responsive person at the other end of the phone line. Have your marketing efforts drive customers to a phone number and your company will sell more!

WRIGHT

Why are you also an advocate of same-day phone follow-up?

HAMILTON

In the event a salesperson is unsuccessful at motivating a customer to buy immediately, same-day follow-up is an important habit of presale service that leads to additional closed sales. Some trainers promote following-up after one day, others after two, and some after three days. Others suggest sending a video from an iPhone. I strongly believe that the best salespeople sell customers while they are hot, and they are hottest the first day they see your products. After the first day, customers begin to cool off. The longer salespeople wait to personally follow up, the less motivated they will find their customers.

Culturally, we as consumers are trained to think about buying decisions overnight. I believe many people, in fact, do sleep on their buying decisions. Even though a great salesperson is focused on motivating the customer to buy today, when customers leave without purchasing, I believe their wheels are turning about whether or not they want to move forward. Chances are they are still unsure because they have unanswered questions. This is not because the salesperson necessarily failed to answer any questions, but because the customer may not have thought to ask some questions while he or she was with the salesperson.

By picking up the phone the same day, ideally the salesperson reaches customer and gets a sense of the customer's thoughts and feelings about the salesperson's products. Second, this habit creates an opportunity for the salesperson to answer any additional questions the customer may have. Third, same-day follow-up gives the salesperson an extra opportunity to overcome any lingering objections. Last, reconnecting with the customer right away is one more positive interaction that affords the opportunity to close for the sale and schedule a return appointment to complete the purchase.

In my trainings, I teach salespeople how to complete a same-day follow-up call. I demonstrate by picking up the phone and conducting a mock follow-up call. I show them what to say and how to say it. This is an extremely effective way of teaching by example.

WRIGHT

How does high quality customer service create additional sales?

HAMILTON

Unparalleled customer service improves the quality of the buying experience a company creates for customers, not only before and during, but after the sale, as well. If you want to assess the strength and value of a company, determine how well it chooses to respond to manufacturing, quality, and customer problems. A company best demonstrates high quality service when it converts mistakes into opportunities to earn customer loyalty.

For example, a company that offers unparalleled customer service answers an 800 number 24/7 and the first person the customer talks to resolves the problem.

I had an experience with one such company, Zappos.com. Zappos is an online company whose trademark is Powered by Service. Its 800 number is displayed on every page of its Web site. I ordered a pair of shoes online. The shoes arrived the next day. I opened the box, and the shoes inside were not what I had ordered. They were the right size and the right style, but the wrong color. When I called the 800 number with my concern, I was not directed through a series of choices on the phone tree or referred from department to department. I reached a representative instantly who said, "I am sorry for the inconvenience, Miss Hamilton." He then sent me the right shoes free of charge via overnight delivery. He requested that I return the first pair of shoes within two weeks. He also e-mailed me the shipping label, saving me the inconvenience of searching through the company's Web site to print a return label. And he made me a VIP customer, which means I will receive free Next Day Air shipping on everything I purchase from the company, forever. Wow! Even if they treat everyone that way, it still made me feel special.

Within twenty-four hours, I had the second pair of shoes in the right color. They created the perfect buying experience from a mistake. This mistake turned into one of those happy accidents where a business endears itself to a customer for life. They trusted me to return the first pair of shoes without charging me for the second pair and gave me two weeks to do it. Now I trust Zappos to do the right thing. I am also a repeat customer and tell others about them. Out of curiosity, I asked the Zappos representative how long the company trains its employees. He informed me that Zappos trains its employees for seven weeks. And it shows!

Now, a pair of shoes is not the same as a high ticket item such as a car or a new home, but some valuable lessons can be learned from my experience. Is a customer's problem a problem or is it treated as an opportunity to do something exceptional? A company's mistake can turn into one of the best opportunities to create a customer for life. High quality service determines the difference between customers who purchase once and customers who purchase repeatedly, the difference between a short-term loss and a long-term gain, the difference between losing money and maximizing profit margins, and the difference between not meeting earnings expectations and exceeding earnings expectations.

A business can measure the results of its customer service in repeat business and referrals. Business and repeat referrals are the least expensive way to create an upward spiral of sales growth and maximum profits. A company offering unparalleled customer service is likely a company worth investing in!

WRIGHT

Are you saying that the "difference is in the details" when it comes to maximizing company profits?

HAMILTON

You've got it, David! Start by creating a commission only compensation plan designed to motivate your sales force to close with urgency which ties their success directly to the company's success. This compensation plan will result in eliminating poor performers and motivating others to improve their skills. Learn your salespeople's strengths and weaknesses and then provide sufficient training to motivate your team to meet or exceed their personal goals while they meet or exceed the company's goals.

Use all forms of marketing to drive potential customers to call your 800 number. Then have highly trained sales personnel who assist buyers in completing their purchases and solving their problems. This formula will result in an exceptional sales team that super charges sales and markedly improves your bottom line. My training, coaching, and sales rallies help companies develop the exceptional sales professionals they need.

WRIGHT

I am impressed. Today we've been talking to Christine Hamilton. If I were a salesperson trying to get by in today's tough economy or a sales manager attempting to get the most from my sales force, I would definitely hire you. It is clear to me that your training would make a real difference in their performance.

Christine, thank you so much for being with us today on *GPS for Success*.

HAMILTON

You are welcome, David. It has been my pleasure.

ABOUT THE AUTHOR

CHRISTINE HAMILTON is the past Division Vice President of Sales and Marketing for Beazer Homes (NYSE:BZH), a national top ten home-builder. During her tenure as vice president, she led the sales and marketing teams to consistently exceed sales and closing goals. Prior to executive management, she was the company's top-selling Certified Sales and Marketing Professional (CSP, CMP) and she also served as a Mortgage Loan Counselor. She is a three-time winner of Major Achievements in Marketing Excellence (MAME) Salesperson of the Year, and won Rookie of the Year during her first year in the homebuilding business.

Christine was also awarded the National Association of Home Builders (NAHB) Silver Award for National Salesperson of the Year for California and Nevada, as well as the NAHB Gold Award for the Best New Home Salesperson in the Nation.

Christine has twenty-seven years of sales and marketing experience spanning the home-building industry, resale Real Estate, automobiles, office equipment, skin care, and food products. She is the author of the book series *Sh*t HOTT Sales™: A Guide to Exceptional Salesmanship*. As an international speaker, trainer, sales coach, and author, her mission is to empower individuals and companies to succeed through maximizing sales.

CHRISTINE HAMILTON, CSP, CMP
SALES POWER SOLUTIONS
5510 Butte View Court
Rocklin, CA 95765
(877) 630-5525
CHamilton5525@aol.com
www.ChristineHamilton.com

CHAPTER FOUR
A Values-Based Approach

An interview with...
DR. STEPHEN R. COVEY

DAVID E. WRIGHT (WRIGHT)

We're talking today with Dr. Stephen R. Covey, cofounder and vice-chairman of Franklin Covey Company, the largest management company and leadership development organization in the world. Dr. Covey is perhaps best known as author of *The 7 Habits of Highly Effective People,* which is ranked as a number one best-seller by the *New York Times,* having sold more than fourteen million copies in thirty-eight languages throughout the world. Dr. Covey is an internationally respected leadership authority, family expert, teacher, and organizational consultant. He has made teaching principle-centered living and principle-centered leadership his life's work. Dr. Covey is the recipient of the Thomas More College Medallion for Continuing Service to Humanity and has been awarded four honorary doctorate degrees. Other awards given Dr. Covey include the Sikh's 1989 International Man of Peace award, the 1994 International Entrepreneur of the Year award, *Inc.* magazine's Services Entrepreneur of the Year award, and in 1996 the National Entrepreneur of the Year Lifetime Achievement award for Entrepreneurial leadership. He has also been recognized as one of *Time* magazine's twenty-five most influential Americans and one of *Sales and Marketing Management's* top twenty-five power brokers. As the father of nine and grandfather of forty-four, Dr. Covey received the 2003 National

Fatherhood Award, which he says is the most meaningful award he has ever received. Dr. Covey earned his undergraduate degree from the University of Utah, his MBA from Harvard, and completed his doctorate at Brigham Young University. While at Brigham Young he served as assistant to the President and was also a professor of Business Management and Organizational Behavior.

Dr. Covey, welcome to *GPS for Success: Goals and Proven Strategies.*

DR. STEPHEN COVEY (COVEY)

Thank you.

WRIGHT

Dr. Covey, most companies make decisions and filter them down through their organization. You, however, state that no company can succeed until individuals within it succeed. Are the goals of the company the result of the combined goals of the individuals?

COVEY

Absolutely—if people aren't on the same page, they're going to be pulling in different directions. To teach this concept, I frequently ask large audiences to close their eyes and point north, and then to keep pointing and open their eyes. They find themselves pointing all over the place. I say to them, "Tomorrow morning if you want a similar experience, ask the first ten people you meet in your organization what the purpose of your organization is and you'll find it's a very similar experience. They'll point all over the place." When people have a different sense of purpose and values, every decision that is made from then on is governed by those. There's no question that this is one of the fundamental causes of misalignment, low trust, interpersonal conflict, interdepartmental rivalry, people operating on personal agendas, and so forth.

WRIGHT

Is that primarily a result of an inability to communicate from the top?

COVEY

That's one aspect, but I think it's more fundamental. There's an inability to involve people—an unwillingness. Leaders may communicate what their mission and their strategy is, but that doesn't mean there's any emotional connection to it. Mission statements that are rushed and then announced are soon forgotten. They become nothing more than just a bunch of platitudes on the wall that mean essentially nothing and even create a source of cynicism and a sense of hypocrisy inside the culture of an organization.

WRIGHT

How do companies ensure survival and prosperity in these tumultuous times of technological advances, mergers, downsizing, and change?

COVEY

I think that it takes a lot of high trust in a culture that has something that doesn't change—principles—at its core. There are principles that people agree upon that are valued. It gives a sense of stability. Then you have the power to adapt and be flexible when you experience these kinds of disruptive new economic models or technologies that come in and sideswipe you. You don't know how to handle them unless you have something you can depend upon.

If people have not agreed to a common set of principles that guide them and a common purpose, then they get their security from the outside and they tend to freeze the structure, systems, and processes inside and they cease becoming adaptable. They don't change with the changing realities of the new marketplace out there and gradually they become obsolete.

WRIGHT

I was interested in one portion of your book, *The 7 Habits of Highly Effective People,* where you talk about behaviors. How does an individual go about the process of replacing ineffective behaviors with effective ones?

COVEY

I think that for most people it usually requires a crisis that humbles them to become aware of their ineffective behaviors. If there's not a crisis the tendency is to perpetuate those behaviors and not change.

You don't have to wait until the marketplace creates the crisis for you. Have everyone accountable on a 360-degree basis to everyone else they interact with—with feedback either formal or informal—where they are getting data as to what's happening. They will then start to realize that the consequences of their ineffective behavior require them to be humble enough to look at that behavior and to adopt new, more effective ways of doing things.

Sometimes people can be stirred up to this if you just appeal to their conscience—to their inward sense of what is right and wrong. A lot of people sometimes know inwardly they're doing wrong, but the culture doesn't necessarily discourage them from continuing that. They either need feedback from people or they need feedback from the marketplace or they need feedback from their conscience. Then they can begin to develop a step-by-step process of replacing old habits with new, better habits.

WRIGHT

It's almost like saying, "Let's make all the mistakes in the laboratory before we put this thing in the air."

COVEY

Right; and I also think what is necessary is a paradigm shift, which is analogous to having a correct map, say of a city or of a country. If people have an inaccurate paradigm of life, of other people, and of themselves it really doesn't make much difference what their behavior or habits or attitudes are. What they need is a correct paradigm—a correct map—that describes what's going on.

For instance, in the Middle Ages they used to heal people through bloodletting. It wasn't until Samuel Weiss and Pasteur and other empirical scientists discovered the germ theory that they realized for the first time they weren't dealing with the real issue. They realized why women preferred to use midwives who washed rather than doctors who didn't wash. They gradually got a new paradigm. Once you've got a new paradigm then your behavior and your attitude flow directly from it. If you have a bad paradigm or a bad map, let's say of a city, there's no way, no matter what your behavior or your habits or your attitudes are—how positive they are—you'll never be able to find the location you're looking for. This is why I believe that to change paradigms is far more fundamental than to work on attitude and behavior.

WRIGHT

One of your seven habits of highly effective people is to "begin with the end in mind." If circumstances change and hardships or miscalculations occur, how does one view the end with clarity?

COVEY

Many people think to begin with the end in mind means that you have some fixed definition of a goal that's accomplished and if changes come about you're not going to adapt to them. Instead, the "end in mind" you begin with is that you are going to create a flexible culture of high trust so that no matter what comes along you are going to do whatever it takes to accommodate that new change or that new reality and maintain a culture of high performance and high trust. You're talking more in terms of values and overall purposes that don't change, rather than specific strategies or programs that will have to change to accommodate the changing realities in the marketplace.

WRIGHT

In this time of mistrust among people, corporations, and nations, for that matter, how do we create high levels of trust?

COVEY

That's a great question and it's complicated because there are so many elements that go into the creating of a culture of trust. Obviously the most fundamental one is just to have trustworthy people. But that is not sufficient because what if the organization itself is misaligned?

For instance, what if you say you value cooperation but you really reward people for internal competition? Then you have a systemic or a structure problem that creates low trust inside the culture even though the people themselves are trustworthy. This is one of the insights of Edward Demming and the work he did. That's why he said that most problems are not personal—they're systemic. They're common caused. That's why you have to work on structure, systems, and processes to make sure that they institutionalize principle-centered values. Otherwise you could have good people with bad systems and you'll get bad results.

When it comes to developing interpersonal trust between people, it is made up of many, many elements such as taking the time to listen to other people, to understand them, and to see what is important to them. What we think is important to another may only be important to us, not to another. It takes empathy. You have to make and keep promises to them. You have to treat people with kindness and courtesy. You have to be completely honest and open. You have to live up to your commitments. You can't betray people behind their back. You can't badmouth them behind their back and sweet-talk them to their face. That will send out vibes of hypocrisy and it will be detected.

You have to learn to apologize when you make mistakes, to admit mistakes, and to also get feedback going in every direction as much as possible. It doesn't necessarily require formal forums—it requires trust between people who will be open with each other and give each other feedback.

WRIGHT

My mother told me to do a lot of what you're saying now, but it seems that when I got in business I simply forgot.

COVEY

Sometimes we forget, but sometimes culture doesn't nurture it. That's why I say unless you work with the institutionalizing—that means formalizing into structure, systems, and processing the values—you will not have a nurturing culture. You have to constantly work on that.

This is one of the big mistakes organizations make. They think trust is simply a function of being honest. That's only one small aspect. It's an important aspect, obviously, but there are so many other elements that go into the creation of a high-trust culture.

WRIGHT

"Seek first to understand then to be understood" is another of your seven habits. Do you find that people try to communicate without really understanding what other people want?

COVEY

Absolutely. The tendency is to project out of our own autobiography—our own life, our own value system—onto other people, thinking we know what they want. So we don't really listen to them. We pretend to listen, but we really don't listen from within their frame of reference. We listen from within our own frame of reference and we're really preparing our reply rather than seeking to understand. This is a very common thing. In fact, very few people have had any training in seriously listening. They're trained in how to read, write, and speak, but not to listen.

Reading, writing, speaking, and listening are the four modes of communication and they represent about two-thirds to three-fourths of our waking hours. About half of that time is spent listening, but it's the one skill people have not been trained in. People have had all this training in the other forms of communication. In a large audience of 1,000 people you wouldn't have more than twenty people who have had more than two weeks of training in listening. Listening is more than a skill or technique; you must listen within another's frame of reference. It takes tremendous courage to listen because you're at risk when you listen. You don't know what's going to happen; you're vulnerable.

WRIGHT

Sales gurus always tell me that the number one skill in selling is listening.

COVEY

Yes—listening from within the customer's frame of reference. That is so true. You can see that it takes some security to do that because you don't know what's going to happen.

WRIGHT

With this book we're trying to encourage people to be better, to live better, and be more fulfilled by listening to the examples of our guest authors. Is there anything or anyone in your life that has made a difference for you and helped you to become a better person?

COVEY

I think the most influential people in my life have been my parents. I think that what they modeled was not to make comparisons and harbor jealousy or to seek recognition. They were humble people.

I remember one time when my mother and I were going up in an elevator and the most prominent person in the state was also in the elevator. She knew him, but she spent her time talking to the elevator operator. I was just a little kid and I was so awed by the famous person. I said to her, "Why didn't you talk to the important person?" She said, "I was. I had never met him."

My parents were really humble, modest people who were focused on service and other people rather than on themselves. I think they were very inspiring models to me.

WRIGHT

In almost every research paper I've ever read, those who write about people who have influenced their lives include three teachers in their top-five picks. My seventh-grade English teacher was the greatest teacher I ever had and she influenced me to no end.

COVEY

Would it be correct to say that she saw in you probably some qualities of greatness you didn't even see in yourself?

WRIGHT

Absolutely.

COVEY

That's been my general experience—the key aspect of a mentor or a teacher is someone who sees in you potential that you don't even see in yourself. Those teachers/mentors treat you accordingly and eventually you come to see it in yourself. That's my definition of leadership or influence—communicating people's worth and potential so clearly that they are inspired to see it in themselves.

WRIGHT

Most of my teachers treated me as a student, but she treated me with much more respect than that. As a matter of fact, she called me Mr. Wright, and I was in the seventh grade at the time. I'd never been addressed by anything but a nickname. I stood a little taller; she just made a tremendous difference.

Do you think there are other characteristics that mentors seem to have in common?

COVEY

I think they are first of all good examples in their own personal lives. Their personal lives and their family lives are not all messed up—they come from a base of good character. They also are usually very confident and they take the time to do what your teacher did to you—to treat you with uncommon respect and courtesy.

They also, I think, explicitly teach principles rather than practices so that rules don't take the place of human judgment. You gradually come to have faith in your own judgment in making decisions because of the affirmation of such a mentor. Good mentors care about you—you can feel the sincerity of their caring. It's like the expression, "I don't care how much you know until I know how much you care."

WRIGHT

Most people are fascinated with the new television shows about being a survivor. What has been the greatest comeback that you've made from adversity in your career or your life?

COVEY

When I was in grade school I experienced a disease in my legs. It caused me to use crutches for a while. I tried to get off them fast and get back. The disease wasn't corrected yet so I went back on crutches for another year. The disease went to the other leg and I went on for another year. It essentially took me out of my favorite thing—athletics—and it took me more into being a student. So that was a life-defining experience, which at the time seemed very negative, but has proven to be the basis on which I've focused my life—being more of a learner.

WRIGHT

Principle-centered learning is basically what you do that's different from anybody I've read or listened to.

COVEY

The concept is embodied in the Far Eastern expression, "Give a man a fish, you feed him for the day; teach him how to fish, you feed him for a lifetime." When you teach principles that are universal and timeless, they don't belong to just any one person's religion or to a particular culture or geography. They seem to be timeless and universal like the ones we've been talking about here: trustworthiness, honesty, caring, service, growth, and development. These are universal principles. If you focus on these things, then little by little people become independent of you and then they start to believe in themselves and their own judgment becomes better. You don't need as many rules. You don't need as much bureaucracy and as many controls and you can empower people.

The problem in most business operations today—and not just business but non-business—is that they're using the industrial model in an information age. Arnold Toynbee, the great historian, said, "You can pretty well summarize all of history in four words: nothing fails like success." The industrial model was based on the asset of the machine. The information model is based on the asset of the person—the knowledge worker. It's an altogether different model. But the machine model was the main asset of the twentieth century. It enabled productivity to increase fifty times. The new asset is intellectual and social capital—the qualities of people and the quality of the relationship they have with each other. Like Toynbee said, "Nothing fails like success." The industrial model does not work in an information age. It requires a focus on the new wealth, not capital and material things.

A good illustration that demonstrates how much we were into the industrial model, and still are, is to notice where people are on the balance sheet. They're not found there. Machines are found there. Machines become investments. People are on the profit-and-loss statement and people are expenses. Think of that—if that isn't bloodletting.

WRIGHT

It sure is.

When you consider the choices you've made down through the years, has faith played an important role in your life?

COVEY

It has played an extremely important role. I believe deeply that we should put principles at the center of our lives, but I believe that God is the source of those principles. I did not invent them. I get credit sometimes for some of the Seven Habits material and some of the other things I've done, but it's really all based on principles that have been given by God to all of His children from the beginning of time. You'll find that you can teach these same principles from the sacred texts and the wisdom literature of almost any tradition. I think the ultimate source of that is God and that is one thing you can absolutely depend upon—"in God we trust."

WRIGHT

If you could have a platform and tell our audience something you feel would help them or encourage them, what would you say?

COVEY

I think I would say to put God at the center of your life and then prioritize your family. No one on their deathbed ever wished they had spent more time at the office.

WRIGHT

That's right. We have come down to the end of our program and I know you're a busy person. I could talk with you all day, Dr. Covey.

COVEY

It's good to talk with you as well and to be a part of this program. It looks like an excellent one that you've got going on here.

WRIGHT

Thank you.

We have been talking today with Dr. Stephen R. Covey, cofounder and vice-chairman of Franklin Covey Company. He's also the author of *The 7 Habits of Highly Effective People,* which has been ranked as a number one bestseller by the *New York Times,* selling more than fourteen million copies in thirty-eight languages.

Dr. Covey, thank you so much for being with us today.

COVEY

Thank you for the honor of participating.

ABOUT THE AUTHOR

STEPHEN R. COVEY was recognized in 1996 as one of *Time* magazine's twenty-five most influential Americans and one of *Sales and Marketing Management's* top twenty-five power brokers. Dr. Covey is the author of several acclaimed books, including the international bestseller, *The 7 Habits of Highly Effective People*, named the number one Most Influential Business Book of the Twentieth Century, and other best sellers that include *First Things First*, *Principle-Centered Leadership*, (with sales exceeding one million) and *The 7 Habits of Highly Effective Families*.

Dr. Covey's newest book, *The 8th Habit: From Effectiveness to Greatness*, which was released in November 2004, rose to the top of several bestseller lists, including *New York Times*, *Wall Street Journal*, *USA Today*, *Money*, *Business Week*, Amazon.com, and Barnes & Noble.

Dr. Covey currently serves on the board of directors for the Points of Light Foundation. Based in Washington, D.C., the Foundation, through its partnership with the Volunteer Center National Network, engages and mobilizes millions of volunteers from all walks of life—businesses, nonprofits, faith-based organizations, low-income communities, families, youth, and older adults—to help

DR. STEPHEN R. COVEY
www.stephencovey.com

CHAPTER FIVE

The Ultimate Competitive Advantage:

Turning the Art of Communications into the Science of Remarkable Results

An interview with...

BART QUEEN & GLENNA GRIFFIN

DAVID E. WRIGHT (WRIGHT)

Today we're talking with Bart Queen and Glenna Griffin. They are highly sought-after speakers, communication experts, and trainers.

Bart is CEO and Glenna is COO of Speak America and Ultimate PowerSpeak. Speak America is a national resource organization for "remarkability," dedicated to helping people create and live lives of intentional legacy. Speak America helps individuals through three key focus areas: ultimate "business speak," ultimate "life speak," and ultimate "youth speak." They believe the result of finding your voice and sharing your gift allows people to find their vocation. Ultimate PowerSpeak is the communications training arm of Speak America. Bart is a valued asset and resource in helping individuals and businesses around the world develop solid communication skills for their professional and personal success. In today's global economy environment, it has never been more important to have the competitive advantage. The ability to communicate your message clearly, concisely, and powerfully is your silver bullet.

Glenna is driven to encourage others to make positive choices and changes in their lives. The power of choice and the power of change can result in outstanding personal and professional success. Through personal and professional experience, Glenna encourages the development of personal communication skills for the discovery of an individual's true voice.

As founders of the Let Your Life Speak Foundation, Bart and Glenna travel the world sharing their communication skills. They recently took the Ultimate Power Speak communication skills to Kenya and worked with a women's political caucus group, high school students, and an orphanage. This global effort has now led to setting a goal of reaching five continents in five years and the launching of National Speak America, Youth Speak Programs. As colleagues, Bart and Glenna believe that when people find their voice and purpose, and have the ability to share that discovery with others, the world truly benefits from the gift.

Bart Queen, Glenna Griffin, welcome to *GPS for Success*.

BART QUEEN (QUEEN)

Thank you, David; it's an absolute pleasure to be with you today.

GLENNA GRIFFIN (GRIFFIN)

Thank you.

WRIGHT

So what are the current issues and complications of poor communication in business today?

QUEEN

David, I think that the foremost thing we're facing today is purely the amount of information coming at us. I know that you mentioned young people. Being able to find the information that is important today from all that is coming at us is extremely difficult. So the question is, with that much information how do you communicate in such a manner that people will remember you? How can you stand out and differentiate yourself? That ability to differentiate yourself today is the one thing that will help you rise to the top.

GRIFFIN

And not unlike what my son experiences with all of his multimedia, when we look to the workplace, we're dealing with conference calls, Web access, people stopping by our office, telephone calls, including text messages and e-mail popping up—all happening at the same time—the level of distraction is sky high. The ability to really focus on what truly makes a difference when we're communicating with somebody influences our personal and professional success in the workplace.

QUEEN

There are two major pieces to that, David. I think of how an individual communicates such as the way I do when running a meeting, giving a talk, or on the phone with a customer. I also think of how the whole organization communicates its message into the marketplace.

WRIGHT

Someone told me recently that he had so much information coming at him that he felt like he was sitting in front of an open fire hydrant with water coming at him while he was trying to drink with a straw.

GRIFFIN

That's a good analogy.

QUEEN

That's a tremendous analogy.

WRIGHT

So what are the top three consequences of poor communication in business and personally?

QUEEN

I think the number one complication for most folks personally is that they lose their ability to influence people. One of my favorite authors is John Maxwell. In his book *The 21 Irrefutable Laws of Leadership*, Mr. Maxwell wrote, "Leadership is nothing more or nothing less than pure influence." If you think about our ability to communicate today, it boils down to: how do I influence others, how do I motivate them to take the action I want them to take, how do I get people to listen to what I have to say if I'm selling something, and how do I communicate my message in such a manner that makes a difference?

An issue that was forefront in the news was a growing number of parents across the country were troubled by President Obama's plan to address elementary, middle, and high school students directly on September 8, 2009. It bothers me that people are concerned about having their children listen to their own nation's President, but it's a great example of the power of communication and what it can do when a message gets out there and is delivered properly. That is a great example of the power of influence through communication.

GRIFFIN

If there is this lack of influence on the personal front that transitions over to the professional front, and if we have the inability to influence people personally, one-on-one, that carries over to the business world. We're not being influential with our colleagues, our teams, our business partners, or our customers. So what is happening in our personal world also carries through to our professional world and our bottom lines are affected.

QUEEN

When I was first beginning to work with one of my clients, I asked the executives what the top three internal communication problems he is facing were. He said, "Two things: number one is that people who work in the organization don't know how to communicate who the company is and number two is they don't know what the company does."

"Well," I said, "what's the major problem externally—outside of your company?"

"As a result of the way we communicate internally," he replied, "the marketplace is confused about the true value that our organization brings to the table."

I actually walked through his business and spoke to five different people. I asked each one of them a very simple question, "What is it that you do, and how do you explain who you are?" I got five different answers. Inconsistency of a message can bring a company down more quickly than anything else because they don't get the kind of mental real estate that their leadership is looking for.

Most companies don't want to take the time to help their employees understand what the top benefits the company brings to the table are and how they express themselves to get potential customers to want more information.

You and I both know that you have about thirty seconds to engage someone. The other interesting statistic that we just came across was that on average, 50 percent of whatever you say will be forgotten. So if 50 percent of whatever I say when I teach a class is going to be forgotten, the question then becomes how do we get people to remember more. We don't have to tell them more—we want them to remember more. But we don't focus on that.

WRIGHT

So why is strategic communication critical to business and personal success?

QUEEN

It is truly the one thing that separates someone from everybody else. Here are a couple of great examples. I'm going to give you a saying and I want you to tell me if you recognize who it is. The first is, "Can you hear me now?" The answer is Verizon. Just in that simple saying, it is evident that Verizon owns our mind. We automatically think of them when we hear that question. Now, that's what I call mental real estate. Here's another one: "Where's the beef?" The answer is Wendy's. Now you and I both know that ad is over twenty-five years old, but today, when I'm in class and ask that question, even young people answer, "Oh, that's Wendy's."

Now here's one from a newscaster. See if you recognize this: "And that's the way it is."

WRIGHT

Cronkite.

QUEEN

Right. Now, here's another: "The rest of the story." Do you know who is famous for that line?

WRIGHT

Paul Harvey.

QUEEN

That type of simple communication of what I call a "seven-factor phrase"—something that you say over and over again—creates mental real estate that stays in people's minds. Think about President Bush and John Kerry. President Bush said that Kerry "flip-flopped on issues." Now, some people may question President Bush's ability to communicate, but in that particular case President Bush won. He stayed on message and flip-flop is what you remember. Obama did the same thing when he said, "It's time for change." He stayed on message and he stayed on track; it was powerful. If you look at some of the other people who were running for office during the 2008 presidential campaign, you can't really remember their core message. Again it comes back to how do I get you to remember more? That takes effort.

If you look up the definition of "strategy," the root word is the Greek word *strategos*, meaning "general." Very few of us take an approach to our communication as a general does. It doesn't matter how many guns we've got or how many men we've got, it's a matter of how we out-strategize the enemy. Take that application to people out there in the sales field—how do they out-strategize the competition in articulating their message differently? We're just not willing to make that kind of effort.

WRIGHT

Will you share with our readers some key goals in communicating successfully?

QUEEN

Absolutely. In my experience, I believe there are three major roles: 1) you have to be able to build trust. If I could write the script for people when they come into their jobs, when they're spending time with their family, when they're with their friends, with their colleagues, and with their customers, the number one thing we have to build is trust. When I work with sales teams, the typical salesperson will sell the company. They then sell the product, tools, solution, or service, and then they sell themselves. But, David, that's not how you and I buy. You and I buy the person first! Then we buy the solution, tool, or product, and we then get the company. If salespeople are selling the product, then the company, and then themselves, they're selling in the wrong order—they're communicating in the wrong order.

I just recently bought a wagon from a gentleman in Canada, sight unseen. I had one conversation with the gentleman on the phone. I absolutely trusted the man because of the way he handled himself on the phone. The number one thing we have to do is build trust.

GRIFFIN

That's related to more than just the sales environment in the business world. All of our relationships—human resources, accounting, marketing, prospective clients, employees, departments, teams—everything we do is built on that fundamental principle of trust. If trust is not there, companies aren't going to be functioning as they should be.

QUEEN

We can even look at keynoters. If those people on stage can get people in the audience to think, "I'm just like them. We share a similar experience," I begin to trust them. The more I trust them, the more I buy into the information that they are sharing with me.

The second key major goal is to build relationships. I am willing to "die on the hill" for this one. I am amazed at companies today when they put an executive up on a stage. They spend thousands of dollars to get their customers in front of the executive. Here is what typically happens (you've probably seen this happen before): The executive gets up on stage, a ton of lights are on the executive's face, and then the auditorium is darkened. How does the executive build a relationship with the listeners if he or she can't see them? You and I don't send our children to school and let them sit in the dark. You and I don't go to a service of faith and sit in the dark—we want to connect with the person who is sharing information with us. Why do we darken the room in business? One of the reasons I think we do it in business is because we let PowerPoint or whatever we're going to put up on a screen be our focus instead of the person who is sharing information. We lose contact with our customers and our guests when we do that.

GRIFFIN

The other reason I think we've lost it in the business environment is the power of getting a video shot of the speaker. So you have an audience of a thousand people who is listening to an executive or keynote speaker in person. There is an opportunity to build a relationship front and center but for the sake of sending out a video with a hope that someone will watch it, the room is darkened and the connection to the audience is lost. You're losing the immediate effect of the speaker who wants to share what he or she has learned. Connecting with the audience is lost for the sake of a potential video production. That's unfortunate.

QUEEN

Glenna and I see this often where someone is trying to serve two audiences. If you are going to create a training tape of some sort, you'd go into a studio with maybe a mock audience and deliver the information in such a manner that it would be recorded for viewing.

GRIFFIN

It's a production.

QUEEN

Right. Most the time, organizations are trying to serve two audiences—a live audience and an audience who will view a recording/videotape. You can only serve one audience at a time. Unfortunately, you sacrifice the live audience for some other type of an audience as Glenna just mentioned.

GRIFFIN

It goes back to losing that moment of influence and that opportunity for influence because you're trying to do too much at one time.

WRIGHT

And number three?

QUEEN

Number three is engagement. What I mean by engagement is the ability to get the listener to respond, listen, and interact. If we can accomplish those things in any office, in a meeting, giving a talk, giving a presentation, doing a PlaceWare session, a webcast, a conference call, we'll win. Most of us do what I have found to be more of a speaker's approach instead of a listener's approach to engagement. How do I as a speaker put listeners in the palm of my hand? How do I get them saying, "Bart, tell me more," not looking at their watches thinking, "When will this be over; how much longer will this take?" We've all sat through presentations like those.

WRIGHT

So what does that communication process look like?

QUEEN

I think there are four major components. Think of a circle. In the center of the circle we'll write the words "communication process." At the very top of that would be "development"—what's the development of the message? How do you create it? How are you going to craft it? How are you going to boil it down to the key concepts that you want to deliver? Once the content has been developed, you move into how do you deploy it? The deployment component has two pieces to it: how do I get it out there? In the sales example, the question would be: how do I get the information out about our new solution, tool, or product in such a manner that customers can use it in their communication situations? Then the second piece to deployment might be an event, a meeting, or conference that you are deploying the information to.

From there we move into the whole delivery piece: How do I deliver the message and how do I deliver it congruently? You and I both know that if the delivery of the message and the content doesn't match, people aren't going to buy what you have to say. The percentage of what you and I would probably call body language—what people actually see—is extremely high. Most of us believe it's all content-based, but studies show that it comes to delivery.

Then, last but not least is how do you sustain your information, how do you keep it fresh, and how do you keep it updated? That takes us right back to the development of the information. Most companies spend all their time on the delivery of the information. They very rarely spend any time on the proper development of the information or key tools that will allow them to deploy in an effective manner.

GRIFFIN

You can see where the development, deployment, delivery and sustaining really comes back to that strategic communication we talked about at the beginning. Everything is very strategic and in line with the overall end goal in mind.

WRIGHT

So what are the three strategic areas to be aware of?

QUEEN

When we talk about this we're really bringing it back down to an individual. The three core areas to pay attention to when anybody is delivering a piece of information are within the delivery of the information. Here we're specifically talking about a lot of body language issues—eye contact, posture, gestures, facial expression, what we call vocal variety, volume, speed, inflection, and the ability to pause, or get rid of your ums and ahs.

The second key area, then, is around knowledge or content. How do you craft your information in such a manner that it makes a difference?

Then third, how do I interact with the people I'm speaking with? How do I keep that engagement high? How do I use whiteboards, chalkboards, flip charts, handouts, PowerPoint, overheads, or other media? Those three areas—your delivery, your content and knowledge, and then your ability to interact—are the three things that you've really got to keep an eye on.

Now those three things only came to light out of my experience with what I call two key "filters." The first filter is being listener-focused, not being speaker-focused. A quick example for that would involve understanding cultural differences. I can look at my audience for three to five seconds, which is acceptable in a western style of communicating. If Glenna and I happen to be in a classic Asian country that has not been westernized, that kind of eye contact should be only one to three seconds, not our standard three to five. If we went into parts of the Middle East (leaving Glenna out of this just for the moment, as a she is a woman), keeping it between men, eye contact should be anywhere from five to eight minutes—it's a lot longer. The rule of thumb then begins with all the three core strategic areas: you have to be listener focused and it's going to vary in every single situation that you're in.

The second key filter is perception versus reality. This is the one where students in our class really struggle the most. For example, we'll get someone, for example, a man, to stand, balanced on his feet, which is about two to three inches apart. Now, his first reaction is to say, "Bart, I feel like I'm really stiff. I feel like I'm a soldier" or "I'm going to fall over." But we'll ask the class, "How does he look?" They'll say, "Wow, he looks really confident. He looks open. He looks approachable." Yet the student repeats his reaction that he feels really horrible. This brings us back to our mantra: *Don't go with how it feels, go with the impact that it creates.* If people will use that perception versus reality concept, and ignore the effect of how it feels, they'll always make the right choice in the way they communicate.

Everything we share in our program is based on those five core principles—the three areas that you need to be aware of and the two key filters.

WRIGHT

So what is the difference between "mind share competition" and "mental real estate"?

GRIFFIN

We talked a little bit about mental real estate when we were talking about Verizon, Wendy's, Paul Harvey, Walter Cronkite—all of those advertising campaigns and individuals that own some mental real estate in our minds. Another cell phone company would have a very difficult task trying to imitate Verizon because the phrase, "Can you hear me now?" is so embedded in our minds and connected to the Verizon brand.

QUEEN

Individuals create mental real estate. There are many times when we're in class and I'll say, "Okay class, we have an opportunity to listen to President Obama speak. Who wants to go?" The class members will all raise their hands. We have no idea what he going to say, but because he owns mental real estate in our mind we're willing to go listen to him.

Now, in a business perspective, many of us may get a meeting request via Outlook and we might think, "Oh, do I have to go to this meeting?" We think it's going to be boring. Somebody else may send out a meeting request, and you think, "Wow, I can't wait to go to that! It's going to be awesome." The difference is mental real estate. Mind share competition is what you're competing with. When you are sharing information, what else is on your listener's mind?

GRIFFIN

Those things can be personal, professional. It can involve the temperature of the room and it can be all kinds of things.

QUEEN

We get a lot of students in class and as soon as you tell them that they can't look at their BlackBerrys or have their laptops open, we're competing with their desire to use them. I'm sure that you've sat in thousands of meetings where someone pulled out his or her BlackBerry when a speaker is making a presentation. That's mind share competition. How do I compete with that? The average adult's listening span is only about four to six minutes; therefore, every four to six minutes we've got to change it up. I've had leaders in companies who will say they're going to do a four-hour demonstration for a customer, and I think, "Are you crazy? Who can stay focused on technology for four hours? It's just not possible. People can barely stay focused on a thirty-minute sitcom."

Sitcoms are truly a good standard for keeping people's attention. They typically run for about four to six minutes, and then there is an advertisement. Then there it runs again for four to six minutes and there's another advertisement. They know very clearly that in order to keep the viewer engaged, in that thirty minutes they're going to have to break it up a little bit. We need to take the same kind of principles used in television and apply them to our communication. How do I keep people engaged? How do I keep them interested? How do I reduce mind share competition as much as I possibly can? You will never, hit zero; it's just not possible.

WRIGHT

So what's the difference in communication style and communication skills?

GRIFFIN

From my perspective, I believe that they go hand in hand. Everybody has an individual communication style. For example, I would never encourage somebody who isn't a particularly funny person to try to be humorous. Everybody has his or her own individual style. Using good communication skills can enhance people's particular style. Everybody can learn the skills sets that create the muscle memory when communicating so that those skills sets can be applied to individual personal styles. That's when you can rock the world with your ability to influence.

QUEEN

Based on what Glenna just shared, here's an example that I think most would recognize. We'll talk about Bill Clinton and, just for the moment, leave politics out of the scenario. Most of the time when I ask a class what their perception is of Bill Clinton as a communicator, they say he's very solid, very charismatic. Bill Clinton very effectively demonstrates the communication skills that we teach in class. Then, on the other side of the coin, let's look at someone like Colin Powell. Most people would say that Colin Powell is more stoic, he's more serious, he's very deliberate in his approach, and exhibits the skills just as well as Bill Clinton, but their styles are distinctly different.

GRIFFIN

And you wouldn't ask one to imitate the other one's style, it wouldn't work.

QUEEN

Often, in class, someone will say, "Well, Bart, right now we all look the same." I reply, "You should all look the same right now until you tweak and twist those skills to match your style."

David, if you and I went to take a golf lesson from a golf pro, and we'd never golfed before, that pro would teach you and me how to hold the club exactly the same way. Six months from now, if you and I really embraced the game, you would probably hold your club slightly differently than I would hold it. This is because we each have developed our own individual style.

We still have to base everything on solid communication principles. We can then develop our own style.

WRIGHT

So what is the number one thing that will make an immediate difference in anyone's communication style?

QUEEN

This concept is simple but we have gotten so far away from it—eye contact. The illustration I give in class is if people were seated around a Thanksgiving table or a dinner table, they would be looking people in the eye when they're having a conversation. When a young child six or seven comes up to you (you'll remember this when your children were little) and they pulled on your shirt sleeve and said, "Dad, Dad, Dad, Dad," that child doesn't stop until you look at him or her. Little children have the concept of eye contact down tremendously. As we get older we learn the extremes—we learn intimidation and intimacy. I believe that as a result of this, we break away from eye contact and we don't engage in a conversation as well.

You've seen this happen. Somebody gets up in front of a group and does what I call "eye spray"—the person looks across the room but is not really connected to anyone. So now take that eye spray and come back to my example of a dinner conversation at the table. You wouldn't eye spray the table saying, "How's your dinner?" You would look someone in the eye and say, for example, "Glenna, how's your dinner?" or "David, what did you think of the prime rib?" You would give eye contact.

The greatest benefit to using eye contact properly is that it gets rid of the ums and ahs. It is one of the neatest little "secrets" that very few people know. You and I are both looking at people when we speak. You and I have heard you shouldn't use ums and ahs, but very few people are taught how to eliminate them. If you would put eye contact in place and if your basic rule of thumb is only speak when you're looking at a set of eyes, you will be amazed at how much more clear your speech becomes, how much more effective it becomes, and how much the retention level goes up for your listeners.

WRIGHT

So what are the top three content tips that will allow me to stand out above all the rest?

QUEEN

Well, one of the very first ones is short sentences. The average person uses medium to long sentences and as a result, the listener can't keep up with it. David, have you ever heard someone give an answer to a question and he or she spoke so long you couldn't remember what the question was?

WRIGHT

Right.

QUEEN

It's the same kind of an idea. Now here is that perception versus reality example again. If I get you to use short to medium sentences, your typical response to me would be, "Bart, I sound like I'm talking to a two-year-old. I sound like the books I read when I was a kid—'See Jane run,' 'Watch spot follow.'" Remember those, David?

WRIGHT

Oh yes.

QUEEN

That's what it's going to sound like to us as we share the information. But listeners think, "Wow, I can keep up with that. That makes sense. I understand what you just said."

GRIFFIN

That goes back to the "don't go with how it feels; go with the impact it creates!"

QUEEN

Absolutely.

The second key point is you've got to reduce the amount of information. You and I both know that "the rule of three" is one of the number one rules to follow. I am constantly telling people no more than three or four key points because people just can't remember more than that. Getting those key points to be three things that are simple, memorable, and repeatable will make a world of difference in having the listener(s) retain the information you are sharing.

WRIGHT

Simple, memorable, and what was the third?

QUEEN

The third was repeatable.

I just worked with an executive who was prepping for a Forbes conference. He decided to use King Kong as his grabber to open his talk. He was only going to speak for ten minutes, but he thought that King Kong and risk had a lot in common. His key points, as he developed his talk, were that people need to assess the risk, to plan for that risk, and then execute the plan. He created the acronym APE to help the audience remember the concepts—Assess, Plan, and Execute. Using those three principles is how you get the ape off your back. So his key points were his opening grabber. They were simple, repeatable, and memorable. To this day, he still has executives calling him and asking him if he can help them with the planning part or with the executing part. It makes a world of difference to how much people can remember.

GRIFFIN

It creates the mental real estate!

QUEEN

Absolutely; one of the biggest benefits is that mental real estate.

The last key delivery tip or content tip that helps you stand out is the use of stories, analogies, quotes, and pictorials. People will remember a story before they'll remember a data dump. How we tell those stories can make a world of difference. As for working with executives or engineers or salespeople, we'll remind them that their story really shouldn't take more than about a minute and a half. After that, they're going to lose their listeners.

So how is it possible to boil a story down to where it's clear, it's to the point, it's repeatable, I can share it, and create the kind of effect that I'm interested in. If we could just remember those three things: shorter sentences, no more than three or four key points to whatever we're sharing, and make sure we have laced stories, analogies, quotes, and references throughout our information, our influence would be doubled.

WRIGHT

I get a lot of questions in my workshops on the visuals. Speakers wonder if they should use visuals. How do I make visuals work for me and not against me?

QUEEN

The very first thing I would point out is a small study by the University of Illinois. Researchers found that those who use visual aids are 85 percent more effective than those who do not. Our question isn't whether we use visual aids or not, the question is how we use those visual aids.

David, I'm sure you've been in a business meeting where someone walked in the door, started the meeting, turned out the lights, and brought up a PowerPoint program. The first thing you and I did is go to sleep; it just gives you license to go to sleep.

How do you create visuals that keep whoever is sharing the information the center of attention? How do I use those visuals to enhance what I'm trying to say, and not be the center of attention? I don't have any quarrels with PowerPoint; I have more quarrels with how people use PowerPoint than PowerPoint itself. Most people use PowerPoint as their notes, not as a visual aid for their listeners.

When we're using PowerPoint, two paradigm shifts have to happen. Most people bring up the first visual and they immediately begin to speak. The challenge with this is that the audience members are trying to absorb the information on the visual, yet the person giving the presentation is speaking. As your listener, I can only do one thing—I can either take in a visual or I can listen to you. So the first paradigm shift is that the speaker has to give the listeners a moment to absorb what was on the visual.

The second paradigm shift I must make is to let the listeners know what is coming. Most people bring up a PowerPoint visual and then immediately begin to speak about it because they don't know what is coming and they have to look at the visual to know what they're going to say. Someone who uses PowerPoint strategically knows what visual is coming up next and leads you, the listener, to it. It is almost like they've taken you by the hand and said, "Walk with me, David. Let me lead you," as compared to saying, "David, let me push you through the information."

Those two simple things make a world of difference in their PowerPoint presentations.

GRIFFIN

I think one of the problems is that as people prepare to make a presentation, they will think, "Wow, I have this wonderful PowerPoint presentation. I spent two weeks developing it." We say, "Okay, how long have you spent working on what you're going to say?" The answer usually is, "I haven't started that part yet." It's the wrong process—they're putting the cart before the horse. How you're going to interact and what the message is to the audience should to be crafted prior to the presentation. But we have just become so accustomed to PowerPoint that we've got the process reversed.

WRIGHT

So tell me, what is the ultimate communication?

QUEEN

The ultimate communication is something that Speak America really tries to accomplish with all the people we work with. Our term for it is "letting their life speak." Today we've spent a lot of time talking about how we make our message more powerful, how we make sure that our delivery is congruent with our message, how we answer questions, use visuals, and how to be strategic. But the ultimate communication we're really striving for is when your whole life speaks—when everything you do and how you live your life speaks to the world. That's where you can live out your purpose. When you live out your purpose you get to share your gift, you have the ability to communicate that gift. Your gift is not only your message, but it's your life. Those are the things that create the ultimate communication.

GRIFFIN

When you're letting your life speak, you are truly able to influence people and that's where we started the conversation—talking about the power of influence. When you are influencing others personally, you're influencing others professionally too, and everybody reaps the benefit of that.

WRIGHT

Well, what an interesting conversation. I could listen to you all day long. I wish we had the time to keep on with this topic of communication. The information you've shared is not only necessary but interesting as well. I really appreciate all the time both of you have spent with me to answer these questions. I think our readers are going to get a lot out of this chapter; I know I have.

QUEEN

David, it's been an absolute pleasure speaking with you today.

GRIFFIN

Wonderful experience!

WRIGHT

Today we've been talking with Bart Queen and Glenna Griffin. Bart is the Founder and CEO of Ultimate Power Speak. He's a valued asset and resource in helping individuals and businesses around the world develop communication skills for their professional and personal success.

Glenna, COO of Ultimate Power Speak, is driven to encourage others to make positive choices and changes in their lives. As colleagues, they believe that when people find their voice and purpose and have the ability to share that discovery with others, the world truly benefits from the gift. I think I agree with that, and I think our readers will too.

Bart, Glenna, thank you so much for being with us today on *GPS for Success*.

GRIFFIN

Thank you, David.

QUEEN

Thanks, David.

ABOUT THE AUTHORS

BART QUEEN and GLENNA GRIFFIN are highly sought-after speakers, communication experts, and trainers.

Bart is CEO and Glenna is COO of Speak America and Ultimate PowerSpeak. Speak America is a national resource organization for "remarkability," dedicated to helping people create and live lives of intentional legacy. Speak America helps individuals through three key focus areas: ultimate "business speak," ultimate "life speak," and ultimate "youth speak." They believe the result of finding your voice and sharing your gift allows people to find their vocation. Ultimate PowerSpeak is the communication training arm of Speak America. Bart, the Founder and CEO of Ultimate Power Speak, is a valued asset and resource in helping individuals and businesses around the world develop solid communication skills for their professional and personal success. In today's global economy environment, it has never been more important to have the competitive advantage. The ability to communicate your message clearly, concisely, and powerfully is your silver bullet.

Glenna is driven to encourage others to make positive choices and changes in their lives. The power of choice and the power of change can result in outstanding personal and professional success. Through personal and professional experience, Glenna encourages the development of personal communication skills for the discovery of an individual's true voice.

As founders of the Let Your Life Speak Foundation, Bart and Glenna travel the world sharing their communication skills. They recently took the Ultimate Power Speak communication skills to Kenya and worked with a women's political caucus group and high school students in an orphanage. This global effort has now led to setting a goal of reaching five continents in five years and the launching of National Speak America, Youth Speak Programs. As colleagues, Bart and Glenna believe that when people find their voice and purpose, and have the ability to share that discovery with others, the world truly benefits from the gift.

BART QUEEN

P.O. Box 80335

Raleigh NC 27623

866-609-2333

www.SpeakAmerica.com

www.UltimatePowerSpeak.com

GLENNA GRIFFIN

P.O. Box 80335

Raleigh NC 27623

866-609-2333

www.SpeakAmerica.com

www.UltimatePowerSpeak.com

CHAPTER SIX

Goals + Planning = Success

An interview with...

KATHRYN JORDAN

DAVID E. WRIGHT (WRIGHT)

Today we're talking with Kathryn Jordan. Kathryn is lead consultant for The Success Associates. In addition, she is the director of Academic Engagement and Career Services at Radford University. Before assuming this role in higher education, Dr. Jordan was the Virginia Managing Consultant for Drake, Beam, Morin, the country's leading provider of human resources consulting services to corporations. In addition to her work as a corporate consultant and higher education administration, Kathryn is a veteran employment expert and pioneer of online human resource solutions. Her background includes specializing in executive level career management.

Kathryn is a strong proponent of the value of self-assessment as a major building block for a proactive career management strategy. She is a nationally certified career counselor and holds memberships in such professional organizations as the American Counseling Association and the National Association of Colleges and Employers. She has been active in the business world as a member of the Board of Directors of the Chamber of Commerce, a member of the Society of Human Resource managers, and as President of Main Street Radford. As a graduate faculty member of Radford University, she has taught students about the career counseling profession, authored numerous articles, and made countless presentations.

Dr. Jordan, welcome to *GPS for Success*.

KATHY JORDAN (JORDAN)

I'm delighted to be here today.

WRIGHT

How did you formulate your principles for success?

JORDAN

The principles began to emerge into patterns during my twenty years of career consulting. As I helped people reach their career objectives, I also began listening to people's stories about their lives. I heard in these life stories some similarities as each explained, for example, why they were so happy at work or why they were unhappy in their personal lives. Many talked about what life decisions made the critical difference to their career success.

The career principles we are discussing today are really the results of years of listening to both people's career narratives and their life stories. Since I grew up in a Scots-Irish heritage where the tradition of storytelling is a means of communicating about important personal themes, I knew those life stories and common themes contained critical points that everyone could use.

WRIGHT

You've had twenty years of experience, from the boardroom to the manufacturing setting, right?

JORDAN

That is right, and I have worked with and listened to people in all walks of life. These were people who were in the early development of their career as well as those who had achieved some outstanding successes. So the secrets I am getting ready to share are definitely ideas from a diverse population such as chief executives, service employees, people working in manufacturing settings, college administrators, students, ex-military, and former stay-at-home-mothers.

WRIGHT

What are the major concepts upon which you have based your principles?

JORDAN

First, the most important thing is that people who clearly understood who they were and what was important to them were also the people most likely to feel some clear satisfaction with their careers. They could tell me what they had accomplished, and why they were successful. Early on I realized that understanding yourself and being able to establish your goals were critical themes.

The next thing I began to notice was that people who were always prepared by continually developing their resume, collecting samples of their work, and developing a professional portfolio were the same people who could easily talk about their accomplishments. These people were prepared, confident, and able to take advantage of an unexpected career opportunity whenever it came along.

In contrast, other people talked about how it was twenty years, fifteen years, five years, since they had been in the search for a job, and they were too busy with day-to-day life to be prepared. These people were also unclear about how to find a job.

For example, it had been so long since they found a job they did not understand the importance of technology in a contemporary search process. It turns out that it is critical for everyone to stay current about how to actually find a job and to be ready to look for another job at any moment.

The last theme I recognized was that almost invariably, successful people talked extensively about their networking relationships. They attributed a lot of their success to the fact that they had a mentor early in their life. They were able to develop personal, close relationships that led to a particular job step or even to an idea that helped develop a new business concept. The final theme then is the importance of developing personal relationships throughout all parts of life and how important strategic business networking can be to career and work success.

WRIGHT

How does someone begin to achieve this career success?

JORDAN

I mentioned previously that some people are intentional and very thoughtful when they begin a career. For instance, they take a moment to analyze how their education can fit into the job market and what organizations are good targets. People who have a plan for their careers usually get there. However, I also learned that at least 50 percent of us are in a career or a work location by happenstance, fate, or chance. We found a job that was available at the time we were looking. It turns out that those people who have a plan for themselves do get ahead more quickly and more efficiently than those who leave their careers to luck and chance.

As people move forward in their careers, they tend to get on the "fast track" of life. They are so busy with life and work that they neglect to take a moment to step back and think about what is great about the job or what they need to learn so they can go to the next level.

The first real secret to career success is that everyone needs to build time into their busy schedules for periodic self-reflection. This should include thinking about what is important to them, what their values are, what they are really interested in, what their skills are, and what they really have accomplished.

One way to start this process is to ask a best friend, a spouse, and/or someone who knows you very well to describe you in two key words. What would they say about you? With that beginning point, expand the two key words into a full-blown self-reflection. Write a career and personal vision statement for yourself. I suggest that everyone needs to do this for themselves at least once a year, and that it is very, very important for achieving success!

WRIGHT

Good point. I think most companies try to do that on their annual report.

JORDAN

They do, and then interestingly, their CEOs do not take the time to do this kind of planning for themselves.

WRIGHT

Exactly. I think it is more geared for management down than for CEOs.

What is the primary component that an individual needs to have for career success?

JORDAN

Probably first and foremost in all of those life stories of men and women—from people who worked in the service industries to manufacturing settings, from people who were CEOs and everyone in between—the most common denominator was that they were confident. They all had a positive self-image; they believed that they were good. What I understood was that if you don't believe in yourself, nobody else would either. No one will hire you or promote you if you do not first know and project that you can do the job successfully.

So it is critical for achieving success to stay positive about yourself. This leads itself to another important point I heard in my conversations. Even if people find themselves in a negative economic climate or organization culture, it is critical to stay positive if they want to be successful. If, for example, people are having problems at home, they must stay positive in a work environment. Just as it is very important to feel good about yourself, it is important to also feel good about where you are working. Even if you don't feel something positive, absolutely don't say anything negative about your work environment.

WRIGHT

How does one deal with the current upheaval in jobs, unemployment, and the global marketplace?

JORDAN

The last six months have definitely been interesting. However, if you look back at the last ten years, the workplace has been in a constant state of change. It is important for all of us to be "change ready," and to recognize that change is a constant in life. The workplace predictions coming from the career futurists predict that most workers are going to have nine jobs and at least three major career shifts during the course of a lifetime. It is very important for people to be resilient and to know that if an employer announced a merger next week, their resume is ready to go! Always have the work portfolio ready to go, and know where the next good job fit or next step is.

This is particularly true in a recruiting season when employers say they are going to hire 22 percent fewer employees than the year before and when the national unemployment rate is increasing and may hit 12 percent or more. Also, with a recession here or on the horizon, people who are "change ready" must be able to adapt their goals. Think about taking a steppingstone job until the ideal comes available.

The job on Wall Street may be a possibility in the future but not immediately. The goal in a turbulent economic climate is to find a job that will build skills and could ultimately lead to other opportunities in the future. So the secret to dealing with change, upheaval, or economic recession is to embrace change and not run from it.

WRIGHT

Is there a single guide that everyone needs to incorporate in coping with career changes?

JORDAN

Yes. In fact, I was speaking to a group of about forty people yesterday and that was one question that came up several times. The ability to embrace change of course, as I have said, is important, especially since we do not really know what job titles will be in demand in the next ten years. The predictions are that even the ways that work and jobs are done will be different in ten years because of the rate of emerging technologies.

To remain employable, the successful person will embrace change, remain confident, *and always be willing to participate in continuing education.* The successful career path will include on the job training or it might include taking an extra class after work. Everyone, no matter what our age or role or life stage, needs to be willing to go back to the classroom and get additional training. This is exactly how people will stay employed. Embrace the notion that everyone can learn and be positive about continuing to grow at every life stage. It can be exciting because it provides opportunities when you build new skills.

A few years ago I spoke to a gentleman who had been a machinist all of his work life. He talked to me about the time when he was asked to learn new computer skills because the lathe machines were now being run by computers. He had originally been reluctant to think about going back to school at age fifty, but by moving forward and taking some classes at the local community college, this man ensured his continuing success. He set himself up for security in his employment role.

Even in fields with high demand like the healthcare field and meeting the needs of a society with an aging population, most nurses in clinical settings will be required to go back for periodic recertification hours. The same is true for teachers and many other fields. Continuing education is setting people up for remaining employed in their field, and it turns out that successful people are never done learning!

WRIGHT

How does one know what jobs and skill sets will be in demand?

JORDAN

Everyone must take responsibility for their career and try to become something of an economic futurist. The nurse and the machinist must read the business news whether it is online or in the paper. Understand the changes affecting your career area. Talk to people about their work and ask questions to find out what is influencing that industry. Your goal is to never be in an industry that is in full decline. If you are in one of these fields, you know there will be fewer and fewer opportunities. I advise everyone, including those individuals not particularly interested in the business world, that everyone's career area will be influenced by the economy. We all owe it to ourselves to at least understand the business headlines and how that translates into our own areas of work.

For example, for the last twenty years there have been articles about the decline in the manufacturing sector, and that the economy of the United States was experiencing a technology boom that was revolutionizing work.

We read about the information exchange revolution; however, many did not want to understand the scope of these changes and just how much this would influence their own workplaces.

So the secret to success is that all of us need to understand these economic and workplace trends, and it is important to be on the front end of understanding those changes in our work environments instead of on the receiving end.

WRIGHT

If people have aspirations for upward mobility in their company, or organization, or field, what skills should they acquire?

JORDAN

Initially, I noticed upward mobility was blocked for many women who were passed over for promotions. In my conversations with them they had not acquired the appropriate managerial or leadership skills to compete effectively for the promotions they wanted. However, in the last ten to fifteen years the "glass ceiling" concept has begun to fade. I have worked with both men and women who were searching for promotions to the next level and upward promotions.

The secret is you can keep yourself on the upward track, if you are always actively looking to acquire either a new managerial skill or leadership competence. If you find yourself in an employment situation and there is a chance to lead a committee, that's the time for you raise your hand and say, "I would like to do it." To be promoted, learn to manage people and projects effectively. Be able to handle money within the organization and look for budgetary responsibilities.

It is also important, while taking on additional responsibility at a place of employment, to observe the role models around you. Who are the leaders you admire? What is it about their leadership skill or what is it about their communication style that you really find effective? What is it that gets them to motivate others to succeed? As you begin to analyze the role models, you will learn there are certain characteristics you will take forward yourself when that leadership moment arrives.

For example, one thing that is critical in the contemporary workplace is the ability to work in a team environment. Successful team leaders will know to create teams, what they need to do or say to motivate team members, and how to recognize and reward teamwork. Typically, they used what they learned while serving on other teams and then implemented those practices when they had the chance to become a team leader.

Another insight from my conversations with people is that many successful people have confronted their perceived weakness and found ways to overcome it. For example, there was a woman who was math phobic and felt she had never been very good with numbers. She pushed herself to learn to manage a large corporate budget at work and became highly successful and promotable. The ability to manage budgets actually became a resume builder for her. She learned that it was important to seek the chance to supervise people, supervise projects, and manage budgets. This woman broke through the glass ceiling once she had acquired these skills and headed into executive positions.

While not everyone wants to be the CEO of an organization and there are many who would be happy to be the vice president or assistant, if you want to move upward in any organization you need to demonstrate managerial and leadership skills.

WRIGHT

You talked about formal learning; are there other ways you can learn to be successful?

JORDAN

Absolutely, and perhaps the best one builds on one of those first themes that I mentioned about how important it is to have good personal relationships. There is a lot of research that demonstrates that people who have reached the upper levels of any organization have a mentor. If you ask them if there were certain things that they can say that definitively helped them, almost invariably they will say they had mentors at some time in their life. I know that finding a mentor, and then ultimately turning around and being a mentor yourself to help the next person, is extremely important.

This mentoring process is life-long and reciprocal. You have different mentors at different points of your life. You may not see mentors you had when you were a young person for twenty years, but they remain part of your ongoing network.

A mentor should always be a person you can ask for advice. The mentor will point out for you things that you should be focusing on or avoiding. The mentor will lead by sharing previous experiences and knowledge. The mentor can give you a "heads up" in advance about an issue or potential problem. The mentor is also someone who can turn to you later on and say, "You know, I've really enjoyed our mentoring relationship and now I need your help." So the mentoring relationship is lifelong and it is mutual—it goes back and forth and is reciprocal. You might help that person or he or she might help you, but the bottom line is that mentoring contributes to success.

An interesting insight, again from my conversations with women, is that many women who began to break through into upper management fifteen years ago had been mentored by a man early on in their careers. Now, in the more recent work environments, women are just as likely to have a successful woman mentor as a successful man as their mentor. Again, regardless of gender, mentoring is very important.

WRIGHT

What are the steps to actually getting the job?

JORDAN

To begin, everyone has to have a resume that is tightly written and focused on their particular accomplishments. I hate to say it, but even the most senior CEOs occasionally need help with their resumes. Typically, they have been so busy leading organizations that often they have not updated their resume in years. At the other end of the age and career spectrum, I always encourage high school students to get started early and have a resume before they graduate.

It turns out that many of the people who have problems finding a job had not reworked their resume in years. This is exactly the wrong strategy if you are planning on career success. Everyone needs to update their resume at least once a year. The resume, and the accompanying self-assessment that must occur before you begin to write, is a reflection of your life's process and your ongoing accomplishments. Just as I've suggested earlier with self-reflection, set your resume rewrites to a calendar date that will remind you to get it done every year. If you let the resume go longer, you're going to forget the accomplishments. Your resume must be ready to go and letter perfect at all times. So building a strong resume is critical to beginning an effective job search.

The second thing that is really critically important to successful job searches is confidence in the interviewing process. Interviewing is an art form. The more you do it, the better you get at responding to the questions. If you are a person just starting out in your career, then a mentor might be the person to practice some questions and answers with before you get to the real interview. Mentors or others in the field can help you anticipate the types of questions in the interview. Remember, great interviewing is related to the applicant's ability to project sincerity, energy, and passion for the job.

Again, those who have broken through to success and expressed satisfaction with their career tell me that they are passionate about their work. So in an interview if you can project energy and you can project passion, you're definitely going to increase the likelihood of achieving the next job and ultimately long-term career success.

A question that often opens a career coaching situation is, "why didn't I get the job?" People really do need to understand why they were not hired in order to enhance their chances for success in that next interview situation. Sometimes the answer can be that the applicant did not do the appropriate research about the organization before the interview.

Practice questions, do your research, and project passion are three great tips for a successful interview in a job search strategy.

It is also important to understand the methods of actually getting a job, including targeting, networking, using recruiters, and responding to advertised openings. As with interviewing, you can enhance your chances of success by linking your accomplishments to the job description. It is important to talk and write about your "fit" for the organization and to be able to ask questions that illustrate this.

WRIGHT

You mentioned in this segment about being passionate. One of the traits that my father tried to instill in all of us was to work toward meaningful work—you become more passionate when it's more meaningful to you.

JORDAN

The first time someone asked me if I was passionate about helping people be successful in their careers I actually had to hesitate for a moment. Up until that question, I had always associated passion with an emotional quality that's more personal. But as I began to reflect on the question, and before I responded to it, I realized in that instant I was passionate about helping people find life and career satisfaction. This is absolutely what gives me my life's energy. It is why I want to get up every day and gives my life purpose. It is this passion that people are seeking. We work to pay the bills, however, we find satisfaction when we can control what we do for work and are passionate about it.

WRIGHT

Assuming that people achieve career success, what else do they need to remember?

JORDAN

The bottom line for men and women, as well as the seasoned worker or young person starting out, is that it's critical to carve out work and life balance. When I use the term "work" in this context, I define it to mean work or effort that can be either paid or unpaid. It is that in which you have invested your life's energy to accomplish. Work is just one part of your career. Career also includes your volunteer efforts and the roles you take on in your family.

The balance concept here is that you've got to give some time to yourself, to your family, and on what you intentionally expend effort to achieve. Finding that balance between work and a personal space is a difficult task. In fact, at different times or stages in our lives, we do need to re-emphasize certain roles. This up and down of career being balanced by times of focusing on the personal is part of the natural evolution of your life's progress. The real secret to career success is to keep work and our personal life in balance.

When you first join an organization, they will want you to give as much of yourself to that organization as possible. You become part of the culture. New employees typically will want to immerse themselves because they are interested and they want to create a positive impression. It is easy to give 125 percent of yourself to a new job. However, remember that any positive taken to an extreme can become a negative. People who do give 125 percent of themselves over a long period can become workaholics. They end up having to trade off something else in their personal lives because there is no longer any time or energy left for other parts of their life's space. Ultimately the balance scale will need to be readjusted.

Finding work and life balance is critical as we begin careers, maintain our careers, and end our career. For example, if you are approaching retirement, take time to develop an avocation interest for the next stage of your life. It ultimately comes to work and life balance and being able to carve out time for yourself and your work.

Those who let work become the most important element of their life end up feeling that a change at work or a disagreement at work is personal affront because they do not have work and personal life balance. Many problems result in the workplace when work becomes all consuming. People know intuitively that work is critical and needed because it can provide financial reward and security, structure to the day, friendships and a sense of belonging, and it influences self-esteem. However, work is not everything there is to life. Work does provide you with a sense of satisfaction and purpose; however, with all of the positives, work must be kept in balance. Remember that all of those personal stories of career success I listened to included the concept that those who were ultimately the most satisfied had successful work and life balance.

ABOUT THE AUTHOR

KATHRYN JORDAN is lead consultant for The Success Associates. In addition, she is the director of Academic Engagement and Career Services at Radford University. Before assuming this role in higher education, Dr. Jordan was the Virginia Managing Consultant for Drake, Beam, Morin, the country's leading provider of human resources consulting services to corporations. In addition to her work as a corporate consultant and higher education administration, Kathryn is a veteran employment expert and pioneer of online human resource solutions. Her background includes specializing in executive level career management.

Kathryn is a strong proponent of the value of self-assessment as a major building block for a proactive career management strategy. She is a nationally certified career counselor and holds memberships in such professional organizations as the American Counseling Association and the National Association of Colleges and Employers. She has been active in the business world as a member of the Board of Directors of the Chamber of Commerce, a member of the Society of Human Resource managers, and as President of Main Street Radford. As a graduate faculty member of Radford University, she has taught graduate students about the career counseling profession, authored numerous articles, and made countless presentations.

Her professional philosophy includes working with clients to develop clarity of purpose and understanding self; understanding contemporary work environments and to identify and implement career steps; integrate both personal and career goals to develop individualized job search strategy; build confidence in the job search process with a development of strong search tools including resumes, vitas, portfolios, cover letters, and reference lists.

With a bachelor's degree from the College of William and Mary in Sociology, a master's degree in Counseling from Radford University, and a doctorate in Education and Counseling from Virginia Tech, Dr. Jordan has worked at both Radford University and Virginia Tech prior to going into consulting. Dr. Jordan resides in Radford, Virginia, with her husband, who is a college professor. She has two grown daughters who live in the Washington, D.C., area.

KATHRYN JORDAN

8217 Sawgrass Way

Radford, Virginia 24141

kathy.jordan@thesuccessassociates.com

www.thesuccessassociates.com

CHAPTER SEVEN
Achieving Greatness Through Life Challenges

An interview with....
JULWEL KENNEY

DAVID E. WRIGHT (WRIGHT)

Today we're talking with Julwel Kenney. Julwel is CEO of JK Personal and Professional Development with more than years of experience. She is a global author of two books: *How to Bring Out the Best in You: The Journey to Personal Transformation and Leadership* and *Bringing Out the Best in You through Life Challenges*. She is the host of *Julwel Kenney Live, Let's Talk Real* radio show. The theme of the show is "Achieving Greatness through Life Challenges." Julwel has an MBA in HR Management, an MS in Organizational Leadership, a BS in Organizational Management, and a PhD in 2010 in Educational Psychology, specializing in Training and Performance Improvement. She is an inspirational and motivational speaker, college professor, life coach, leadership developer, performance improvement, and HR consultant. Julwel is a member of ASTD, Society of Human Resource Management, International Society of Performance Improvement, Toastmasters International, International Speakers Network, and Phi Delta Kappa International. She is a true professional, experienced global speaker and connects with her audiences. Her services add great value and they transform organizations to achieve effective results to bring forth positive change in performance, productivity, and profitability. She has been married to her husband, Keith Kenney, for more than twenty-three years.

Julwel Kenney, welcome to *GPS for Success: Goals and Proven Strategies*.

JULWEL KENNEY (KENNEY)

Thank you very much.

WRIGHT

So the first question is about the importance of life challenges. How important are life challenges?

KENNEY

Life challenges are very important. Life challenges come to make you, not to destroy you. They build character in you and they take certain characteristics out of you. Life challenges are to be used as lessons learned and as opportunities you can use to help others as well as yourself in any situation. They are tests that each of us must pass in order to learn what life is trying to teach us because if you don't pass the test the first time, trust me, you will repeat the test again. This is why many people wonder why they keep going around in circles; it seems as though they cannot get off the crazy cycle. It is because they have not passed the test; therefore, the next time the test comes, it seems to be harder the next time around.

Once you have learned what life is trying to teach you in a particular situation, trust me, you will conquer it and be ready to move on to the next level. However, the key is to know that if you pass the last the test, you can definitely pass the next one that comes your way.

There are five C's that must be used to conquer life challenges. The first C is Communication, the second C is Courage, the third C is Confidence, the fourth is being Change, and the fifth C is Choice.

One must always remember that your decisions today will affect your choices for tomorrow; therefore, never make decisions based on your emotions or moods but on facts. When decisions are based on emotions or moods, there are consequences and repercussions to those decisions; however, when decisions are made based on facts you can reap a harvest of benefits.

WRIGHT

So how do life challenges prepare you for your destiny?

KENNEY

Life challenges prepare you for your destiny because they strengthen your weaknesses and by building characteristics in you and taking negative characteristics out of you if you allow it. Most of the time, when we experience certain challenges, we do not expect them. If you are not prepared and ready for them, and do not know who you are or whose you are as a child of God or creation of God, these challenges will knock you off your feet. For example, due to the economic challenges that almost everyone has experienced, many people have lost their jobs, lost their homes and cars, and others have lost their life's savings. Since many people experienced these challenges that they were not prepared for and did not know how to handle, they have taken their life and other people's lives too.

When I do not know what to do I use the acronym P.O.P., which means the Power of Prayer because I learned to go to my Source and ask God for help. I know that He will give me direction and put the right people in my path at the right time, the right place, and in the right situation to take me through a particular challenge and show me the direction in the way I should go. That is how I excel and succeed through life's challenges. God told me in His Word, "In all thy ways acknowledge him, and he shall direct thy paths"—Proverbs 3:6 (KJV).

WRIGHT

Do life challenges build you or destroy you?

KENNEY

Life challenges do not come to destroy you but to prepare you for your destiny. The challenge is how you handle the situation, which will determine the outcome. This is why you should not make any decisions based on your emotions or moods. Always remember that you are a diamond in the rough; therefore, look at yourself as being that ugly, hard piece of coal before it is made into a beautiful diamond. The coal is heated to a very high temperature and then undergoes an enormous amount of external pressure. The process of the coal being heated under pressure, cut, and shaped continues until the coal turns into the beautiful diamond it was intended to be.

You are going through the same process of being made into a beautiful diamond. Your situation is that the fire is purifying you. The hotter the fire in your situation, the more unproductive characteristics that are being burned out so that when you are taken out of the fire for a moment, new characteristics are being created in you. As a result, you must go through the process of being made before you can achieve the destiny God has planned for your life. Based on God's promise, "For I know the plans I have for you, says the Lord, thoughts and plans for welfare and peace, and not for evil, to give you hope in your final outcome"—Jeremiah 29:11 (Amplified).

This is why we encourage you as a leader to allow life's challenges to bring out the best in you instead of the worst. You were created with every tool you need to win, especially when you ask God for help. According to Psalm 121:1–2, "I will lift up mine eyes unto the hills, from whence cometh my help. My help cometh from the Lord, which made heaven and earth" (KJV). Always ask God for help in every situation and you will win no matter how tough, rough, or unmanageable it may seem. The key is that since He made Heaven and Earth, everything and everyone is under His control and He will work out the situation for your good. This will happen because God made a promise to you, "And we know that all things work together for good to them that love God, to them who are the called according to his purpose"—Romans 8:28 (KJV).

WRIGHT

What are the benefits of using life challenges?

KENNEY

You must use life challenges to help you to succeed beyond your expectations by taking the limitations off yourself and God. Life challenges are to help you to develop spiritually, personally, and professionally. Their purpose is not to destroy you but to make you a better person, even though the experiences seem like they will kill you at that time.

You must remember that the decisions you make today will affect your choices for tomorrow; therefore, you must not make decisions based on your emotions or moods but on facts. It is very important to be a problem-solver in order to excel and succeed in life. Always weigh the facts, not your emotion or mood during a crisis. When you make a decision based on your emotion or mood there will be consequences and repercussions that you will have to live with and experience. It is important to remember the bottom line of any life challenge is to learn the lesson life is trying to teach you at that moment so you will not have to repeat the lesson again. Thus, your decision to become a problem-solver instead of a peace-lover will open up doors to be the peacemaker that will bring about effective and efficient results.

You may wonder what is the difference between a peace lover and a peacemaker. Good question. A peace-lover tells someone what he or she wants to hear and not what the person needs to hear to succeed through life challenges. A peacemaker tells someone what he or she needs to hear to ensure that the person does succeed through life challenges. You must make a decision which role you will play to succeed through life challenges, as well as to help others.

When you allow life challenges to bring out the best in you, these six Es will become a major part of your characteristics: You will be effective, efficient, encouraged, enriched, excellent, and empowered.

WRIGHT

So what have life challenges done for you?

KENNEY

Excellent question! Let me just say that life challenges helped me succeed beyond my own expectations and imagination by taking the limitations from myself and God. They have taught me how to be like an eagle in staying focused on my goals and not on anyone or anything that will distract me from achieving the greatness God has planned for my life spiritually, personally, and professionally. Thus, when life challenges came as a storm, I learned to act as an eagle and soar through the storm until I was above it. I knew that the storm was only a temporary inconvenience for a permanent improvement. Therefore, the stronger the storm, the stronger my wings became so that I could spread my wings to soar into the destiny planned for my life. I learned to ignore negative comments that were not in my best interest. They represented pigeons that made me lose focus, since eagles do not hang out with pigeons.

As a result, I have been able to use my life challenges and experiences to help, empower, motivate, enrich, and encourage individuals to build a relationship with God, not to settle for mediocrity but to strive for excellence. I've also been able to write books to inspire others to cultivate and nurture their leadership abilities into leadership skills. In addition, I used life challenges to stimulate others to achieve the greatness within them by increasing their education and to never stop learning.

WRIGHT

So how do you handle challenges that are pushing you into the next level?

KENNEY

When you are facing challenges that are pushing you into the next level, the best way to handle them is to go with the flow; otherwise you may be missing an opportunity of a lifetime that will help you achieve the greatness in you. The challenges you experience are not always negative, even though it may seem like it at that time. You must remember that greatness comes through much pain, sacrifice, and discipline and is not achieved overnight.

For example, I always loved the corporate environment and the challenges it presented because it forced me to grow personally and professionally. The stimulation of working in the matrix of a fast-paced organization with varying workloads, board meetings, team meetings, organizational goals to achieve, and interacting with a diversity of individuals presented such excitement and enrichment for me. When I was laid off and could not find another job, I was so confused. I asked God, "Why were all the doors closing in obtaining another position in the corporate industry?" I had all the credentials, education, experience, leadership, interpersonal skills, and team-building skills necessary. My skills could bring forth effective results in achieving organizational goals and objectives by increasing the performance and productivity needed to ensure profitability—the bottom line for any organization. I asked God, "What are you trying to tell me and what am I to learn from this situation?"

When I stopped complaining, I realized that I was too close to the mirror and could not see or hear God's direction for my life because I was trying to control it. After I stepped back from the mirror, I was able to see that God was pointing me into a totally different direction to fulfill the purpose He had ordained for my life.

Presently, I am so excited to be living my best life and purpose by fulfilling my purpose and passion as a professor, coach, leadership and development consultant, trainer, motivational and inspirational speaker, businesswoman, author, and, most of all, an evangelist/elder who motivates people to change their lives and not settle for mediocrity. It is my passion to inspire individuals to achieve the greatness within them to fulfill their God-given destiny by using life challenges to bring out the best in them and not the worst. When you are passionate and love what you do, you will never work a day in your life.

WRIGHT

Most people try to avoid challenges. From what you have shared, it sounds like we should embrace them.

KENNEY

I encourage individuals to embrace challenges, especially professionally and personally. You cannot avoid challenges, because if you try to avoid them, trust me, you are going to run around the corner and another one is going to be right there waiting. As previously mentioned, challenges do not come to destroy you. Challenges are to help build you; therefore, this is why it is important to embrace them instead of trying to avoid them.

It is extremely important to not focus on the challenges or situations, but on your goals to achieve the greatness intended for your life. If you focus on a challenge it will distract, discourage, and disappoint you because the negative is being magnified more than the positive. Thus, it is extremely important for you to transform your thinking on a continual basis to stay focused on your goals and soar through the storm of life's challenges. It is imperative that you do not get diverted by "pigeons" that are hanging around but stay focused, keep learning, and strive for excellence.

For example, when eagles are on a tree branch and can see the storm coming, they will soar through the storm until they are above it. Therefore, when you embrace the storms (life challenges) you will not allow fear to enter into your mind or heart because you know that your experiences are teaching you a lesson. You will also be more aware of how to handle the next storm and how to help someone else through their storms. Always remember the acronym FEAR: False Evidence Appearing Real. Consequently, embracing life challenges will keep you learning about yourself so that you can continually strive for excellence and not settle for less than the best in order to bring out the best in you.

WRIGHT

So what life challenge experiences can you share that have pushed you to achieve?

KENNEY

I must be honest, from my experience, I ran into so many individuals who acted as if they were excited for my achievements yet, the more I achieved, the more these same individuals began to reject me. Rumors started to spread that were untrue; people tried to make me lose focus of my destiny and vision. Since I grew up around individuals who spoke negatively about me and to me in organizations, churches, immediate family, close associates, co-workers, and business associates, it taught me how to handle jealousy, confrontation, and rejection. Those experiences prepared me for today. I have learned to use these challenges to empower me and energize me to succeed. Since I am a results-oriented person, I love to speak by action—actions always speak louder than words. Therefore, I do not concentrate on the negative, but on the positive.

Do not allow yourself to be dismayed or lose focus when situations arise. Thank your enemies because they are being used to push you into your destiny, achieve greatness, to build character in you and take negative characteristics out of you. You are not responsible for what people do or say to or about you. You are responsible for how you respond. It takes a lifetime to build a reputation, but a moment to lose it because, as I said earlier, your decisions today will affect your choices for tomorrow. Again, make sure you make your decisions based on facts and not your emotions.

As a leader, you will definitely experience personal life challenges and professional challenges. Challenges will come especially when you will not allow yourself to be controlled by others or do what they think is traditional and familiar; remember that effective leadership creates positive change. It is imperative that you use each life challenge to bring out the best in you so that you can soar as high as an eagle into your destiny, spiritually, personally, and professionally. Always remember God's promise and plan for your life, "The thief cometh not, but for to steal, and to kill, and to destroy: I am come that they might have life, and that they might have it more abundantly"—John 10:10 (KJV).

So do not allow anyone or anything to steal, kill, or destroy your destiny. Do not give anyone power over your life. Always keep it moving and if individuals do not celebrate or appreciate your successes and gifts, do not waste your time and energy associating with those individuals; they will drain you and cause you to doubt yourself and gifts. Associate with those who celebrate and appreciate you, motivate you, and help you achieve your goals, destiny, and greatness. As you lead, you should stay focused and live the abundant life God designed for you today.

WRIGHT

So what challenges have you overcome to help you accomplish the success you have achieved?

KENNEY

I can think of many challenges I have overcome. One main challenge that I will talk about is growing up in the South Bronx educational system when social promotion was extremely high and a part of the normal school operations. I was one of those students who struggled with proper writing skills due to not learning correct English during my high school years. As I entered college, my professors handed me back my papers marked up in red because of all the grammatical errors. One of my professors even told me to drop out of college because I needed to learn how to write proper English. I was dismayed by his comment and I asked God to help me learn how to write effectively to finish my bachelor's degree.

While I was at work one day, I met Marcia Richards; she saw me crying at my desk. She asked why I was crying and I told her that I was struggling with writing my class paper for college. Marcia asked to see what I was writing about and began to teach me how to write an effective college paper. After we completed the paper, Marcia volunteered to tutor me in English and writing throughout my bachelor's degree program so that I could achieve my educational goal. The tutoring took a lot of time and sacrifice but I knew that I would reap the benefits because this challenge was only a temporary inconvenience for a permanent improvement. Also, I knew that God put Marcia in my path at the right time, in the right place, and in the right situation to prepare me for my destiny.

As a result of learning how to overcome my writing challenges and not being ashamed to ask and receive help, God has blessed me to write three books titled, *How to Bring Out the Best in You: The Journey to Personal Transformation and Leadership, Bringing Out the Best in You Through Life Challenges: It is Your Time to Achieve,* and to co-author the book in which this interview will appear. Therefore, I have learned to commit my work to God so that I can have great success. The Bible says, "This book of the law shall not depart out of your mouth, but you shall meditate on it day and night, that you may observe and do according to all that is written in it; for then you shall make your way prosperous, and then you shall deal wisely and have good success"—Joshua 1:8 (Amplified). God's promises are a part of every aspect of my life and the reason why I am successful. The writing challenge I experienced pushed me to achieve beyond my own expectations and imagination to cultivate and nurture the greatness in me to become successful.

It is imperative that you do not focus on your faults, weaknesses, or challenges, but on what you want and need to accomplish. When I realized that I was able to conqueror my writing challenge, my confidence built and I knew that God had a greater plan for my life—to help and motivate others to achieve the greatness planned for their lives. Because I stayed focused and knew who I was as a child of God and knew my purpose—and realized that I was not born just to live, but born to achieve, and not just achieve but to achieve greatness—I learned throughout the years that greatness comes through much pain, sacrifice, and discipline. Thus, I was determined to stay focused, energized, and empowered to cultivate and nurture my leadership abilities into leadership skills so that I could achieve the greatness and purpose planned for my life.

WRIGHT

From your viewpoint, what does success really mean to you?

KENNEY

Success to me means achieving the destiny, purpose, and goals that you were born to accomplish in order to excel beyond your own expectations and imagination. When you are successful, you know that you are doing your best and not settling for less. When you are fulfilling your purpose, you become passionate about what you are doing and accomplishing to bring forth rich self-actualization and satisfaction, which makes you feel successful. In addition, when you are happy with yourself, have peace within, enjoy being with family, and are financially and educationally stable—according to your goals—all those things bring forth success.

Lastly, success to me is giving yourself room to fail so that you can learn how to achieve to succeed. You will then feel enriched, empowered, energized, and effective. I totally agree with Eagan (2004)—feeling successful you will:

- Enjoy life and feel good about yourself;
- Feel as though your life really makes a difference;
- Feel complete and fulfilled;
- Experience a full and satisfied life;
- Experience a more stable marriage and a better understanding and relationship with your spouse;
- Spend less time and energy in unproductive activities;
- Enjoy and get more pleasure out of life;
- Experience a high level of personal satisfaction, confidence, and significance to soar as an eagle;

- Be able to take control of your life and make your dreams a reality;
- Unlock and fulfill the greatness within;
- Be disciplined and determined to fulfill your God-given destiny;
- Maximize your strengths and minimize your weaknesses;
- Become extremely comfortable in who you are;
- Be empowered to use your gifts and talents to the best of your ability;
- Have great relationships with virtually no jealousy, envy, or strife, knowing you are not in competition but are to complement every relationship;
- Understand what makes you and others react;
- Become an expression of how God made you;
- Not have to compete or compare yourself to others;
- Be able to strengthen and mature in your natural gifts and talents, thereby making you more successful, valuable, and profitable.

This is why success to me is to never stop learning—it is a lifelong process. I also believe that leadership is a lifelong process as well; therefore, leaders must never stop learning in order to stay successful and maintain a charismatic leadership style that makes people want to work with and associate with them.

WRIGHT

Well, what a great conversation. I really appreciate all the time you've taken with me this afternoon to talk about the importance of facing challenges and adversity. I, too, believe in the "refiner's fire;" I'm glad you pointed that out. I really appreciate what you have included in our discussion I'm sure that our readers are going to get a lot out of this chapter.

KENNEY

Thank you very much.

WRIGHT

Today we've been talking with Julwel Kenney. Julwel is CEO of JK Personal and Professional Development. She is an inspirational and motivational speaker, a college professor, a life coach, leadership developer, and a performance and HR consultant. She also host of *Julwel Kenney Live, Let's Talk Real* radio show.

Julwel, thank you so much for being with us today on *GPS for Success: Goals and Proven Strategies.*

KENNEY

Thank you very much for having me.

ABOUT THE AUTHOR

JULWEL KENNEY is CEO of JK Personal and Professional Development with more than years of experience. She is a global author of two books: *How to Bring Out the Best in You: The Journey to Personal Transformation* and *Leadership* and *Bringing Out the Best in You through Life Challenges*. She is the host of *Julwel Kenney Live, Let's Talk Real* radio show. The theme of the show is "Achieving Greatness through Life Challenges." Julwel has an MBA in HR Management, an MS in Organizational Leadership, a BS in Organizational Management, and a PhD in 2010 in Educational Psychology, specializing in Training and Performance Improvement. She is an inspirational and motivational speaker, college professor, life coach, leadership developer, performance improvement consultant, and HR consultant. Julwel is a member of ASTD, Society of Human Resource Management, International Society of Performance Improvement, Toastmasters International, International Speakers Network, and Phi Delta Kappa International. She is a true professional, experienced global speaker and connects with her audiences. Her services add great value and they transform organizations to achieve effective results to bring forth positive change in performance, productivity, and profitability. She has been married to her husband, Keith Kenney, for more than twenty-three years.

JULWEL KENNEY

Maywood, NJ 07607

866-511-4743

julwelkenney@jkpartners.org

www.julwelkenney.org

CHAPTER EIGHT
Stretch, Push Yourself, and Reach Further

An interview with...
LES BROWN

DAVID E. WRIGHT (WRIGHT)

Today we're talking with Les Brown, internationally recognized speaker and CEO of Les Brown Enterprises, Inc. He is also author of the highly acclaimed and successful books, *Live Your Dreams* and *It's Not Over Until You Win.* Les is former host of the *Les Brown Show,* a nationally syndicated daily television talk show that focused on solutions rather than on problems. Les Brown is one of the nation's leading authorities on understanding and stimulating human potential. Utilizing powerful delivery and newly emerging insights, Les's customized presentations will teach, inspire, and channel any audience to new levels of achievement.

Les Brown, welcome to *GPS for Success: Goals and Proven Strategies.*

LES BROWN (BROWN)

Thank you very much. It's a pleasure to be here.

WRIGHT

Les, you've been a role model for thousands of people down through the years because of your triumph over adversity. Tell our readers a little bit about your early life and who was responsible for your upbringing.

BROWN

Well, I was born in a poor section of Miami, Florida, called Liberty City. I was born on the floor of an abandoned building along with a twin brother. When we were six weeks of age, we were adopted. When I was in the fifth grade I was identified as EMR (Educable Mentally Retarded) and put back into the fourth grade. I failed again when I was in the eighth grade.

I attribute everything that I've accomplished to my mother. Whenever I give a presentation I always quote Abraham Lincoln by saying, "All that I am and all that I ever hope to be, I owe to my mother." I saw a sign once that said, "God took me out of my biological mother's womb and placed me in the heart of my adopted mother." I love my adopted mother's faith, her character, her drive, her dedication, and her willingness to do whatever it took to raise seven children by herself. She only had a third grade education but she had a Ph.D. in mothering.

WRIGHT

If I remember correctly, you were diagnosed at the age of thirty-six with dyslexia. How did that happen?

BROWN

No, I was never diagnosed with dyslexia; but I was in special education from fourth grade all the way through my senior year in high school. My formal education ended at that time; but I became very much interested in personal development tapes and books because of a high school teacher who challenged me to do something in a class. I told him I couldn't do it and he insisted that I could.

Finally, I said, "I can't because I'm Educable Mentally Retarded."

He said, "Don't ever say that again. Someone's opinion of you does not have to become your reality."

This teacher's name was Mr. Leroy Washington and he's still around today. One of the things he emphasized to all of his students was that you don't get in life what you *want*—you get in life what you *are*. What you achieve—what you produce in life—is a reflection of your growth and development as a person. So you must invest in yourself.

He often quoted scripture by saying, "Be ye not conformed to this world: but be ye transformed by the renewing of your mind . . . " (Romans 12:2). He said most people fail in life because "they don't know that they don't know and they think they know"—they suffer from mental malnutrition. He said take the time each day to develop your mind, read ten to fifteen pages of something positive every day, and find some goals that are beyond your comfort zone that can challenge you to reinvent yourself. He told his students that in order to do something you've never done, you've got to be someone you've never been. He told us the possibilities of what you could achieve by developing your mind and developing your communication skills (because once you open your mouth you tell the world who you are). You can really begin to climb the ladder of success and do things that will literally amaze you.

WRIGHT

So your education is self-education.

BROWN

Yes.

WRIGHT

Listening to tapes and reading books and that sort of thing?

BROWN

Yes. Going to seminars and then testing and experimenting. I think it's very important that people experiment with their lives and find out what it is that works for them—what gives their lives a sense of joy and meaning. What is it that brings music to your life? That way you're able to discover some talents, abilities, and skills you don't even realize you have.

WRIGHT

I remember reading your first book, *Live Your Dreams*. This bestseller is helping people even today. Can you tell us what you're trying to say in this book and why it is important?

BROWN

What I'm doing in *Live Your Dreams* is challenging people to look at their situation and ask themselves some crucial questions. Is life working for me? Is it really giving me what I want?

When most people get out of high school, they end up doing things that other people want them to do. Albert Schweitzer was asked a question, "What's wrong with humankind today?" He replied, "Men simply don't think." He meant that statement in a generic sense. Men *and* women simply don't challenge themselves to think about what it is that really makes them happy and gives their lives a sense of meaning, purpose, power, and value.

I want to challenge people to think about what it is that really gives their lives a sense of meaning and power. Once you determine that, assess yourself. What are your strengths? What are your weaknesses? What is it you bring to the table of life? What help? What assistance? What training? What education? What resources? What do you have to tap into that will help you to become the kind of person that can produce those results?

Then next is to commit yourself. Don't ask yourself, "How am I going to do it?" The "how" is none of your business—what is most important is to get started—the how will come. The way will come. Everything you need to attract—the people, the resources, and the assistance—will come to be available at your disposal.

WRIGHT

What do you think about goal-setting? There has been so much written about it lately.

BROWN

I think it's very important that people set goals because what that does is allow you to focus your energy. It helps you to put together a game plan and a strategy and an agenda for your life. If you don't have an agenda for your life, then you're going to be a part of somebody else's agenda; therefore, you want to set some goals. There's a quote I love very much that says, "People who aim at nothing in life usually hit nothing dead on the head."

WRIGHT

Oh, my.

BROWN

Yes, so you want to have some goals you are setting in each area of your life. You want to monitor those goals after you put together a plan of action to achieve those goals. Break those goals down into manageable increments: long-range and short-range goals, three-month goals, thirty-day goals, and weekly goals. You should have daily tasks and activities you engage in that will move you in the direction of your goals. Dr. Robert H. Schuller said something that is true, "By the yard it's hard, but inch by inch anything is a cinch."

As you begin to look at the big picture and come back to where you are right now, looking at the completed big picture of where you want to go, then you can begin to put together a strategy of things and activities you need to do each day to move you in the direction of those goals. As you get closer to those goals you have set for yourself in the various areas of your life—your physical life, your emotional life, your spiritual life, your financial life—then you can begin to push the goals back. Continue to stretch—continue to push yourself—and reach farther.

WRIGHT

A few years ago you had a nationally syndicated television talk show. It's next to impossible to get a show of that nature on the air. Tell us the circumstances that helped to get your show on the air.

BROWN

I believe I'm coming back, I don't think it's impossible to get back on again. I wanted to go in a different direction. During the time I ventured into it, television was based upon a formula the executives were accustomed to which they'd always implemented—the show must be based upon conflict and controversy. So you had Phil Donahue, Oprah Winfrey, Sally Jesse Raphael, and Geraldo. My show was based upon solutions. I believed you could have a show that was not based upon conflict and controversy—you could have a show where you would look at what challenges people are facing and who has gone through a challenge and come out on the other side? Talk to that person and find out how he or she got there. Interview a guest who is in the middle of a challenge and find one who's just approaching that challenge. Have an expert work the person through that process during the hour of the show, asking what is it that brought you here? There's an old saying that goes, "Wherever you find yourself, at some point and time, you made an appointment to get there."

The other thing is that success leaves clues. What we must do is talk to someone who's had the same problem you've had and find out from his or her experience what is it you can do to implement a game plan. What help and support will you need to work through this problem?

The *Les Brown Show* was very successful. It was the highest rated and fastest cancelled talk show in the history of television. It was cancelled because, even though it had successful ratings, the producers of the show wanted me to do a show based upon conflict and controversy and sensationalism—fathers who sleep with their fourteen-year-old daughter's boyfriends—and subjects like that. I decided to be true to my concept and not venture off into those other areas to do those Jerry Springer type shows, so they cancelled the show and brought someone else in who was willing to cooperate with what they wanted.

WRIGHT

Did you learn any lessons from your highly competitive talk show?

BROWN

Yes I did. The lesson I learned was I should have been the executive producer. I was hired talent and "the hand that pays the piper calls the tune." Had I been the executive producer of my show like Oprah Winfrey, then I could have done what Oprah did after she saw the success of my show—she changed direction and used the formula I'd come up with and the rest is history.

If I had it to do over again I would've put my own production company together, continued to do the show I was doing, and would've found someone else to syndicate the show nationally. If I couldn't find someone to syndicate the show nationally I would've set it up to do it locally and then rolled it back out nationally myself.

WRIGHT

I bet you still get stopped on the street by people who saw your commercials on the PBS station for many years. Those were some of the best produced I've ever seen.

BROWN

Well, thank you. We've gotten a lot of response from PBS. We just did one show four months ago called, *It's in Your Hands*. In fact, I end the show with my children because five of my seven children are speakers as well; they're also trainers. What we're doing is teaching people how to become responsible for their careers, their health, and for their family life. The response has been very, very successful on PBS.

WRIGHT

So you're growing your own speakers, then.

BROWN

Yes, and I'm training speakers—I'm more of a speech coach. I've developed a reputation as a speaker, but I have a gift of helping people tell their story and to position it so it has value for an audience. I have people's stories create special, magical moments within the context of their presentation so that those stories can create a committed listening audience and move them to new heights within themselves.

WRIGHT

Yes, you don't have to tell me you're a sought-after speaker. Some time ago we were planning a speaking engagement in Ohio and the two people who were requested more than any others were Stephen Covey and Les Brown. They really came after you, so you do have quite a reputation for helping people.

BROWN

Thank you.

WRIGHT

A lot of our readers have read many books that advocate focus in their career. I know you've done several things and you've done them well. Do you advocate going in one direction and not diversifying in your career?

BROWN

I think that you have to find one area you want to focus on and as you develop momentum in that area and reach a certain measure of success, then you can branch off into other areas.

WRIGHT

Les, you had a serious bout with cancer several years ago, right?

BROWN

Yes.

WRIGHT

How did this catastrophic disease affect your life?

BROWN

What cancer did for me was help me live life with a sense of urgency that tomorrow is not guaranteed. It helped me reprioritize my life and find out what's really important. When something major like cancer happens in your life, you spend more time focusing on those things. So, even though I always practiced and advocated that people live each day as if it were their last, my cancer battle helped me to focus even more so on priorities. That's what I began to be about the business of doing—thinking about my legacy, spending more time with my children, my grandchildren, friends I cared about, and working on the purpose I've embraced for my life.

WRIGHT

My wife was going through cancer at the same time you were, I remember. I heard her say recently that even though she doesn't want cancer again, she wouldn't give anything for the lessons she learned going through it.

BROWN

Yes. It helps; it gives new meaning to life, and you value things you used to take for granted.

WRIGHT

So, you gained a lot of insight into what's important?

BROWN

Oh, without any question I did.

WRIGHT

Your book, *It's Not Over Until You Win*, was long awaited, of course. Would you tell our readers what it's about and what you're trying to say?

BROWN

I think what people must do is challenge themselves to overcome the inner conversation that has been placed in them through their conditioning, through their environment, and their circumstances. We live in a world where we're told more about our limitations rather than our potential. We need to overcome and defeat that conversation.

If you ask most people if they have ever been told they can't achieve a goal they envision for their life will say, "Yes." My whole goal is to help people learn how to become unstoppable. Yes, it's going to be difficult—it's going to be hard. You're going to have obstacles thrown in your path. You will have setbacks and disappointments. But you must develop the mind-set of a winner. You must come back again and again and again. You must be creative and flexible, versatile and adaptable, and never stop until you reach your goals.

WRIGHT

I read many years ago that 98 percent of all failure comes from quitting. Would you agree with that?

BROWN

Yes, I agree with that without any question. Most people become discouraged and they see delay as a denial. I encourage people to go back to the drawing board in their minds, regroup, and get some fresh thinking. Einstein said, "The thinking that has brought me this far has created some problems that this thinking can't solve."

Sometimes we have to allow other people to be a part of the process—to look at the situation we're battling with new eyes that can help us overcome the challenges we're facing.

WRIGHT

As I have said before, you have been a role model for thousands of adults as well as young people. Do you have any advice to give our readers that would help them to grow in body, mind, and spirit and live a better, fuller life?

BROWN

Yes. I think it's important for people to raise the bar on themselves every day. Look at your life and understand and know you are greater than you give yourself credit for being; you have talents and abilities you haven't even begun to reach for yet.

Jim Rohn has a quote I love, "When the end comes for you, let it find you conquering a new mountain, not sliding down an old one." So, therefore, we have to raise the bar on ourselves constantly and assess ourselves.

The other thing is I believe it's important we ask for help, not because we're weak but because we want to remain strong. Many people don't ask for help because of pride. "Pride cometh before a fall" because of ego. E-G-O means edging God out.

I think that you also have to ask yourself, what is your plan for being here? Most people take their health for granted; but living a long, healthy life is not a given—pain is a given—you have to fight to stay here. You have to have a plan of action to stay here. So what is your plan for being here? Put yourself on your to-do list. Develop a plan of action on how you're going to take better care of yourself and spend more time with people you care about. Focus on living the goals and dreams you've envisioned for yourself that are the calling on your life.

WRIGHT

Down through the years, as you've made your decisions, has faith played an important role in your life?

BROWN

Yes, faith is very important. I think you have to believe in yourself, believe in your abilities, believe in your dreams, and believe in a power greater than yourself. There's a quote I love which says, "Faith is the oil that takes the friction out of living." Do the best you can and leave the rest to a power greater than yourself.

WRIGHT

Les, you don't know how much I appreciate you being with us today for *GPS for Success: Goals and Proven Strategies.*

BROWN

Oh, thank you so much.

WRIGHT

Today we've been talking with Les Brown, an internationally recognized speaker and CEO of Les Brown Enterprises. He's the author of *Live Your Dreams* and *It's Not Over Until You Win.* I suggest you run down to the bookstore and look for both of them. Les has been a successful talk show host and as we have heard today, he is now coaching speakers.

Thank you so much for being with us, Les.

BROWN

Thank you, I appreciate you very much.

ABOUT THE AUTHOR

LES BROWN is an internationally recognized speaker and CEO of Les Brown Enterprises, Inc. He is also author of the highly acclaimed and successful books, *Live Your Dreams* and *It's Not Over Until You Win*. Les Brown is one of the nation's leading authorities in understanding and stimulating human potential.

LES BROWN
Les Brown Enterprises
P.O. Box 27380
Detroit, Michigan 48227
800-733-4226
speak@lesbrown.com
www.lesbrown.com

CHAPTER NINE
It's All About the Market

An interview with...
KEITH THIRGOOD & HELEN WALTER

DAVID E. WRIGHT (WRIGHT)

Today we're talking with Keith Thirgood and Helen Walter. They are co-founders of Capstone Communications Group, a marketing company specializing in helping businesses get more business through innovative marketing ideas and materials. They founded Capstone in 1982 to develop marketing solutions for businesses. They advise clients on marketing issues and develop successful marketing campaigns, brochures, logos, advertising, Web sites, and all the other legitimate tools organizations use to get more business. Capstone's clients have ranged from multi-nationals such as Northern Telecom, Cantel, and Environment Canada to midsize manufacturers and software developers to small entrepreneurial companies in the speaking industry, consulting, and high tech.

Keith and Helen, welcome to *GPS for Success: Goals and Proven Strategies*.

KEITH THIRGOOD (THIRGOOD)

Hello David.

HELEN WALTER (WALTER)

Hey, David!

WRIGHT

I understand that you began as entrepreneurs, artists, and photographers. How did the two of you become involved in marketing?

THIRGOOD

Well, we didn't learn marketing by going through an MBA course; we learned it by studying the best marketing minds available at the time. Then we spent a lot of time testing their ideas on ourselves, in the real world of small business. We found that when they didn't work, we lost money. If they worked, we made money.

So, for the first five years in business as photographers and producers, we lost as much money on marketing as we earned. Then things began to turn around and we gained more and more new clients as our marketing worked better and better. When prospects and clients saw our marketing materials they asked where we had them done. When they found out that we did it all, they asked us to do the same for them.

WALTER

David, I can tell you that we certainly read as much as we could because we thought we'd find a lot of answers in books written by the founders of the great agencies. But what they were saying was: "Spend only $10,000 on a trial marketing effort and take these ideas to your board of directors." I thought, "Only $10,000?," This was more than I had in the world. I also thought, "What board of directors?" Maybe I could take my ideas to my cat and say, "Well, how do you feel about not having cat food for the next three months because we're going to spend your cat food money on a trial marketing effort?"

Their advice just wasn't practical for a small business, so we had to figure it out for ourselves. There just wasn't any literature on how a small business like ours could do something that would make a difference. We knew that our bigger competition had bigger budgets and bigger backers. They were different from us. So we decided to figure out how we differentiated from them, and that started to give us some answers.

WRIGHT

So how long did the transition from audio visual production and design to marketing consultation and design take?

WALTER

It happened over a period of three to four years. We began to sense a change in the climate of commerce—the economy changed and technology was changing. We also had a general sense that what we're currently doing would probably *not* be what we'd be doing in the next little while. So just like a tugboat pushing a great big ship in the harbor, to change direction, we began to incrementally change what we were doing.

THIRGOOD

By 1989 we pretty well completed the switch from what we had begun doing to concentrating on marketing.

WRIGHT

With such a different background from most marketing advisors, does your approach differ from the mainstream?

THIRGOOD

As we don't particularly watch what our competitors are doing, I'm not sure how different we are. However, I believe there are three fundamental pillars at the core of every successful marketing effort. The first is the *image* projected by the effort, which is quite important. The *message* is equally important, however, in our opinion, the *market* is the most important of the three, and it tends to be the most neglected by businesses.

WALTER

As a professional speaker, I knew that what was working in my talks was emotion—people respond hugely to the emotional content. That doesn't mean I was talking about being emotional or that I was delivering my message in an overtly emotional manner. What I mean is there was an emotional connection they made to what I was saying. It was like they were saying to themselves, "You get me, you *so* get me." I kept hearing that over and over again and I thought that this is what we need to have happen when someone looks at a logo or brochure or Web site. With an emotional connection, their first response would not be, "You're selling me" or "I don't get your jargon," but, "Oh god, you so get me. You get me as nobody else does." I think that's where we differ from everybody else. And the emotional connection most often comes from the visual—the image—followed by a concise statement that resonates rather than sells.

WRIGHT

So when you refer to image, exactly what do you mean?

THIRGOOD

Well, image refers to the visual, auditory, tactile, and attitude aspects of a marketing effort. It encompasses the colors you use, and the shapes, photos, and graphics. It includes things like the way a company's people dress, they way they answer their phones, the timeliness of their correspondence, their tone of voice, and manners.

WALTER

In the last few years it's come to be called branding—walking the walk, talking the talk. It's how people see you, 24/7. I think a lot of companies make the mistake of thinking that the logo or a single ad is it—that's their image out there. They don't realize it's the whole package.

THIRGOOD

As a business, you have to consider the influence of the image you're building or the image that's being created without your direct involvement because that's what will happen—you either build your own image or it will be determined for you. Is it the right image for your target market and your industry? Image is more than just that little logo.

WALTER

David, I came across three lines that were real eye-openers. They refer to individuals; however, they work just as well for companies. First there's the image you make for yourself. It's a vision you've invented. It's how you see yourself. Then there's how other people see you. That's the impression you make. (Sometimes we make an impression we don't intend, which means we haven't been paying attention and attending to our image.) Then there's the image that you worry other people have of you. That's the one that keeps you awake at night.

WRIGHT

What about a company's message? Is your advice the same as everyone else's—don't talk about features, talk about benefits?

WALTER

Well, that's old school and we certainly did preach that right up front, but it's like the ante at the poker game—you can't get into the game without it, so yes, you have to talk benefits. But it's not the whole game.

THIRGOOD

And the majority still talks about their company's features and neglect its benefits. However, to really stand out in the market today, we believe benefits are no longer enough. We believe every marketing effort needs to identify the core emotional issue of the company's product or service. This is what Helen alluded to earlier. Companies need to make sure that the target market gets it loud and clear. We don't mean that every marketing effort has to be a sob story; however, every effort needs to understand, and play to, the emotional rationale behind the purchasing desire.

WALTER

And one of the best ways to deliver both the benefits and the emotions turns out to be storytelling. It constantly amazes me because—telling as many stories as I do, and telling them as often as I do in my talks—I start to wonder if people don't tire of it. But they don't, they want more, and they want the same story again. I think some people don't believe that they have a story when, in fact, every product and service has a story behind it or, more likely, a story behind the desire in the market. Telling those stories can set a company apart and far ahead of their competition.

For instance, I happened to be giving a talk, and when I got to the part about stories and emotions, one of the people in the audience said, "Well, I'm a concrete engineer; I don't think there is any emotion behind that." You know, my first thought went to 9/11 and I thought, "Really?," I also thought about some bridges that have collapsed in recent years.

"You know," I said, "I can get awfully emotional about concrete. And if you had a powerful story behind how good concrete engineering has saved lives, that would be more powerful than saying, 'We've got great concrete.'"

WRIGHT

You've mentioned markets a number of times. Everyone talks about having a market; what do you say that's new about markets?

THIRGOOD

I don't think our take on markets is new; it's simply that we believe target marketing is neglected. Conversely, it's also talked about a lot. The biggest failure surrounding target markets is that many businesses still don't know what a target market is. The second biggest failure is the belief that everybody can use my product or service, therefore everybody is my market. Businesses, for the most part, can't seem to get past gross segmentation; they say things like, "High tech is my target market." That's not even a market, let alone a target market. It's simply an entire segment.

We could best illustrate what we mean by a target market with a folk tale. I'll let Helen tell you the story.

WALTER

Once upon a time there was a manufacturer of good, rugged air bags. The company decided to sell to the general automotive industry because its leaders saw a clear need for air bags in the market. The problem was, their air bags cost more than normal, non-rugged air bags.

One day the air bag CEO woke up and realized that perhaps they should try selling to the manufacturers of off-road and military vehicles; that must surely be a target market. So his salespeople approached VPs of production for this perceived target market and described their amazing air bags—they were rugged and inflated in half the time of their competitors' air bags did.

"So what?" the VP said, obviously unimpressed.

"Well," the salespeople said, "it's obvious—your customers get to walk away from a head-on crash, even in harsh off-road conditions.

"So what?" the VP repeated. "How does that help me on my production line?"

Then the salespeople realized they weren't addressing the VP of production's needs, so their "obvious" benefit was meaningless to him (or her). So the salespeople added to their marketing document the fact that installation came in at half the time and only needed one line worker to install, compared to other air bags.

Then the salespeople took their air bag marketing up to the VP of Finance. After their pitch of personal safety and functionality in the desert, and speed of installation, the VP of Finance said, "So what?"

It turned out that all this person really wanted to know was the financial benefits of the air bag. So the salespeople added this to their marketing approach.

Then they pitched the VP of Marketing on their product and they talked about the financial savings, the speed with which it could be installed. They instantly bored the marketing guy, who started thinking about lunch before the salesperson got around to mentioning customers walking away from crashes because of the air bags. They forgot that the marketing VP only wanted to hear about how it made customers' lives better.

Finally, with a multi-benefit marketing document, they tried to see the CEO about their new air bag. However, the CEO took one look at the multi-page marketing document and determined that it wasn't worth the investment in time it would take to read it. So they never did get their chance to give their pitch.

The moral is: even when you think you have a target market, to be truly successful, look for the targets within that market. These individuals have their own buttons and respond to their own issues. Forget everybody else's. General marketing doesn't hit home if you try to be all things to all targets; you can even repel them. If you're a good fisherman, you know that if you're going after trout, you use trout bait. Leave the other lures at home.

THIRGOOD

We have a tool we often use to help a client reach the right target with highest effect. We call it, our Awareness Scale™.

WRIGHT

What is the Awareness Scale?

THIRGOOD

It's a way of understanding how people in your target market think, their level of awareness of your industry, your benefits, and your company. Once you've come to understand what your target market is, you can improve your effort by choosing within that market an awareness level to go after.

We use a lot of stories to explain things, so here comes another folk tale. This is our fishmonger story.

WALTER

Imagine for a moment that I'm presenting an idea to a large audience of businesspeople. I ask them to pretend they are all fishmongers and they all want to sell more fish. And let's pretend that everyone on my left is of the unaware mindset, everyone in the middle is of a doubtful mindset, and the ones on my right have a go-getter mindset. Now I reveal that a good way to market fish is to use a newsletter. Do they all respond identically because they're all fishmongers? Hardly. The people on the left side of the room will be *unaware* of the value of newsletters. They don't get it, so they say, "Never heard of such a thing. Isn't a newsletter what you wrap the fish in after you sell it?"

The middle group will have heard of newsletters. They can see it might be a good idea, but they've got issues and their favorite phrase is always, "Yeah, but." They set up barriers between themselves and doing any particular marketing effort. They are full of doubts.

The audience on my right would not only know about newsletters, they're actively using them to market fish. These people are aware and engaged and they only want to know who creates the most effective newsletter.

THIRGOOD

We call the ones on the left, the *Unaware*, the ones in the center the *Doubters*, and the other ones the *Aware*. Many leaders of businesses seem to think that they must educate their audience. However, the only audience here that needs real education is the Unaware. The problem with sending an educational message to the entire target is that the Aware group will say, "We already know what we're doing, don't waste time educating us." The Doubters will say the same. What the Aware audience needs to see is how you differ from everyone else in your business. However, if you sent a differentiation message to the Unaware, they wouldn't care that you're better because they still think you wrap the fish in newsletter paper. And the Doubters need a message that helps them overcome their fears.

You can see that each of these submarkets needs a different type of message. So many businesses try to include all three in one piece of marketing. The messages they send are like giving people a bowl of minestrone and telling them that if they're interested in peas then find your own peas, if you looking for carrots, then find your own carrots. That's asking people to do their own homework and nobody is willing to do homework.

WRIGHT

There is a lot of hype surrounding the so-called social media, Web 2.0, and other modern "miracle cures" for marketing problems. What's your take on these?

THIRGOOD

As with every other miracle cure and magic bullet that we've read about over the past thirty years, there is more hype than substance in the claims.

Electronic social media is essentially like old fashioned networking. When you strip away the hoopla it's still just about meeting people, helping people, getting noticed, and winning hearts and minds. You do the same thing with traditional networking (assuming that you do traditional networking correctly)—you help people by answering their questions, sharing your knowledge, volunteering, and becoming noticed.

One of the biggest problems with social media is learning the rules of each group. At the moment, many businesses still react to social media with fear or they see social media as simply another advertising medium, like newspapers. They're not—they're not called *social* media for nothing. And it takes time and dedication to be part of it.

As for Web 2.0 it's mostly technology chasing a market. It's driven by people who sell the solutions, who advise on the solutions, or people who write about the solutions. Web 2.0 is simply an additional level of functionality for Web sites.

Despite what many gurus say, you don't have to have an all-singing, all-dancing Web site to succeed. What you do have to do is to look at the needs and, more importantly, the desires of your target market and see if your site is answering them. Does it need 2.0 to answer them? If not, don't use it. But if Web 2.0 type tools make things easier, then add them. Otherwise, don't drive yourself crazy trying to keep up with a moving technological target. Unless you sell Web 2.0 technology or are in the entertainment industry, you don't automatically need these tools.

WALTER

One of the other things we recognize is that marketing is very much about mindset. Your target market is a mindset. And people's mindsets and attitudes change depending on their location and the environment they're in. Recently we heard one of the engineers from Google reveal that their research shows that the average Google user goes through about ten pages a day, on average. When they go to someplace like Facebook or Myspace, or any of the social media, they go through a hundred pages a day. What that could mean to a marketer is that you're in something like a bigger mall and your prospects are going through it in a bigger hurry. You aren't going to be as easily noticed, as you would be in another environment where there are fewer distractions and people aren't focused on different activities.

WRIGHT

Do you have any last words to sum up what a small or mid-size enterprise can do to improve their chances in today's market?

THIRGOOD

I'd say the number one thing most small to mid-sized enterprises can do is re-think their target market—are they addressing the people they should be speaking to, and is what they're saying in the right tone, and are they saying the right things? If those answers reveal new information, review your marketing material in light of what you've learned and determine what needs to be changed.

WALTER

They should determine if they really need a full-scale overhaul of their marketing or if just a tweak will do, because often there are elements that are good and we don't want anyone throwing the baby out with the bathwater.

THIRGOOD

Get started on the new you. In marketing books this is called "branding" and is often wrapped in mystery or doesn't go deeply enough. I think that if a small business follows the steps we've been talking about it will reach branding nirvana.

WRIGHT

Well, what a great conversation. This is an interesting subject. Because I've owned many businesses in my lifetime, and I've really had trouble at different times and in different markets, the information you've given here has been helpful. You've give me a lot to think about.

THIRGOOD

Well I'm glad we could be of value.

WRIGHT

I appreciate all the time both of you have spent with me today to answer these questions. I wish you the very best as you continue to help people.

WALTER

Thank you very much; we hope the same for you.

THIRGOOD

Nice to talk to you, David.

WRIGHT

Today we've been talking with Keith Thirgood and Helen Walter who are co-founders of Capstone Communications Group, a marketing company specializing in helping businesses get more business. They help develop marketing solutions for organizations and they advise clients on marketing issues. They develop successful marketing campaigns such as brochures, logos, advertising, Web sites, and all the other tools organizations need and use to get more business.

Keith and Helen, thank you so much for being with us today on *GPS for Success: Goals and Proven Strategies*.

WALTER

Our pleasure.

THIRGOOD

Cheers.

ABOUT THE AUTHOR

Keith Thirgood and Helen Walter are co-founders of Capstone Communications Group, a marketing company specializing in helping businesses get more business through innovative marketing ideas and materials. They founded Capstone in 1982 to develop marketing solutions for businesses. They advise clients on marketing issues and develop successful marketing campaigns, brochures, logos, advertising, Web sites, and all the other legitimate tools organizations use to get more business. Capstone's clients have ranged from multi-nationals such as Northern Telecom, Cantel, and Environment Canada to midsize manufacturers and software developers to small entrepreneurial companies in the speaking industry, consulting, and high tech.

KEITH THIRGOOD & HELEN WALTER

Capstone Communications Group

15 Wilson Street

Markham

905-472-2330

www.capstonecom

CHAPTER TEN

Stop Running From and
Start Racing Toward Your Destiny

An interview with...
SCOTT SCHILLING

DAVID E. WRIGHT (WRIGHT)

Today we are talking with Scott Schilling. Scott is the founder of TalkingWithGiants.com—a cause committed to illuminating the path to self-discovery. Scott's true desire is to serve others in all aspects of life. His life purpose statement reads: To inspire and empower others to serve humanity by living their life's purpose in spirit, love, and joy.

Scott brings over thirty years of experience in sales, marketing, speaking, and training to the financial and service industries, business owners, corporations, and entrepreneurs. Through his affiliations with Fortune 500 companies, innovative start-up companies, and high-paced individuals, Scott brings a wealth of knowledge, sales, marketing, implementation strategies, education, and expertise to the podium and to print. Scott's books to date include *Talking with Giants!, Heart-Centered Selling, Extreme Excellence, Conversations on Success,* and *Wake Up . . . Live the Life You Love.*

As an Internationally accomplished and entertaining presenter, Scott has spoken to thousands of attendees across a range of industries. Scott's goal is to maximize the potential and God-given talents of the individuals and organizations he encounters. Delivering content in an "easy to understand and digest style" makes his presentations extremely valuable, enabling them to be implemented by his students quickly.

Scott, welcome to *GPS for Success.*

You are an internationally renowned speaker, author, trainer, philanthropist, and fitness enthusiast. With all of the opportunities that come your way, why did you want to be a part of *GPS for Success?*

SCOTT SCHILLING (SCHILLING)

It's an honor to be asked to participate in *GPS for Success!* I've been very fortunate to have many mentors come into my life over the years. They have shared their secrets of success with me and for that, I am tremendously grateful. I made the commitment to each of them that if they would invest in me, I would in turn invest in others—I would share the lessons learned from them and the new lessons that developed out of putting their teachings into action. Ultimately, this is one way of "paying it forward."

Book projects like *GPS for Success* provide a proven vehicle to share some great insight (pardon the publishing pun) into how anyone who wants to get ahead in life can get ahead. It is always a joy to be part of a book like this and it's an easy way to give back to those who are searching. Being committed to never-ending personal improvement, I love to learn myself, so I have a real soft spot in my heart for those who love to learn as well.

We all have been granted infinite capabilities by God. It is ultimately up to us to develop and refine those talents and capabilities in whatever direction our true heart's desire leads. Learning about and then listening to your personal inner GPS (guidance positioning system) will take you exactly where you want to go, once you acknowledge the destination you desire to achieve.

WRIGHT

In your quest for constant improvement, what is the most enlightening thing that you have learned lately?

SCHILLING

It has to be the value of physical fitness. We all live in a world full of so much stress and pressure coming at us from so many different directions, we tend to absorb "toxins" from these various sources. In most cases, we don't even realize it's happening. Some of these toxins are physical, others are mental, and still more are environmental. Bottom line, most of them manifest in our physical plant—our bodies and with that, all sorts of issues arise.

We were born perfect beings. It is the various things that happen to us, things we have been exposed to, or that we've had to accept throughout our lives that change what once was perfect into something that rarely is running at its optimum. It takes a concerted effort to keep it as pure as possible. And if we don't, "dis-ease" will rear its ugly head. The issue is that disease takes place over a number of years in most cases and happens so often that we don't even recognize it happening. The changes are gradual and seemingly insignificant at the time. But it's like anything that accumulates over time, a pound here and a pound there turns into an issue left unchecked.

The exciting part is that we can all live a more fulfilling and wonderful life when we recognize that we are 100 percent responsible, totally in control, and can do something about it. Many times, unfortunately, it takes a traumatic event to raise our awareness. Fortunately for me, I didn't necessarily have to have something happen to me personally to wake me up. Hopefully, my participating in a book like *GPS for Success* will help raise awareness and send a wakeup call needed for you to take action before something major happens to you personally.

WRIGHT

So how did you personally recognize this?

SCHILLING

It was pretty easy and involved a combination of a number of things. First, my brother developed some health issues that raised my awareness to a family trait of potential heart and circulation issues. With that came a possibility of diabetes. Quite frankly, I wanted no part of any of these in my life. All of these potential issues were well within my personal control. If it was to be it was up to me!

Secondly, all I had to do is look in the mirror. Being out on the road speaking over two hundred and fifty times per year over the last four years, I had ballooned up to two hundred and fifty-six pounds on my six-foot, one-inch frame. I had over 30 percent body fat. This is nothing I'm proud of by any stretch. The time on the road had taken its toll. Now, I'm not blaming the road for what had happened to me. I was an active (or better put inactive) participant. I take total responsibility for my actions. Nobody held a gun to my head and made me eat the wrong things, stay up too late, or stay away from the hotel gyms.

People talk about comfort foods or taking it easy on yourself because the road is hard enough. That's all a bunch of hooey! You made the choices and you are receiving the consequences of your actions. No matter who you are or what you do for a living, it's pretty easy to get caught up in the stresses and pressure of it all. I believe inherently, everyone wants to do and be the best they can. Because of that internal desire, things get out of balance. And when we are out of balance, we tend to respond to the more immediate issues that are pressing us right then and there. To a certain extent, it's human nature. We come programmed with a fight, flight, or freeze response. We tend to fight the stresses head on, take flight from the things that relieve that stress, or freeze and simple get bombarded.

Physical fitness is a sneaky one because you don't get out of shape in a day. It comes from a series of days of eating too many of the wrong things, not sleeping enough, and not exercising to expand our conditioning. Getting out of shape is easy because it takes no effort—literally. And applying no effort consistently enough causes everything negative to build up throughout your body.

The good news for me is that I took back control and you can too, once you make the decision to do what you need to do to be physically fit.

WRIGHT

Was there anything that woke you up?

SCHILLING

It wasn't any one thing, it was many things. For over a year I had chest pains. None of the pains were really severe but should a person have any to begin with? I was becoming more and more fatigued at the end of the week and it was taking me longer to recover. Basically, I started having to limit my activity with family and friends on the weekends because I had to regroup my energy getting ready to head out again the next week. Then there was the fact my brother had four stents put in his heart, coupled with the onset of diabetes. I can assure you, I wanted none of that!

It came down to becoming aware—opening my eyes, taking off the blinders, and looking around at what was happening. It is truly amazing how freeing it is when you take back control of your own destiny. It is truly empowering. By taking 100 percent responsibility, you take control of your power. You allowed it to get to the level it has reached. Now you have the power to do something about it. It is really just that simple.

WRIGHT

So what did you do about it?

SCHILLING

The first thing I did is something anyone in this situation has to do—make the decision to do something about it. Believe it or not, it all starts with deciding to improve your situation. It is that easy!

I made the decision about what I wanted to accomplish—being fit for the rest of my life. After that decision was made and "out of the way," the rest started to fall into place.

WRIGHT

Is it really as easy as simply making a decision to change?

SCHILLING

Absolutely, after becoming aware that there needs to be improvement, deciding to do something about it is the next step. We were created and given "free will." With our will, we can truly accomplish anything in life that we want to accomplish.

Sometimes people get discouraged or they feel everything is against them. Even when I talk to people today they say, "You just don't understand my situation" or "It may have been easy for you but it's just not that way for me." It breaks my heart to hear people resign themselves to the fact that they are just along for the ride and have no control of their lives. Again, that's a bunch of hooey!

It's your life, you control it, and you are in charge. If you don't like it or where it's going, do something about it! Nobody fed me from across the room with a slingshot. And they haven't done it to you either. Why are you giving any of your God-given power to other things like food, schedules, or lack of discipline? Use your power for good—you!

We have all been so amazingly blessed with potential and opportunity to live as fulfilling a life as we can imagine. We live in an abundant universe with infinite possibility. Doesn't it make sense to grab your piece? As Napoleon Hill said many years ago, "Whatever the mind can conceive and believe the mind can achieve!"

WRIGHT

What else did you do?

SCHILLING

I recognized that the easiest way to be successful in any area of life or business is to put a system in place. In the trainings I facilitate, I share a concept called SYSTEM, an acronym that stands for "Save Your-Self Time, Effort, & Money"! Who wouldn't want that? You have to put a system in place that supports the desired result.

In fact, as I prepared to take on my fitness challenge head on, I developed an acronym for the entire fitness process. It is A DREAM I . . . LIVE. People tend to remember acronyms easily and it's always good to create the path of least resistance to help them be able to implement what they have learned.

A DREAM I . . . LIVE is a desire that I believe most people want in their lives. If they want it, it makes sense that they will not only remember it but will also put it into action for their benefit. Simply put, it's a seven-step process that anyone can put into action and use to achieve success. The process, while being truly successful in the fitness realm, also translates across all areas of life.

The "A" stands for Awareness. We have to become aware of our true situation, call a spade a spade, and be totally honest about where we are at the moment. Sugar-coating is what got you here—literally! Become aware of your situation.

I learned a long time ago from one of my mentors Jack Canfield, author of *The Success Principles* and co-founder of the *Chicken Soup for the Soul* series, a simple formula. It is Growth = Awareness + Inspired Action. With that, awareness and honest evaluation of where you are at this moment are essential to the growth process.

The "D" stands for Decide on Your Future. This is your life and you are the pilot. You can have anything you want in life, you just have to find someone who already has what you want and do what he or she does. For goodness sake, this is your life, why not design it the way you want it?

Most people today don't even know what they want out of life. It's pretty hard to "model" something when you don't even know what you want to model. Take a moment, stop, think, and make a decision as to what you want your life and your ultimate fitness to look like.

The "R" stands for Restructure Your Activities. This calls for making the changes necessary to be consistent with where you want to go, not where you are today. Your focus needs to be on the future because we get what we focus on. If you focus on the past and how you got here, that is exactly where you will stay. You have to look forward to what you want the outcome to be.

Let's relate this back to the title of this book, *GPS for Success*. A GPS is a Global Positioning Satellite system. It knows where you are and the minute you program it with where you want to go, it will give you the route to follow. The "R" is your route to achieving success.

The "E" stands for Execute the Plan. Most people fail because they don't create a plan in the first place. This is followed closely on the failure scale by not following the plan once it is created. As the old saying goes, failing to plan is planning to fail. Create a plan and execute it. Remember, it didn't take you three weeks to get out of shape, don't set unrealistic expectations and believe you are going to be back to being totally fit in three weeks. Like life, this is a marathon not a sprint. Gaining overall fitness will take time. That's okay, God's timing is perfect! You will right size accordingly.

The other half the growth formula is inspired action. Executing the plan is taking action toward the desired result. You have to get into and stay in motion. It provides progress toward your desired result and constant feedback along the way.

The "A" stands for Analyze the Results. You have to "inspect what you expect" so there has to be the ability to measure your progress. This is what keeps you going at those times where you may fall into some stinkin' thinkin'. Everyone has lulls in activity and desire; don't be so hard on yourself. But don't use it as an excuse to bail out of what you are really looking to accomplish. You'll feel really great about yourself and your progress when you see the pounds and inches peeling off in all the right places. There are many other vital signs that improve including cholesterol numbers, blood pressure, and blood sugar levels, you name it. These are all easy ways of identifying progress.

It doesn't matter whether you are talking about how to measure personal, professional, or business success—if you can't measure it you can't evaluate it. And if you can't evaluate it, you don't know how to improve it. It is just that simple.

The "M" stands for Modify the Plan and Re-Execute. It is unlikely that everything you put into action initially is absolutely perfect. And even if it is, the body has an amazing way of adapting to it. You have to throw your body a curve every once in a while to keep things going on the right track.

Flexibility in what you do, how you do it, and to what degree you do it will keep your progress moving forward. It will also add variety that is so often described as the spice of life. Don't you want some extra spice in your life?

The "I" stands for Inspire Others to do the same. I truly believe we have been put on this Earth for two reasons—to have a fabulous life and to help as many people as we possibly can. Because you will become the pinnacle of fitness, you will naturally inspire others to do the same. It may not be something that you thought about as you embarked on this course, but from personal experience I can tell you that people really look up to those who are fit and in shape. That in itself should inspire you!

It is an absolutely awesome feeling to have people you have never met before come up to you and ask, "How do you stay so fit?" It is an automatic opportunity to do good in the world and share an area of expertise that so many need to hear about. You have become the change you desired!

And "LIVE" stands for Love, Invest, Value, & Enjoy life. We all have been so amazingly blessed, it is absolutely fantastic to be able to Love those around us, Invest in the greater good, Value everyone's gifts, and Enjoy our life to its fullest.

Life is truly worth living. We live in such wonderful times full of opportunity and promise. And just in case your world is exactly as you want it to be right this minute, you have the power to make it different and better. So why not live it such a way that you can experience it to the max? That's my desire for everyone!

WRIGHT

You are writing another book to share this recipe for success aren't you?

SCHILLING

Yes, it is titled *Talking with Giants in Health and Wellness*. It details how people can take back control of their bodies and, more importantly, their lives. When I set out to become fit, I never thought I would write a book on the subject or the process. The response from so many people has been very gratifying. I am repeatedly asked how I accomplished taking back control of my fitness and, more importantly, my life. It became evident that writing it all down in an easy to understand, layman's version of fitness could help as many people as possible.

Helping people is consistent with who and what I am. I want to truly inspire and empower others to live their life's purpose to serve humanity in spirit, love and joy. If writing *TWGHW* can help even one person live a better life, the mission has been accomplished.

WRIGHT

Why should people read *TWGHW*?

SCHILLING

Everyone should read *TWGHW* for a number of reasons, actually. The lessons they will learn regarding gaining fitness in their lives physically parallel taking back and gaining control of their finances, their relationships, their time, and virtually everything in their lives. The principles in this book go way beyond simply getting fit physically.

The balance alone that can be learned will take them to a new level. Today too many people are living someone else's version of their lives. People are not taking control and making decisions to live the life of their dreams. And if you don't make those decisions, someone will make them for you and you end up living their definition of your life. And it's usually not nearly as fulfilling as it could have been or you would have liked it.

WRIGHT

It really sounds like it encompasses retaking control of mind, body, and spirit. Is that true?

SCHILLING

Absolutely! As I mentioned earlier, I believe we have all been put on this Earth for two reasons—to have a fabulous life and to help as many other people as we possibly can. And if you are not having a fabulous life and not even helping yourself, it's pretty obvious that you are not helping anyone else either. I believe we have all been put on Earth for a higher purpose. We have been given the perfect physical plant when we are born and then we go about messing it up. Not purposely mind you, it just happens, if you don't pay attention along the way.

To live a totally fulfilled life it really takes having control of your mind, your body, and your spirit. The power contained within the minds of each and every one of us is amazing. We have so much capability but unfortunately, most people don't develop it and therefore don't use it. And even those who do work to grow the mind's capabilities, probably only use a small percentage of what could be developed. Very few people have mastered the mind to the levels capable, including me. This is exactly why I will always be a passionate learner.

When it comes to our bodies, they were perfectly designed and meant to be at equilibrium—perfect balance. And yet we allow outside agents to invade our beings and take over a potentially perfectly operating machine. It's not too hard to figure out that if we don't do some preventative maintenance along the way, the machine will not work as well for as long as it could have. That doesn't sound like an option to me.

And as for spirit, I believe we are all connected to a higher source in the beginning. It is how we nurture and grow that connection that brings us greater satisfaction in life. For me that source is God. For you it might be Buddha, Allah, The Universe, or whatever is right for you. When you disconnect from your source, there is a feeling of something missing. It's really a shame because it doesn't have to be that way. The exciting thing is you can take and keep control of your mind, body, and spirit by paying attention and taking the required actions to stay at your original perfection.

WRIGHT

That is some amazing wisdom. Where does it come from?

SCHILLING

I look at the great sources of inspiration I have had in my life. It started with my parents. My dad worked for the same company for forty-six years—from age seventeen until sixty-three when he retired. That consistency taught me many great lessons along the way. He also loved public speaking and was an avid member of Toastmasters International. He used this passion to speak in behalf of the United Way for many years as a volunteer. I never really understood his desire to give back when I was younger, but now I totally get it. And I thank him for the example he set as I was growing up.

My mom is eighty-eight and still works forty hours a week to this day. She too showed me a path of dedication and commitment to the people she worked for and the causes she surrounded herself with. When my daughter graduated from high school and my mom came to the graduation, she showed us her new gold watch that had been presented to her by Florida Hospital for twenty-five years of volunteering. She started volunteering for them when she was sixty! Who says it's too late to contribute or give back?

I have an amazing wife, Peggy, who has been a sounding board and helped me refine my thinking consistently throughout our marriage. It's great to be married to my best friend, biggest supporter, and ally in my desire to improve myself while helping others.

I have been blessed to be exposed to some of the most amazing mentors teaching today. They include Jack Canfield, T. Harv Eker, Janet Switzer, John Childers, John Dealey, Dr. Fabrizio Mancini, and many more. They have all been extremely gracious in sharing their education and wisdom with me. Learning from the best of the best has been an absolute honor. Many have taken me under their wings and shared their most private details on success and business. They have shared their heart with me and it has given me the desire to do the same for others.

I've also had the great fortune to meet and be treated by some of the great healers around the world. These have been experiences that have been truly life-changing. We all have such great potential for good when we unearth our inner brilliance. The energy we can unleash is phenomenal.

WRIGHT

Is that why you have also launched TalkingWithGiants.com?

SCHILLING

You betcha! TalkingWithGiants.com is a worldwide "Portal of Good." It is your "Access to the Experts," the true giants of our time. The desire is to "illuminate the path to self-discovery." It is naïve to think that any one person has all the answers. In fact, many years ago one of my teachers drilled into our heads that we didn't have to always have all the answers, we just needed to know where to find them.

I guess to a certain extent, that's what I see TalkingWithGiants.com being. A resource of all things good that can help people get from where they are to where they want to be. Most people today work in a competitive model where they keep their things theirs and will only share if and when they get some kind of immediate return for it. I understand the need for revenue and growing your business. It's essential to stay operating. At the same time, I believe you can accomplish both and do it in a collaborative way that lifts all parties. A rising tide lifts all boats. I love to be in a harbor of tall ships!

My belief is that by working together, we can all achieve more. Mark Victor Hansen once said to me that TEAM meant Together Everyone Achieves More. It makes sense. When we pull together we have significantly more strength than when we try to pull alone. The strongest cables in the world holding up the most massive bridges and structures ever made by man are a weaving of many individual single strands together to give a combined strength far surpassing the capability of any single strand. There are many brilliant people we can all learn from. My goal is to create that encouragement and opportunity to make that knowledge and those resources available to anyone who has the desire to seek them out.

WRIGHT

So TalkingWithGiants.com is a place where anyone can come to find the resources needed to be successful across all aspects of life?

SCHILLING

Exactly! If what people need is something I have expertise in, I can supply that expertise to help them move forward. But if they need expertise in other areas, I have been blessed to meet and get to know the best of the best in many areas outside my expertise. It's a desire to prove quality solutions from the heart and minds of the best experts available to the challenges people need most.

People are out there searching for answers these days to so many different questions. The exciting part is that the answers to all those questions exist but sometimes they are hard to find. Or the places that the answers exist are not as trustworthy or known for their "quality" approaches. The desire is to have TalkingWithGiants.com to be a quality resource to obtain the answers while having the comfort that the people providing those solutions not only talk the talk but walk the walk.

WRIGHT

What drives you to want to supply this information?

SCHILLING

It's a "pay it forward" mentality. I've said it repeatedly—we have all been amazingly blessed and live in an abundant universe. God has provided enough for each and every one of us—and then some. It only makes sense to share the good.

Along the way, the commitment of TalkingWithGiants.com (TWG) is to "double tithe" from the revenue that is created. As more giants are added, there will be more causes for us to support. Why not help people achieve their dreams while giving back by contributing and helping other people develop some dreams?

Currently, TWG supports the United Way, Habitat for Humanity, American Red Cross, The Juvenile Diabetes Foundation, The Autism Society, SPCA, and many, many more charities and organizations that are doing tremendous work to improve our world. It's exciting to see them succeed!

Not only can we help supply people quality solutions, but we can become a solution by donating to many worthy causes that need support in our tougher economic environments today. This is win-win-win. The people who need answers get them and win, TWG generates donations that allow the ability to support causes needing support, causes achieve funding to do their good works to those who need it so they win, and the giants gain greater reach with their solutions so they win—truly a win-win-win-win!

WRIGHT

Is there anything else you'd like to share with our readers?

SCHILLING

Absolutely! You can be anything you want to be, live the life you want to live, help the people you want to help, and be the change the world needs today. If each of us reaches out, collectively we can make our world an absolutely amazing place. As long as that possibility exists, and there are people on Earth who have the desire and are willing to expend the effort, we can live truly fulfilling and happy lives.

We are coming into a time of greater social consciousness. That in itself is wonderful and exciting. Let's all participate together to make our world a better place. It's not really that hard. Maybe it starts for you with a "rampage of appreciation," thanking everyone and anyone you come across. Or having the "attitude of gratitude" and being truly grateful for all the blessings in your life. We all have so much to be thankful for. It's really comes down to focus and your level of commitment to engage.

You can reach me by visiting my Web site or you may e-mail me. My contact information is available on the About the Author page. I'd love to hear from you. We have newsletters that keep you up to date with what the "Giants" are up to, where they are appearing, their special offers, and many other kinds of valuable information. We also have many *free* gifts from the "Giants" available to be passed along as a thank you for your support and desire to continue to grow personally.

Finally, simply let me finish with a huge *thank you!* I greatly appreciate the opportunity to share with everyone. Please let me know how I can be of service to you! It truly is an honor!

ABOUT THE AUTHOR

SCOTT SCHILLING is the founder of TalkingWithGiants.com—a cause committed to illuminating the path to self-discovery. Scott's true desire is to serve others in all aspects of life. His life purpose statement reads: To inspire and empower others to serve humanity by living their life's purpose in spirit, love, and joy.

Scott brings over thirty years of experience in sales, marketing, speaking, and training to the financial and service industries, business owners, corporations, and entrepreneurs. Through his affiliations with Fortune 500 companies, innovative start-up companies, and high-paced individuals, Scott brings a wealth of knowledge, sales, marketing, implementation strategies, education, and expertise to the podium and to print. Scott's books to date include *Talking with Giants!, Heart-Centered Selling, Extreme Excellence, Conversations on Success,* and *Wake Up . . . Live the Life You Love.*

As an Internationally accomplished and entertaining presenter, Scott has spoken to thousands of attendees across a range of industries. Scott's goal is to maximize the potential and God-given talents of the individuals and organizations he encounters. Delivering content in an "easy to understand and digest style" makes his presentations extremely valuable, enabling them to be implemented by his students quickly.

SCOTT SCHILLING

4020 N. MacArthur Boulevard, Suite 122-183
Irving, TX 75038
972.659.8941
scott@ScottSchilling.com
www.ScottSchilling.com

CHAPTER ELEVEN
The Simple Road to Success

An interview with...
JUDY MACKENZIE

DAVID E. WRIGHT (WRIGHT)

Today we're talking with Judy Mackenzie, MBA, Certified Human Resources Professional and Professional Certified Coach. She founded TEVO Consulting Inc. in 2007 to provide services and guidance to small and medium sized businesses. Her primary goal through TEVO is to support companies in reaching their strategic goals by developing leadership and people management systems that allow employees to be at their best. She believes that engaged employees are fundamental to business success, and designs support and management systems to help leaders and companies achieve their full potential. Judy specializes in leadership coaching, which is the culmination of twenty years of executive HR experience in private, public, and not-for-public sectors, as well as a social work history that gives her a unique set of experiences from which to draw.

Judy is a consummate change agent and has enhanced her vice president roles in human resources by being strategic in her thinking as well as outcomes-oriented in her approach. Judy takes a practical no-nonsense approach to her work.

Judy, welcome to *GPS for Success: Goals and Proven Strategies.*

MACKENZIE

Thank you very much David, I'm glad to be here.

WRIGHT

So why is it that success seems far away for so many people?

MACKENZIE

For many people, success seems like searching for the Holy Grail. They feel like they are always looking but it is so elusive. One of my favorite quotes sums this up nicely:

"Would you tell me, please, which way I go from here?" said Alice.
"That depends a good deal on where you want to get to," said the Cat.
"I don't much care where—" said Alice.
"Then it doesn't matter which way you go." said the Cat.
—Lewis Carroll, *Alice's Adventures in Wonderland.*

Success is a state of mind! It is the result of setting goals and reaching them. It sounds so simple, yet this very statement has frustrated many great plans. The stumbling block seems to be the series of actions that are required to get you from your plan to actual results. It is so easy to become overwhelmed by all the details, by the number of changes required, and even to get lost on how and where to start the change.

This chapter will take you through the basic steps that are fundamental in creating any change in your life. More importantly, through a series of questions and activities, we will help you uncover what stops you from accomplishing your goals and consistently sabotages your plans for success. By stimulating your ability to self-observe, we will help you uncover the *unconscious decisions and assumptions* that are present in your everyday thinking and are responsible for derailing your success.

Follow the questions and activities presented in this chapter and you will learn how to program your thoughts and decisions so they are geared for success.

WRIGHT

Judy, you make it sound so simple but sometimes I just don't know where to start. Will you help me with that?

MACKENZIE

Let's get started.

GOALS—THE STARTING POINT

To achieve success, you need a goal—a desire for a tangible object or state of being; a strong desire. We're not talking about comments that frequently pepper our conversations such as, "Oh, I wish I could—" Goals are set for something that you really, really want and are willing to work for. More importantly, goals are what you are willing to struggle for and not give up easily. In order to create a goal that stands a reasonable chance of being accomplished, you have to explore your personal style, feelings, challenges, and opportunities in some depth.

How well can you identify goals contrary to wants? Try this exercise: Make a list of things you want. Now beside each one, using a scale of one to ten, write how much work and sacrifice you believe you are prepared to experience to have that goal. One is "not lifting more than two fingers to accomplish it" and ten is "prepared to work like Lance Armstrong does to win the Yellow Jersey—day in and day out, every day—no matter how I feel." Take your time, think honestly about the item you want, and try to imagine how much you would be willing to give up to attain that item.

Now review your list. Are there goals that have a "work and sacrifice" score less than eight? Then throw them away—they are just "wishes" and are wasting your mind space and energy. Let them go. Now pick the one that you want the most. Now you have a goal.

WRIGHT

Okay, that is making sense so far, but now I'm sitting with a goal and it seems so far away. What's next?

MACKENZIE

The next step in the process is visualization. Now that you have identified what you want, now is the time to visualize it. Can you see yourself having accomplished goals? Having fulfilled this desire? This is the time to give your imagination free reign. Really flesh out this visualization as fully as possible. What would you look like? What would you feel like? How would you feel differently?

Now take this visualization and put it onto paper. Describe in enough detail that you will recognize what it will look like once you have achieved your goal. You've heard it many times because it is true: if you can see it, you can create it.

If you are a highly visual person, create a collage of images that show your mental picture. Comb through magazines and pull out pictures that inspire, show, illustrate, and allow you to see and feel your goal. There are many places to find images—on the Internet, in art stores, photographs. If you have some skill at drawing, you can even draw what your success looks like.

If you aren't as visual, find a phrase or grouping of words that brings this goal to life for you. Put it in a place where you can see it every day. Look at it every day, say it aloud, and experience all the feelings of that goal.

It is so important that you experience the feelings, feel the joy, image how your life will be different, more fulfilled, richer, and all the other emotions that go along with success and happiness. Let me give you an example of how *not* visualizing career goals almost derailed a promising career.

I worked with a young manager who, although hard working, was having difficulty keeping her staff. Viewed by her superiors as having much potential, her inability to keep staff was becoming a serious problem and had the likelihood to seriously derail her success.

I sat down with her and asked what she thought were the reasons for such high turnover. I also asked what she thought a good manager looked like. She replied that a good manager had all the answers and that her role was to show the team how to do their work because she was technically so much stronger than they were. She felt that if she showed them exactly how to complete the task, they would learn from her. This didn't turn out to be the case. She found that each time a problem came up, they would immediately come to her for the solution. She couldn't understand why they didn't learn from her demonstrations.

She also found that she had so little time in her day to give to her staff that when they ran into an issue it was more time efficient to just fix the problem rather than coach them through it, enabling them to think more independently. A cycle of dependency was created, which resulted in staff leaving due to their dissatisfaction with their manager.

She was convinced her "lack of time" was the principal issue. It entirely escaped her that her inability to empower her staff to think for themselves was the real issue. She didn't see that they demanded her "mothering "approach to problem-solving and that her staff were fearful to do a procedure differently in case it didn't suit her style.

The time management issue was so huge for this young professional that she couldn't see how to get around it. We used this issue as the basis for personal change. After a number of coaching sessions using the methodology I will show you in this chapter, she was able to transition into having her staff be more accountable for their work.

She ultimately created an environment where outcomes were measured as opposed to her traditional method of micro-managing every detail. This freed up significant amounts of time for her to spend in other areas of her busy schedule.

She deeply wished she had been able to make this change sooner but realized that without being really clear about what she wanted to accomplish, she just couldn't see how to make the changes. She had settled for an obvious "external" problem that she thought was lack of time.

Through questioning and self-awareness she discovered how her own unconscious beliefs were driving her and sabotaging any chances she had to make a real change.

I can't stress enough how setting the destination of your learning journey will have a huge affect on your life. How will you know that you've arrived if you don't have the specific destination in mind?

Many years ago I journaled what success looked like for me. At that stage of my life I was very focused on career and learning, and my goals reflected this. I had been reading about the power of visualizing and used the athlete approach of seeing the end game to focus me on the process. So I put my wishes and thoughts on paper about what I wanted to accomplish in three- and five-year intervals. I put big, hairy, audacious goals (acronym: BHAGS) in my journal. I was a bit uncomfortable with some of my big thoughts, but in the spirit of visualizing, I continued on.

I broke down my journal into money goals, where I would live, what my house would look like, and what my life would be like when I accomplished my goals. I put pictures in this book to support my goals. Then I moved across the country and put this journal into a container and didn't think about it for some time.

Several years later, I reviewed the early pages of this journal. (I keep all my journals—sometimes they are just plain entertaining.) I found the goals with dates and accomplishments assigned to each one. I was totally astounded when I realized I had exceeded each of these goals significantly. I remember thinking at the time these BHAGs were really stretch goals for me, but what was the danger in thinking big? My approach became "go big or stay home," and it worked for me. The power of goals has been with me ever since.

This is a very important step, so please take your time and work through the visualization of what you are looking for—this is the starting point for building success in your life. This is how you plan your trip. You likely wouldn't go to the Yukon if you didn't have a reason to go there. However, once you realize this is where the best gold panning activity in North America is located and that this is a significant goal of yours, then you start to make your plans. You have to know where you want to go so you can put that into your modern day map called a GPS.

Congratulate yourself at this point. By detailing your goal and creating a visual/verbal support system to keep it alive, you have likely gone further and are closer to actually accomplishing your goal than you have probably ever done in the past. You have put valuable time into the process and developed a clear, visual identification of where you want to go. How many times have you thought you wanted to accomplish something, but then you got distracted? If you think this hasn't happened to you, I challenge you to consider that perhaps you aren't being entirely honest with yourself.

WRIGHT

Boy, can I relate to that coaching story! I have had that same experience earlier in my career. I wish I'd had a coach to help me through that then. I am really seeing how identifying goals and then visualizing them makes them so much more real. What's next?

MACKENZIE

Now, David, we are going to go deeper.

PEEKING UNDER THE HOOD

So far, you have identified your goal and created a visual support system to keep it alive and real in front of you on a regular basis.

Now it is time to delve further. Ask yourself questions that will aid in uncovering your motivation and your commitment to your goals. This will help you understand the "what and why" of your goals.

The answers to these questions provide key support for the upcoming journey. They are the gas stations along the way, if you will. These questions require thought and introspection and are best dealt with when you have time to think through your answers. If you journal, this is a great opportunity to understand your motivation, fears, style, and distracters.

The distracters or disrupters will be dealt with in some detail, as these can be unexpected surprises that often get in the way of many good plans.

It is my goal to assist you with some guideposts on your journey to make your search through this new territory less risky. These guideposts will be in the form of questions. When we ask questions, we evoke a response reflex that gives us information, power, knowledge, and energy. You are early in your goal journey, and now it is time to ask yourself some questions that will give you the information and generate the energy you need to set your course.

Some questions to consider are the following;

1. Is this goal possible and achievable?
2. What if you don't achieve your outcome, what will you do?
3. Is your focus on what you have or on what you don't have?
4. Is your outcome actionable?

5. Can you see yourself very clearly accomplishing your goal?

6. What has got in your way in the past in achieving this goal?

7. Is that barrier still there?

8. How will you deal with it now?

9. What is different now?

10. What do you need in the form of information or other support systems to achieve this goal?

It is important to remember to frame your questions to create a solution or an answer to the question and *not* to find blame or fault. Questions, when asked in the spirit of curiosity, open up possibilities for us. When they are placed in a negative way, they limit or close us off from feeling the experience and gaining the required momentum to move forward in our journey. They basically put the brakes on while trying to move forward.

YOUR INNER CRITIC A.K.A. THE GREAT SABOTEUR

During this exercise it is quite likely that you've encountered questions that don't feel comfortable. They seem to trigger an automatic flow of negative thoughts, comments, and opinions that wash over you like a dense fog. That flow of negativity comes from your inner critic or that voice that keeps giving you all the reasons why you can't be successful. This voice is not unique to you—all people have the internal negative "naysayers" but some have more effectively managed to silence them. I am going to call these irritating and negative messages that come to us in a fairly steady stream our Inner Critic.

It is not uncommon for the inner critic to be victorious over our rational minds. How many New Year's resolutions get laid to rest after the first five days of starting them? Have you ever talked to an ex-smoker after he or she has been smoke-free for a year or more? Did the person tell you how many times he or she had tried and failed before? It's a common tale.

Being an ex-smoker myself, I remember only too well the number of times I failed to quit this insidious habit and was very angry with myself each time, which only reinforced my inability to achieve the goal to quit. I would tell myself I was weak, unable to focus, and that I had failed. So each time I tried to quit, those messages were very close to the surface, which left me feeling that success was a long way off because I had failed so many times. I felt like I had lost the battle before it was even started. So when the first challenge came to me to test my commitment to quitting smoking, I would hear the messages in my mind of weakness and failure as opposed to success and strength.

When I finally succeeded in quitting smoking, I realized that I had combined together a number of activities to help me quit. Not only did I have the desire to quit but I was also able to visualize myself being smoke–free. I could image the fresh, clean smell of being smoke-free and how it would look, as well as all the other advantages of being smoke-free. You can tell I was young because my biggest concern should have been my health, but that was not what the real issue was for me at that time. I had to dig down deep to uncover what was really bothering me about smoking.

To further motivate myself, I calculated in detail the significant cost savings and planned how I would use that money to treat myself in other ways that would give me pleasure (as I was convinced that I would miss the pleasure of smoking).

Knowing myself, I also planned for the bumps and curves in my path to being smoke-free and had my support systems close by. I visualized it, planned it out, knew what it looked like when temptation had gotten the better of me in the past, and planned for some discomfort. The visual was on my refrigerator, and I looked at that image in challenging times.

Of course my inner critic behaved like a demon over the course of the first year. It was relentless in its efforts to get me to cave in. It would tell me to "just smoke to avoid all this pain and discomfort." But, after a while, the voice wore out its welcome. I knew that I wouldn't spend time with anyone, not even a friend, who spoke to me like that. I wouldn't spend time with someone who worked so hard to sabotage my good intentions; so, I reasoned, why would I put up with it from my own inner critic?

We did part company on that topic after a period of time but it still lingers to challenge my commitment to other goals even to this day.

Our inner critic is the accumulation of our fears, beliefs, and limiting messages given to us over the years. It is the voice that keeps us locked into non-productive and unwanted behaviors for years. Its singular goal is to keep us safe—100 percent safe and free from any pain. It will use any past failures or mishaps as evidence why we should not do that action, try a new approach, or even think a new thought. If you want to live in a cocoon and never change anything in your life, then your inner critic will be happy—but you won't be.

Your inner critic never gives you positive messages like "don't try that, you are likely to be successful." This critic is just that—highly critical. It is so afraid to try anything that it will actually send you enough messages to immobilize you, When you hear messages that are restrictive by nature and are judgement-based such as "they will never promote you" or "you can't possibly get into law school," that is your inner critic expressing fear of change. The inner critic doesn't leave room for solutions. In its thinking it is trying to get you to back off or to retreat. Inner critics are often totally out of control and are entirely based on fear.

WRIGHT

I know exactly what you mean, Judy. There have been many times when that voice that sees the negative to everything has gotten in my way. Do you have some thoughts as to how you can put those ideas to rest or make them into good ideas?

MACKENZIE

David, there are concrete steps you can perform to begin taking control of your inner critic.

First, try writing the negative "critical voice" thoughts into a journal as they occur to you. Many times, the written word will expose thoughts and show how extremely negative and unfounded they are.

Another approach is to divide a page into two columns. In the left column, write the inner critic statements and in the right column, write the opposite statement that answers the question in a positive note. What could happen?

For example: You want to apply for a new job with a new company that is fifty minutes from your home. The left-hand column would have the inner critic statements such as: *"That is way too far. I would have to get up forty minutes earlier than I do now and I hate mornings."*

The right-hand counterbalance statements could be: "This *would allow me to take the train and not have to deal with traffic anymore, giving me the opportunity to read the books I haven't had time to read."*

For every negative statement you come up with, you must create a positive one. The power of this exercise is that it will get you out of the habit of negative thinking and will give you experience in creating possibilities. Don't be fooled—this exercise takes a lot of practice, as many of us have had *years* to perfect our negative, self-sabotaging thinking.

I highly encourage you to get in the habit of counterbalancing your negative thoughts each time you have one. It gets easy very quickly if you stick with it. I often reflect at the end of the day on three thoughts that I reframed (turned around) in the course of that day. That way I don't forget them once I have created them.

The following list of questions is for you to think about. It is designed to give you more information about your thinking process and to help uncover unconscious beliefs, opinions, and judgements. Reflecting on these questions may enlighten you to possibilities and remove some barriers at the same time.

1. Have you chosen success?
2. Do you believe you deserve this?
3. What are you willing to do to accomplish this?
4. How will your life be different when you have it?
5. Are you willing to ask for the help you need?
6. Are you willing to listen to others' opinions?
7. What will keep you from being successful?
8. What beliefs need to shift for you to achieve your goals?
9. How is negative thinking serving you?
10. What will it take to move forward?
11. Do you believe your current perspective is helping or hindering you?
12. What is the most uncomfortable part of change at this time? Is this real or imagined?
13. Is this important to you? How important is it?
14. What is the worst thing that can happen if you did this?

15. What are you resistant to and what is this sabotaging your plan or dreams?

WRIGHT

These are some great questions. There are few that really make me think about things differently. The power of the question is often untapped, don't you think?

Up to now we have been talking about understanding yourself and self-assessment. Sometimes people have weak spots or "blind spots" that they are not aware of. How do you take this into consideration? It is like the blind spots when you are driving; you don't realize they are there until you bump into them. That creates a whole other set of issues.

MACKENZIE

David, you are so right. This is one of my favorite quotes.

"Know Thyself" according to Socrates

So far, we have been working on pre-trip planning. We've visualized clearly where we want to go (set our goal). We've illustrated it so clearly that we will know immediately when we've arrived (imagery). We've even reflected on why we want to travel this journey so at the first sign of a detour, traffic jam, or congested spot we aren't tempted to give up and go back home (motivation and stamina).

Before we get in the car and start driving, it is critical to make sure we can go the distance. It is time to look at the gap between what we have and what we need to start our journey and sustain it.

This is one of the most difficult tools to master for many, as it involves self-awareness, self-assessment, and external input through feedback and formal assessment tools. In a nutshell, you need outside information on the validity of your plan.

Did you know that self-assessment is most accurate in your strength areas, but less accurate at weaknesses and least accurate in interpersonal skills and how you affect others? This is the reason it is wise to plan for this reality to ensure you are on track with what you really need at this stage. So how do you get to know yourself? Follow the map.

In viewing the gap, you may need some outside assistance. Some of us have blind spots, often unknown to ourselves but well known by others. They will forever remain blind spots unless we invite others to give us feedback and accept it graciously, even though it is hard to hear and may hurt or challenge our belief system.

Blind spots are often failure points or derailers, and they are pervasive. Many times our friends or colleagues are not comfortable giving feedback in these areas because they are afraid of the repercussions. The sad part of this cycle is you can't change behavior you aren't aware of, and you can't become aware of blind spot behavior if you are not open to constructive feedback.

Where do you see yourself in this cycle? Do you ask for feedback and receive it graciously, or do you ask for feedback and then attempt to maintain your position without looking at it from a different point of view? When was the last time someone you trust gave you feedback and you used it to build a new skill set or strength set? You likely have had success in this area at some point, and you can be assured that it was not catastrophic.

It is fear that holds people back from asking for and acting on feedback. It is a personal change process that can be unsettling. This is where a professional coach or mentor is valuable, as they can help you explore areas for development and growth that you are completely unaware of and in a structured way that allows you to make necessary changes in an environment that is safe.

I once worked with an executive who had a very large blind spot in her ability to communicate effectively with her staff and colleagues. She felt very confident that she was extremely strong in this area and relied heavily on the fact that she had a graduate degree to prove it. The company sponsored a 360 feedback process[1] as part of the development planning for the next year. Naturally it was not a surprise to see the results for this executive, but she

[1] 360 feedback is when you ask people who surround you (thus the 360 degree name) such as managers, secretaries, colleagues, clients, and anyone else appropriate, to share feedback.

was furious. She used every excuse she could find to lay blame with the assessment tool, to challenge the intellectual ability of the respondents to understand the assessment questions, and other unflattering assumptions. Not once did she think that perhaps this was her blind spot and that she had been given the gift (as painful as it might be) to develop this skill further.

Unfortunately, her response continued to isolate her from her staff and she ended up leaving the company. This de-railing behavior was not something she was able to address. While this is an extreme case of a blind spot getting the best of someone, it happens more often than you would think.

There are many indicators of blind spots, but the most frequent is when someone is passed over for a promotion or is given negative feedback on a performance appraisal that he or she didn't see coming. These can be the result of some behavior that falls into that blind spot category that has never been addressed. Other derailing behaviors are defensiveness, unwillingness to adapt to new ideas, arrogance, and being overly ambitious, just to name a few. If you hear feedback of this nature, and you choose to ignore it, I would ask you to reconsider, as these are behaviors that will not serve you well.

Some people have failure points or derailers that they are aware of and still, they choose to keep them.

Consider some of the following questions if you feel you have some of these behaviors and you have not considered them problems:

1. How does behavior help you get you where you want to go?
2. What stops you from change?
3. What would happen if you tried a new approach to this behavior?
4. What is the best thing that would happen and what is the worst thing that would happen? Do you know this for a fact or do you just think you know it?

These are just a few questions that will help you delve deeper into some fears, outdated belief systems, and some stuck behaviors. Remember, what *you think about, you bring about.* You are a very powerful being under your layers of cautious self because you have the ability to create the future—your future.

EXERCISE: LIST OF STRENGTHS

Research tells us that most people are able to identify their strengths with accuracy. If you are a very modest type person you may need some prodding or discussion to get a full list of your strengths. This is the time to really dig deep because once you identify your strengths in a number of areas such as personal, professional, spiritual, community, and family, you will have a solid base to transition some of these skills to other areas.

This is not the time to feel embarrassed about "tooting your own horn." First, this is an exercise in self-discovery. To be successful, you must recognize *both* your strengths and weaknesses with a fair degree of accuracy. Otherwise you can easily get lost on a detour without any signposts to help you get back on track.

If you struggle to find strengths in a number of areas, you will need outside help. We have already spoken about the benefit of having significant people in your life give you feedback. These significant people are co-workers, friends, family, and managers. They know you best, and as long as you believe they have your best interests at heart, you can trust their feedback and comments.

Another way to get private feedback is by 360 degree feedback instruments. There are many companies who use these types of tools on a regular basis to develop their staff, but you can also buy or create your own. There are inexpensive, even free survey systems such as Survey Monkey, Zoomerang, or Survey Builder that you can investigate on the Internet.

WRIGHT

Those are great resources and tips you have shared with us. You are telling me there is a number of different ways to get to "self-awareness." Now that I am aware of some issues that I didn't know before, I feel that I have to start over again. What are your thoughts on this?

MACKENZIE

David, you don't have to do this alone.

BUILD YOUR RESOURCE LIST TO LOOK AT WHO AND WHAT YOU NEED TO DEVELOP YOUR DESIRED SKILLS.

Now it is time to look at the number of resources you have available to you. Who are the people you can count on to help you? Where can you get more training and build your skill set? Where is there more information for you to research and clarify? Resources are all the many tools you will need to develop new skills that will move you toward accomplishing your goal(s).

Did you know that of all the many resources available to you for skill development, the largest amount fall within what is called the "on-the-job experience"? This type of experience ranks the highest in terms of successful skill acquisition and is available to you for no extra cost, just focus and effort. Many companies have numerous opportunities available to develop new skills, however, these often require you to "step up to the plate" and go searching for ways in which to participate. Make it known that you are available for extra job rotations, that you are ready and willing to volunteer— to donate time for company projects. You can look to see if there are committees and other corporate activities for you to serve on that are above and beyond the regular call of duty. There is no shortage of places where people can use an extra pair of hands and a generous donation of committed time and support.

The opportunities within your existing role or a new role are staggering when you think of it from this perspective. At the same time, look around you and identify who is doing what you would like to do or demonstrates skills you would like to learn. Rather than start from scratch, investigate learning options such as coaching or mentoring. Keep in mind, however, that successful and talented people are busy and likely to be more willing to help if they see you have done your homework and have created a clear and concise plan. Make your story a compelling one and make sure they also see the same possibilities that you do.

I have mentored many people over the years and have seen a wide range of personal approaches to mentoring. I am very willing to share my stories and pass on lessons, but what I did not enjoy or engage in is when someone came to me with the hope that I would put together their plan for them to execute. This told me they really didn't know what they wanted and therefore they didn't know what they wanted or needed from me. On the other hand, I've had some very organized and well thought-out plans presented to me that allowed me to tap into my experiences to add value. It was also a pleasure to work with these people, as I knew they had put in thought and effort, which showed their personal commitment and ability to solve problems. This gave me good insight into their approach to life and learning.

THE SCHOOL OF HARD KNOCKS

One very valuable resource that many people dismiss far too quickly is "the school of hard knocks." This is the learning we acquire from experiences that didn't turn out the way we wanted them to. We often call these situations "failures" and many times we are tempted to bury these experiences deep and out of sight. The only failure is a lesson not learned.

That is the loss of a significant learning opportunity. When our experience doesn't match up with our expectations, it is a chance for us to re-evaluate what we *think* we know with what we call *reality*, and this is very valuable learning.

When you lose a job, are passed over for a promotion, or struggle with co-workers, there are valuable lessons to be learned, about you, about others. These lessons can have a positive affect on your future through active evaluation, learning, and adjusting.

You make choices in everything you do, which is a very hard statement for some to hear. If you win or lose, you can take comfort and strength from knowing that at least you made the choice. If you find yourself often being "hard done by," review the five questions a few pages back and search deeply for answers within. An external coach may be helpful in providing a different perspective and setting a positive trajectory.

Reading and attending courses is another key method of learning skills to attain goals. There are so many great books and courses out there that give insight into the next steps to take or introduce you to new thoughts and theories. The key is to take this learning and embed it into your thinking.

When you read a book or take a course, the question that should be on your mind is: how can I apply this today, tomorrow, and the next day? Journalist, author, and pop sociologist, Malcolm Gladwell shares the following thoughts in his book *Outliers,* that "after 10,000 hours of practice you can master anything." Now that may seem a little daunting but habit does take time to build. At least twenty-one days of practice are required to build a degree of comfort with a change. My point is that change does not happen overnight, and you will need to plan for how you will integrate your new learning and stick with it.

This is often the reason that courses are listed so low on the transformational change scale (that is the change that actually makes a difference in how you behave) because once the course is finished and the binder is put with pride on your bookshelf, you will become immersed in the three hundred e-mails you missed while you were at the course. In the blink of an eye, the course content is lost as you return to your crazy schedule. Sound familiar?

You have now identified what you need to develop, through your use of significant others, assessments, and self-analysis. To keep track of your plan and the resources required, you could create a simple table as illustrated below.

Skills I need to develop	Job Experience (What) (75% – 90%)	Significant People (Who)	Books What do I need to read?	Courses Needed to add to my technical skill set
Example: Conflict management skills	Working through department issues	Joe Black company conflict negotiator In legal department	Conflict Resolution for Supervisors	Conflict Resolution 101 at XYZ College

Create a five-column page with what you need to learn on the far left. This is the research phase of the journey. What do you need to know? Who do you need to talk to? What do you need to read? Do you need to take courses? What experience can you get in your current job, community, or church?

Completing this exercise will take you off autopilot and move you quickly into self-awareness.

HITTING A BUMP IN THE ROAD

So many of our journeys start off wonderfully; we are happy and excited, we have our map in hand, exciting pictures of all the wonderful times we'll have, and a car packed with all the food, drinks, and entertainment we need for the trip.

Then we hit the first bump—a large pothole, a serious detour—that does not have adequate directions to get back on our planned trip and before we know it, we either turn around and go home or worse, pull over to the side of the road and sit stewing for ages about why this should be happening to you! Sound familiar? People often fail to plan for the unexpected. They set off in a bubble of optimism and hope, but then give up when all doesn't go according to plan.

This is the serious part of your plan. Be prepared by planning for the difficult times. Be ruthless with your self-examination and know where your challenges may come from. Who can you call on to help you when the going gets rough? What will pull you through when you feel like quitting? Be creative and don't leave any back doors open. Be prepared to give up things, to sacrifice what "used to be," and to have some discomfort from time to time. This is how you accomplish your goal.

When I finally decided to quit smoking, I knew that initially I would have to stop some social activities with my friends who smoked. I knew that after a short while in their company, I wouldn't have the same will power to resist my foe—cigarettes. My inner critic would have a field day reminding that I was weak and that one cigarette would be fine in this social situation. I would even bargain with myself that I would only smoke on Thursdays or when I was with a specific friend. Finally, I had to get more creative than my inner critic and if I was to feel the sweet joy of success I had to do things very differently. I have been smoke-free for thirty years, and I use my successful experience in this major change process as the foundation for changing almost everything.

BE ON THE LOOKOUT—KEEP YOUR EYES ON THE ROAD

After a while, it's easy to get complacent and start to lose focus. When you take your eyes off the road, you know what happens then—you wind up in the ditch or worse.

When working toward a goal, even as you plan for bumps and derailers, you also have to monitor your progress on a regular basis and *at the first sign of trouble,* deal with it. Many times we tend to shrug it off and say, "Oh well, just this one time" or "It's not really important—just once can't hurt." That is listening to your inner critic. It will soothe you and work at eroding the new behavior you have worked so hard on. Remember—the inner critic's job is to maintain the status quo and it will use any argument it can.

So monitor your progress. Be on the lookout for broken commitments, missed actions, and unfilled promises. They are the early indicators that your plan needs some tweaking—some minor adjustments. Go back to the lists of questions and work through them. Practice developing self-awareness and take control of your journey.

WRIGHT

Judy, this has been great. I am coming away from our discussion with some great ideas on how to work on achieving my goals in a step-by-step process.

Will you just recap your steps for me to make sure I have it straight? I don't want to miss any nuggets, as you have shared so many great insights here.

MACKENZIE

I would be happy to, David.

Five Simple Steps Coupled with Huge Insight Equals Success
1. Set your goal.
2. Visualize and make your goal concrete.
3. Identify and confirm all necessary resources.
4. Put your plan into action.
5. Celebrate your success.

These five simple steps to charting your course will be more easily attainable with the self-awareness component built into each step. If you take anything from this chapter, it is my hope that you will appreciate how to use feedback—even the tough stuff—to get you where you want to go. It is also vital to remember that everyone learns these lessons through "the school of hard knocks" or feedback of some sort. Some people have learned early on in their life that listening actively to feedback is a source of rich learning, but the largest majority of us have not because it is often too painful or the confusion about what to do with the information is too great. As a result, we often become resistant to change, which leaves us in the dust. If there is something out there you want, I suggest you follow these steps and try something new. The worst that can happen is you will learn something new.

WRIGHT

I really do appreciate all this time you've taken to go over these questions with me. It's been a real learning experience for me.

MACKENZIE

Perfect, great, thank you so much.

WRIGHT

Today we've been talking with Judy Mackenzie. Judy is a Professional Certified Coach and Certified Human Resources Professional. Her primary goal is to support companies in reaching their strategic goals by developing leadership and people management systems that allow their employees to be at their best. She specializes in leadership coaching, which is the culmination of twenty years of her HR experience. She sounds like she knows what she's talking about—at least I'm listening and I hope our readers are too.

Judy, thank you so much for being with us today on *GPS for Success: Goals and Proven Strategies.*

About the Author

Judy Mackenzie, MBA, Certified Human Resources Professional and a Professional Certified Coach. She founded TEVO Consulting Inc. in 2007 to provide services and guidance to small and medium sized businesses. Her primary goal through TEVO is to support companies in reaching their strategic goals by developing leadership and people management systems that allow employees to be at their best. She believes that engaged employees are fundamental to business success, and designs support and management systems to help people and companies achieve their full potential. Judy specializes in leadership coaching, which is the culmination of twenty years of executive HR experience in private, public, and not-for-public sectors, as well as a social work history that gives her a unique set of experiences from which to draw.

Judy is a consummate change agent and has enhanced her vice president roles in human resources by being strategic in her thinking as well as outcomes-oriented in her approach. Judy takes a practical no-nonsense approach to her work.

Judy Mackenzie

West Vancouver, Canada

judy@tevoconsulting.ca

www.tevoconsulting.ca

CHAPTER TWELVE
Develop a Disciplined Life

An interview with...
DR. JOHN GRAY

DAVID E. WRIGHT (WRIGHT)

John, you've built a successful career as an expert giving relationship advice. I recently read a statement attributed to you: "A wise woman is careful not to pursue a man more than he is pursuing her." Will you explain why?

JOHN GRAY (GRAY)

When women make themselves too available to men, men get lazy. It's old-fashioned wisdom, but on a new level. We can understand it biochemically as well. Men bond with women when their testosterone levels go up. When there's a challenge, testosterone levels go up. But when things become easy, testosterone levels go down—so there needs to be a sense of the man initiating his own behaviors as to a woman doing it all.

The easiest way to make a man lose interest in you is to do everything for him. The most exciting thing to a man is when he feels that he is making a difference in a woman's life, as opposed to her doing everything for him.

WRIGHT

That makes sense. Perhaps definitions were different several years ago when I was single. Today, how does one determine if he or she is dating or in a "relationship"?

GRAY

Quite often women believe that when they are having sex with a man that they are having a monogamous relationship with him. They just assume that is his value system, and that's not always the case. I encourage women to assume that they're having a committed, monogamous relationship after a man has told them so.

The next question that comes up from women is, "Well, how do you bring up such a subject?" The best way to do it is to let him know at some point that you're not interested in having sex unless you're in an exclusive monogamous relationship. When he's ready to make that step she should tell him how she feels about it. That is certainly one approach.

WRIGHT

If someone is not sure that the person he or she is dating is "the one," how can that person get some help to sort through that uncertainty?

GRAY

Certainly feeling uncertain and doubting is a natural course of action in the dating process, and it's the first realization that's important. Sometimes people think, "If I don't know for sure, then maybe this is definitely not the right person for me."

One insight that is very important is that you could be with the right person for you, but still go through a period of feeling doubt and uncertainty. It's just a natural process, and while you are in that process it takes time before a part of you begins to sense that you're with the right person, or you begin to sense that you're with the wrong person. It just takes some time.

Couples who rush into making a commitment often make a mistake, and then feelings get hurt, so it's best to go slow when in doubt and not to assume that something's wrong.

WRIGHT

In the event of a cheating spouse or a lover, what should people do to learn to heal from infidelity in the relationship?

GRAY

It's an important concept to recognize that we all get our hearts broken, our partners make mistakes, and we experience disappointments. A part of growing in real love is the ability to forgive our partners for mistakes. People simply don't think sometimes and they make mistakes. By talking about it and sharing, people can understand what their mistakes are and make changes and grow from that. It's certainly a personal choice that some people make to simply exclude somebody who would ever cheat on them.

If someone has children I always encourage them to recognize that having an affair is a mistake, and people make mistakes—it's not a horrible, horrible mistake, it's just a mistake.

If someone's violent (that's more of a horrible, horrible mistake), even then it's forgivable if the person was to get help and recognize that he (or she) has a problem and overcome that problem.

The main question about being with someone is that after you have opened your heart and you've been hurt, if you take time to heal your heart, do you still want to be with him or her? That's the question. It's not for me or any other person to tell you whether you should be with that person; it's always an individual choice within the heart. The problem is that some people get caught up in this thinking that if someone makes a mistake then for sure I don't want to be with them. It's quite unrealistic to ever expect perfection in this world.

WRIGHT

In your writings you suggest using a relationship advisor or coach for those who need help. Will you explain the process?

GRAY

The process is simply talking with somebody who will ask you questions to help you to get in touch with your feelings. You can express your feelings without feeling that you're going to be judged or your feelings are going to hurt somebody or you're going to be held accountable and stand by those feelings. Often feelings need some room to flow and change as you grow in awareness. It's often not safe to show this with someone you're in a relationship with—the person might hold you to those feelings. So you go to a counselor to talk about those things.

Today it's becoming very popular to talk to coaches as well. One of the differences between a counselor and a coach is that a counselor is trained more academically in the process of analyzing what dysfunction you might have, and in providing a means to reflect on what's happening in your life related to things in your past. The counselor might even do more work on your childhood to rebuild self-esteem issues.

A coach is someone who is there to hold you accountable to do the things that you say you want to do by asking you questions. A coach can also become a sounding board who will ask you about what your feelings are, what happened, what you think should happen, what you think should not have happened, and what you think can happen. This type of exploration helps people find within themselves the wisdom to make better choices in their life. It also helps to motivate them to make better choices and follow up with action. So the coach tends to be more practically oriented.

A Mars/Venus coach adds to it an aspect of providing education as to the various insights of how men and women are different, how their emotional needs are different, and how they can motivate each other to be the best they can be in a relationship, rather than unknowingly pulling out the worst about the individuals in a relationship. I'm a big believer in education first, and then in coaching to motivate people. But often people don't even know what's going on, and some basic insights can help them make better choices and decisions. A coach can then assist them in staying motivated to achieve that end.

WRIGHT

I've heard the divorce rate is 50 percent. Is that true? And can a counselor or relationship coach actually help save a marriage?

GRAY

I've seen counselors ruin marriages, and I've seen counselors help save marriages. There are different forms of therapy. If you're in therapy and it doesn't feel right to you and you don't feel like you're making progress, you're probably in the wrong kind of therapy for you. There are some kinds of therapy where the opportunity is created for two people to sit and talk about how they feel with each other. This can result in arguments and fights in the counseling room just like the fights they have at home.

My Mars/Venus counselors are trained in ways to assist individuals in learning new ways of interacting, new ways of expressing their feelings, and new ways of avoiding arguments and fights. I think this is very important for a therapist to do. A Mars/Venus coach is going to focus more on assisting individuals in taking responsibility for how they're contributing to the problems in their relationship. This can simply be having someone to talk with to share what you're feeling. Sharing your feelings can sometimes bring about enormous insight into a situation, as well as helping you to feel better.

When you feel better you're able to respond in a more positive way. Our Mars/Venus coaches and counselors repeatedly receive stories and testimonials of couples who feel that their marriages were saved.

WRIGHT

I went on your Web site and I looked at some of the things that you're doing. I was really impressed. One thing that caught my eye was the Relationship Test. Does the Mars/Venus Relationship Test really work? What do you actually test?

GRAY

There are different areas of relationships which could be stronger or weaker. What a Relationship Test does is allows you to become more aware of what you're experiencing every day. Often people do not take the time to sit down and reflect on what's working here and what's not working. Our lives are often so busy that we're just going from the *next* thing to the *next* thing to the *next* thing, and we don't sit back and reflect on what's working and what's not working.

By doing the test and answering the questions, you're having to take that time and reflect upon what really is going on in your relationship. The irony in relationships is sometimes couples will be fighting in counseling or they'll be fighting at home, and they don't even know what they are fighting about. They don't even know how the argument started! Everything was fine, and suddenly one little thing happens and one or the other is flying off the handle and they just don't know what to do about it.

Often these flying off the handle experiences are like the water boiling and turning into steam. Long before it boiled, it simmered, and long before it simmered, the water was heating up. So there's a process that leads up to uncontrolled experiences in relationships. When you become more aware of what's not working in a relationship long before it's boiling, you have a chance to easily make adjustments in your behavior.

When taking a Relationship Test you're able to see many places where you have confusion or you don't understand what is going on. Talking to a relationship coach you can ask questions, particularly in the problem areas. You can talk about what's going on so that you can make sense of what's going on in your relationship.

Often when we don't know what's happening or don't know how to correctly interpret what's happening because it doesn't make sense to us, we then assume the worst rather than assume the best. And what our Mars/Venus coaches do is help to point out the *good* reasons why people do what they do, and strategies to help bring out the best in them.

WRIGHT

Every time I hear a talk show host ask a guest about the most important attribute a person needs to have when considering a relationship, the answer from males or females are always the same: "A good sense of humor." Is that really true?

GRAY

Well, that's what everybody says, but when difficulties arise in relationships the women then complain that the men are not serious. Or the man could complain that the woman isn't serious. Generally it's the number one thing on the list for women to say "a man's sense of humor," and when I hear that I want then to educate that woman to recognize that she's looking for the wrong thing. The last thing you need is for a man to entertain you. What you want is a man to provide security for you, to be attentive to you, and to understand you. In that place of safety, then you will naturally be expressive of your femininity, which is actually quite entertaining to men. It's the woman who brings joy to life, not the man. So when women are looking for men to bring joy to their life, women are often just feeling insecure as though they can't provide enough, and they are looking to a man to provide that role.

I have a wife and three daughters. When I travel with them it's amazing how entertaining they are! The nature of femininity is that women talk, they share, they look, they comment, they respond, they laugh a lot.

But what *is* good for a woman to look for in a man is not entertainment. She may think she's looking for that, but she'll find herself being disappointed again and again. What she should be looking for is a man's sense of humor in that he doesn't take things too seriously. That's extremely very attractive to women. Not taking himself too seriously means that he's not defensive about things and he doesn't claim to be perfect or expect or demand that she believes him to be perfect. That is a very healthy attitude and attribute in a man. If he can, in a sense, "lighten up," that constitutes a good sense of humor. That is what creates a sense of security for a woman.

If women want men to entertain them all the time, not only will they be disappointed, but it puts way too much pressure on men—they'll come on really strong and then women will lose interest because men are just not entertainers.

WRIGHT

Is it possible to be too cautious setting your criteria too high when choosing a life partner?

GRAY

I think the idea that you are getting at is very healthy to examine. I hesitate to say, "Lower your expectations and find your ideal partner." That sounds like you're not getting the best. What is going on today with both women and men is that they have very unrealistic expectations of what they require and what they want in a partner.

Life is often a gradual process of humbling them and helping them recognize what's realistic and what they are really looking for. We often look to the cover of a book rather than to the substance of the book, hence the old saying, "Don't judge a book by its cover." In our society we have become somewhat superficial in how we look for people. It takes a little maturing before we begin to realize who a person is is much more than how they look or how they react in certain situations or what they have or what they can do.

And yet those are all a part of the picture. I focus on helping couples change their expectations just in a sense of what a healthy relationship looks like. It doesn't mean that he's being romantic all the time, and it doesn't mean that she's happy all the time—two people really need to learn how to be happy on their own and then want to share that happiness with someone. That becomes the foundation of a relationship. When we are looking to someone to fill us up and make us happy, we will be disappointed later on. When we are somewhat happy and fulfilled in our own life, then we can find extra happiness through sharing our happiness with someone else. When that happens we are much less needy and our expectations tend to be much more realistic automatically.

WRIGHT

Almost everything you've said has hit me personally, especially the aspect of education. You see people who say, "This is my life-long partner" and they talk about all kinds of things, but it seems like you're talking about education.

GRAY

I feel that what's missing most in the world today when it comes to relationships is insight and education into understanding how to create healthy relationships. And why we need this education now more so than a hundred years ago, is that people didn't take courses even fifty years ago in improving their relationships. That's because there were hundreds of years of tradition where women had certain roles and men had certain roles. Men interacted in certain ways and women interacted in certain ways. As long as everybody acted according to those established patterns, everyone got along quite well.

Then the world changed. Now the world is different and yet no one has defined new roles and how men and women are supposed to interact and what works best for them. To a certain extent there is no "best"—it's a world of tremendous freedom and choice and we have to define those roles ourselves. But in defining those roles there's a certain amount of freedom to create those roles, and there's also a certain lack of freedom.

I might wish to walk through a wall, but I just can't—certain realities don't change. So in this world where we are "making up" relationships in a new way, there are certain realities that have not changed. There are certain ways that men interact and there are certain ways that women interact. There are certain needs that women have and certain needs that men have. The needs men and women have are different. By understanding those differences we can then realistically work with those differences to support each other better at this time of enormous change and enormous stress in our lives due to that change.

And what is interesting is that men and women react differently to stress, so most of the differences that cause frustration between men and women are simply differences that we don't understand, and those differences that we don't instinctively relate to are particularly how men and women react to stress.

For example, men will often become quiet or distant under stress, whereas women will want to open up and share and talk under stress. And then, taking another step that stresses even more, women will then *not* want to talk because they'll feel that they've tried to talk and no one listened so they begin to close up, and then they have no way to effectively cope with stress.

On the other hand, you've got men who tend to naturally pull away and mull things over to feel better under stress. If they are really under a huge amount of stress, these men don't even take the time to pull away. They go into a more talkative mode—they just want to complain and point out how they are victims in life. This becomes very distressing to women, and they go further and further away. That's what I would call "role reversal," which is another problem occurring today.

There are a lot of combinations in men and women and we just don't understand how to make sense of it, but by having a basic understanding of how men and women are different and how they cope with stress differently, we can then be better equipped to support our partners when they are under a lot of stress.

For example, if my wife doesn't want to talk about something, I can be helpful to her and be cooperative, which will lower her stress level. She will then begin to open up and talk, which will lower her stress level even more—as long as I make it safe for her to talk.

If a man is stressed and is complaining a lot and talking a lot, then what a woman can do is instead of trying to be a good listener, she can simply ask him to talk with his friends and give her some room to do what she wants to do. She should not encourage him to talk about all the things that are going wrong in his life. As she leaves him alone he will then be able to cope with stress better. He will then "come out of his cave" so to speak and be much more friendly to her. Women have to recognize that when men are in a bad mood or when they're stressed out, it's not up to her to do anything for him. Men have to come out of this primarily on their own, otherwise they tend to become weak.

So these are primary differences that a woman wouldn't think of. Another example is if a woman's feeling stressed out and he comes to her and asks her questions to help open her up and give her support, it will actually empower her. And doing so empowers the man. But when a woman is too much like a mother to a man, it will weaken him and she will resent it later as well, that's a no-win situation.

WRIGHT

I have known you for several years and I have always been impressed by your ability to stay on the leading edge of the subjects you are passionate about. Have you found any new information about relationship-building in the past few of years that might help people make fewer mistakes in the search for love and companionship?

GRAY

I think that in a sense I was touching on that a few minutes ago when I mentioned the subject of stress. Stress has become so high that not only do men and women have strong stress reactions, they actually go further into a role reversal where women are so stressed that they feel they have to do everything themselves and they become very much like a man. Men become so stressed that they begin to complain about their lives and feel like they're not responsible for their lives anymore. This is the wrong direction, and yet it's a natural stress reaction.

Today we are experiencing unprecedented amounts of stress with longer commuting hours and higher costs of living, balancing work and home life, increased information, and cell phones, talking, and being connected to work all the time. All this is putting a huge new burden on our lives and on our relationships.

What I have done is help to point this out, which can help couples enormously. Couples can recognize that there are ways to lower stress. If we are going to have more dramatic stress, there are more dramatic ways that couples can lower the stress levels for each other. Those ways happen to be women learning to ask for help—that's a real big issue—and men being more responsive to give help. That's not to say they have to do it every time she asks as if he's supposed to "jump to it." There are times when you are supposed to take your rest, so there needs to be understanding of that.

Women often resent having to ask for help, and that is something that has to change. She has to recognize that when you grow up in this world you have to learn how to ask for things, particularly in the business world. Likewise in relationships, if a woman wants her partner to change his natural mode of behavior she needs to *ask*. She shouldn't expect him to be like a woman who would just tend to think about everything that needs to be done until overwhelmed doing it—men typically don't fall into that role. So she needs to ask him, and when people ask others to do something, when they do it they need to let them know it's appreciated.

This is a new skill for a woman. While women sometimes resist this, once they practice it they realize, "Wow, this isn't that hard, and it works!" So that's one way to lower stress in life—if women are not feeling supported to *ask* for it in a way that will work rather than the way that they do ask, which often doesn't work. Practice "realistic expectations." Instead of complaining that "I can't walk through this wall" and "Why doesn't the wall open up for me?" you've got to find the door and learn how to open it!

The second important area to lower stress is in the realm of communication. Women want more sharing and more communication and men aren't providing that. There's a way that men can provide it—if women cooperate. As I said before, women should ask for what they want. Maybe a woman could say something like, "I'd like for you to listen to what is going on in my life." Let him know that he doesn't have to say anything. In fact, I encourage that in the beginning—he should say nothing, and let her talk for five or ten minutes. She then thanks him for listening, and then walks away. While this seems very unnatural, it is a super stress reducer once people start to experience it. It's quite amazing.

I didn't invent this—this is what has been going on for years in the therapy office. Women come in and they talk about what's going on in their lives and they feel better. The therapist doesn't say much at all. And the better the therapist, the less the therapist says and the more questions the therapist asks.

So the secret here is learning how to talk about what is bothering you without expecting a solution or without expecting your partner to "fix" you or fix the situation in some way. So she can set up that conversation and she will feel better; he'll feel better too because he helped her. And men like helping their wives.

The third area is romance. Again, in this area couples stopped having romance, and romance is actually one of the most strong and powerful stress reducers. It's just that when we're under stress the last thing we think about is romance, both for her and for him. Yet the difference is women will often think about how much they miss it. They're not necessarily feeling romantic, but they often complain that "he's not romantic," implying that she wants him to be romantic so she can feel good again. I understand that and I respect that. And I have a solution for that, but it's not waiting for him—you have to ask! Now, what woman would ever think to ask for romance? Well *you* can. It's a very simple thing.

To solve this problem women have to learn how to ask, and men have to learn how to respond. Women then have to learn how to appreciate that, and the solutions do occur. Women can't expect a man to be a mind-reader. He doesn't know what's going on inside her head and in her heart. Asking for romance is something so foreign that women need a few examples of it and then they can get the hang of it.

For example, she shouldn't say, "You're not romantic, we don't experience romance anymore, we never go out anymore, we're not having fun anymore." Those are just negative complaints. Instead she needs to focus more on what's positive. For example, "Hey, this particular band is playing in town this weekend. Would you get tickets for the concert?" The woman asks the man— that's it. It's a very simple thing. The woman could say, "Oh, we haven't gone out this week, would you get tickets for this or that?" or simply, "Would you pick a movie and we'll go see the movies?" or "Would you make reservations and let's go out to eat?" The man could say, "Where would you like to go?" The woman could say, "Whatever you want to pick."

Women can start defining romance as letting him decide where to go, her asking for it, him deciding, and her having a good time just being with him! And gradually that moves into more discretion about what you're going to do and so forth. This process will begin to restore the woman's confidence in the man. All the woman needs to do is to just ask and let him know that whatever he does will be fine.

Just as it was in the beginning when he was so romantic, men often become unromantic because they try, but after a while women start picking out what he did wrong. And men will think, "Well she's so picky I'll just let her decide." And that's the end of romance because part of what reduces stress for women is that she does not have to decide. And when a woman comes back to the realization that having the man make some decisions and she doesn't have to decide will actually lower her stress enormously. It also lowers a man's stress enormously when he knows that whatever he decides she's going to like, as opposed to feeling that he's going to put his best out thee and she's going to step all over it by pointing out what he did wrong. She doesn't mean to do that, but that's the net effect.

So these are extra additions, extra awarenesses, and insights that can help couples to cope with the extra stress they're experiencing in their lives today.

WRIGHT

If you had to "bottom line" the reasons for the success of your Mars and Venus books, products, ideas, and counseling help, what would the main reason be?

GRAY

I think that because the world has changed, people are eager and hungry to have a new way of understanding the world in a positive light. When we don't understand what is going on around us, we just assume something's wrong. By learning the new insights regarding how men and women are different, and how we look at the world differently in a *positive* way, they are released from having to blame their partners or blame themselves. They are motivated to find creative solutions that make their relationships better. So in one aspect, what I do is give people permission to make mistakes, and give them insight to solve the problems.

WRIGHT

An interesting conversation! I always learn so much when I talk with you. It's just incredible. I really do appreciate this time that you've spent with me today, and I really think the readers are going to get a lot out of it.

GRAY

Well, thank you so much. It's a pleasure.

ABOUT THE AUTHOR

DR. JOHN GRAY is the author of fifteen books, including *Men Are from Mars, Women Are from Venus* (Harper Collins 1992), a number one best-selling relationship book. Over thirty million Mars and Venus books have been sold in over forty languages throughout the world.

Dr. John Gray, a certified family therapist, is the premier Better Life relationship coach on AOL. In 2001, he received the Smart Marriages Impact Award. John Gray received his degree in 1982 from Columbia Pacific University. He has authored fourteen other best-selling books. His book, *The Mars & Venus Diet & Exercise Solution* (St. Martin's Press 2003), reveals why diet, exercise, and communication skills combine to effect the production of healthy brain chemicals and how the need for those chemicals differ between men and women.

An internationally recognized expert in the fields of communication and relationships, Dr. Gray's unique focus is assisting men and women in understanding, respecting, and appreciating their differences. For decades, he has conducted public and private seminars for thousands of participants. In his highly acclaimed books, audiotapes, and videotapes, as well as in his seminars, Dr. Gray entertains and inspires audiences with his practical insights and easy to use communication techniques that can be immediately applied to enrich relationships and quality of life.

Dr. Gray lives with his wife and three children in Northern California.

JOHN GRAY
www.askmarsvenus.com

CHAPTER THIRTEEN

Life Transitions

An interview with...
SHARON HENIFIN

DAVID E. WRIGHT (WRIGHT)

Today we are talking with Sharon Henifin, CLC. Sharon has worked in sales, systems management, marketing, and training in corporate America for over thirty years. She is co-founder of Breast Friends, a national non-profit organization that helps women survive the trauma of cancer—one friend at a time. A breast cancer survivor since 1993, Sharon has worked personally with hundreds of newly diagnosed patients and their family members. Sharon understands the difficulty women face when diagnosed with something as serious as breast cancer. She helps women find normalcy in their lives after trauma. In 2008, Sharon became a Certified Life Coach to expand her influence by helping women through all sorts of transitions, including cancer, divorce, empty nest syndrome, career changes, and more.

Sharon, welcome to *GPS for Success*.

What are life transitions and how can they affect people's lives?

SHARON HENIFIN (HENIFIN)

Life transitions happen to everyone. They can be anything that changes your status quo. They are stages we all go through no matter what our age, occupation, or gender. They are events that change the course of our lives. Some of these life events are by choice and some are thrust upon us. Some of these transitions result in loss and some in gain. Either way, the positive and negative emotions need to be processed.

It's surprising to most of us to experience sadness and feelings of loss when the transition is an event we requested or were looking forward to.

A good example is a friend of mine who moved across the country for a very exciting job. She considered it the job of a lifetime. Even though this was a wonderful opportunity for her, it was a big adjustment. She found it extremely difficult to leave her friends and family. She was accustomed to having her loved ones around to support her through all her past life events. She knew that she would be facing unfamiliar territory and found she had a difficult time processing her emotions. Making this transition, once perceived as a great opportunity, gave her the hardest time as she adjusted to her new circumstances.

A major birthday, like turning forty or the big "Five O" can create a life-altering event. Those birthdays can symbolize the end of an era. Being old enough to receive senior citizen discounts may throw you into an emotional upheaval. It could be a birth of a child, or when your "baby" goes off to college. Many couples are excited to start the next stage in life when the kids have moved on and created their own lives, yet sorrow and distress can be also experienced.

A friend told me how difficult it was for her when her last child went off to college. She prided herself in being a great mom, putting her kids above most. She found when they were gone, she lacked purpose and she felt useless and unproductive. She couldn't find peace and happiness without her children around. Once she could take the focus from her perceived loss and concentrate on her future, she started to dream again. She was able to look at this break from her kids as a new chapter where she wasn't tied to their needs. As painfully as it originally was, she had the time to look inside and decide what she needed to make her happy once more. She decided that since she was a great nurturer, she would put her talents and time into helping other children by becoming a mentor. This way she is making a difference in many more young peoples' lives besides her own small family.

Other life transitions might include getting married or getting divorced. Even though a divorce from an abusive spouse may be the best solution in the long run, that move can be terrifying. I know a woman who was married for many years to a man who was an alcoholic. She loved him, but because of his addiction, her life was in ruins. The only sane option was for her to leave the marriage and strike out on her own. Even though this was the healthiest and wisest long-term decision, it was by far the hardest decisions she has had to make in her life. It wasn't made without a lot of heartache and doubt. Her self-esteem had been so damaged that she wondered if she could make it on her own. Before she could embrace her new life and move on, she needed to go through the stages of grief and acceptance.

Transitions may come as a life-threatening illness or death of a spouse, a child, or even a parent. All of those things can be the beginning or the end of a time in our lives. They don't even have to be as enormous as these, but they all signify a change in our lives and our thinking.

Oddly enough, even winning the lottery can lead to major life transitions. Once seen as a normal person, the lottery winner is suddenly faced with relatives who had barely spoken to them before, or they are approached by "friends" in search of a loan or gift. They are inundated with offers to "make them even richer." They will consider quitting their job. Yes, even the lottery winner will face transitions.

Life transitions affect our lives in various ways. Some transitions are forced upon us like the loss of a job. It may have been a job you disliked but it paid the bills, or it may have been a job you wanted to leave but couldn't find the motivation to quit. When that choice has been taken away from you, it may affect you in different ways. You may get a sense of relief or it may put you into a panic. It may allow you to look inside and find you can live on less money and will open you up to a job that will bring you real joy. You may find opportunities you haven't considered while meeting the demands of a less fulfilling job.

A woman I know took a job to be closer to her family. It seemed like the ideal job, but after two weeks, she was laid off. After moving to be closer to her grandma, her grandmother passed away unexpectedly. It seemed that all the reasons for instigating the move and all the changes were no longer valid. She started questioning her motives, her decision-making skills, and her ability to keep a job. However, the next job she discovered ended up being the best job she ever had and found it very fulfilling. She felt appreciated; she was able to take on more responsibility and received several pay raises within a year. None of this would have happened had she not taken and lost the previous position.

Life transitions can throw us into a deep depression or create a new opportunity for happiness. Even the worse life events can result in growth and meaning in the long run. I have found that to be the case with my breast cancer diagnosis. I feel it has allowed me to find my passion and in turn help others to find theirs. Breast cancer was the turning point in my life, and I was able to turn this experience into a positive outcome.

WRIGHT

Why is it important that we learn how to deal with life transitions in a positive way?

HENIFIN

Life transitions create situations where people often have a difficult time moving forward. One important thing to understand is that one part of your life needs to end before another part can really get started. Some new beginnings can be very exciting for us, but at the same time they're very scary. Being able to move through life transitions requires us to let go of the past and be able to move into the future with openness.

When we stay in the past, we can get stuck and have trouble moving forward. Fear is a big reason we can't move on. It might be fear of the unknown or fear of failure or even fear of success. We all face these kinds of fears at one time or another, and we need to acknowledge them and then push through them. We need to find the confidence to handle the changes we face.

I know a guy who made some poor choices in his career and lost a great career because of these choices. His was in a high-paying job that gave him flexibility and confidence. When he lost this job, he couldn't face his responsibility in the choices he had made and blamed others for his job loss. Unfortunately, this was over twenty years ago, and he is still holding a grudge and reeling from the aftermath of this event. He wasn't able to move through this life transition, and it has tainted his life ever since.

It's important to deal with life transitions because we can become stagnant and have trouble reaching our ultimate life goals. Some of us have put our lives on hold, allowing others to make decisions for us, forgetting our dreams and passions and merely existing day to day.

To avoid our lives becoming stuck, we need to learn how to deal with life transitions in a positive way. One way is to embrace the event. Write down some of the less desirable things that happened because of the event. Now find the blessings. Even the most difficult situations will have positive aspects.

Many women I talk to who have gone through a cancer diagnosis find in themselves strength they never knew they had. They realize their inner strength has always been there, but they didn't tap into it until other tools failed them. They had to reach down deep into their character and rely on their own strength. They needed all the strength they could muster mentally, spiritually, and physically.

You are stronger than you know; but until you are challenged, you may not realize the depth of that strength.

WRIGHT

What life events have affected you personally?

HENIFIN

One event that affected me greatly was the passing of my mom. She had been sick for many years and had isolated herself to the point where the only people at her funeral were in attendance for my benefit, not hers. I remember walking away from her memorial service thinking how sad it was to live seventy-six years on this Earth and not have left much of a legacy. I was the only person who would really miss her. She didn't affect many people's lives, especially later in her life. What a lonely and sad way to go. I remember feeling that I needed to make a difference in other people's lives, thus finding and living my purpose in a more active, profound way. I believe God put all of us on this Earth for a reason, I don't believe my mom was ever able to find her purpose, and I didn't want to leave this world the same way.

Another event that affected me greatly was when I got married in my late twenties. I married a man who already had two children, so I became an instant stepmom. Then we had our own daughter very quickly. So within a year and a half I was the mother of three. Those years were filled with transitions—some very exciting and wonderful and some very difficult. Unfortunately, thirteen years later I went through a divorce, finding myself a single mom, but without the blood ties to the stepchildren I helped raise and couldn't imagine being without. Those years of transition were difficult but I'm glad to say, I have remained close with all three of my kids and celebrate the times I spend with all my children and now grandchildren.

Probably the pinnacle event of my life was being diagnosed with breast cancer. I had just turned forty; I was the first one in my circle of friends to go through a life-threatening diagnosis. I didn't know if I would live or die. I didn't know if I'd see my kids graduate from high school or grow up and have their own families. The only person I knew who had cancer was an aunt who passed away after many surgeries and chemotherapy. A friend of my youngest daughter lost her mom from breast cancer before we got to know her, so seeing it through her and her dad's eyes was very scary. My cancer treatment included six surgeries and six months of chemo. Luckily I can say, "I'm a long-time survivor."

These are a few of my life events that have shaped me into the person I am today. We all go through transitions of our own and it's important to understand how to deal with them when we're facing those challenges.

WRIGHT

How are you using your personal experiences to change your life and the lives of others?

HENIFIN

When I was diagnosed in 1993, it was a pretty scary time. I was able to get through it and move on. Then three years later, a very good friend of mine was also diagnosed. Through her diagnosis we realized how important support and friendship are when you're going through a devastating event like breast cancer. Unfortunately, women are wonderful caregivers but we are lousy at asking for help, or even accepting help when it's offered. Women are very capable of doing most things themselves; but when faced with a cancer diagnosis, it's really important for friends and family to rally around and be a good support system. I was able to help my friend, Becky, through her diagnosis by doing a few simple things like keeping her name and contact information in front of our other friends to remind them to check on her, to send her a card, or to pick up the phone and call her.

In 2000 Becky went through another scare. When we were waiting patiently for another biopsy, we talked over lunch about what was missing in the world of cancer. We had an interesting conversation that launched the idea of Breast Friends and set us in motion to help support other women going through cancer while also teaching their friends and family members how best to support their loved ones. We decided to start a non-profit organization. Please visit our Web site for more information: www.breastfriends.com

We've been able to touch the lives of many women and their friends and families through their breast cancer experience by giving them hope and by offering ideas on how to help. We have expanded to other types of women's cancer since then and are working toward our big goal—"No woman should go through cancer alone." By being a good supporter, being proactive, and doing things without being asked, women going through a cancer diagnosis will feel less lonely and isolated during their treatment and beyond. We hope to expand Breast Friends around the country to help us get closer to our goal.

WRIGHT

What is life coaching?

HENIFIN

Life coaching is a wonderful way of taking people from where they are today and moving them forward. I became a certified life coach in 2008. I'm a cheerleader by nature, so when I researched the life coaching certification I felt it was something I was meant to do. With life coaching, I use techniques to help people examine their own lives and values, and to help them create a road map to move closer to their life goals.

I realized that it would be a wonderful addition to what we are already doing at Breast Friends. With my work, I have found when women go through an experience like cancer, it changes them from the inside. Life is not the same. Cancer, like other life transitions, allows us to look at our lives and assess our values—to decide what's important and what's not. Our priorities seem to change when we have a glimpse at our mortality.

I use life coaching to help cancer patients who have finished their treatment. When the doctor says, "Congratulations, you've finished your treatment, I'll see you in three months," patients often feel they should be happy. But underneath they are scared. While they were actively fighting the disease, they had a purpose. Now that they are done, the fear of a recurrence seems to haunt them. Every ache or pain seems to trigger anxiety and the feeling of dread. Family and friends are excited to have them back, yet they aren't really back. They are still dealing with side effects and lingering fears, and feel they will never be their old selves again.

Life coaching techniques help them embrace what they have experienced, find the blessings and even the humorous aspects of their cancer, and help them create a plan to move forward. It is very helpful to get women together in a group environment to discuss these perfectly normal fears. They realize they aren't alone in their feelings. They meet others who feel the same way, which makes it easier to move forward. It encourages them to move from patient to survivor and, better yet, to "Thrivor."

I believe we're born with God-given strengths and talents. We are sometimes unaware of our gifts until something happens to challenge us during one of our life transitions. Our job may work for us until we are forced to look at what really makes us happy. Then we realize that the money is the means to an end, but there is more to a happy life than material possessions and what money can buy. Life coaching encourages all of us to look at our dreams and find our passions. I'm able to use life coaching to help women find their passion and create a life using their gifts while I use mine.

One of the outcomes of a major life event is the ability to look inside and assess what's important. It can help us look deep and decide what is important to *us,* instead of what's important to society or to our parents or boss. You will be asked, "What is of value to me?" "What is non-negotiable in my life?" What values can you not live without? Is it love, security, integrity, etc.? Life coaching techniques and exercises help you uncover your passion and dreams.

Unfortunately, many of us have forgotten how to dream. Our childhood aspirations are gone or crushed. It's time to dream again and life transitions can give us the wakeup call we need to dream and find our passion. I feel honored to be able to help others find their dreams and create a road map of baby steps to reach them.

WRIGHT

How does life coaching help people thrive after a life transition?

HENIFIN

A life transition can stop us in our tracks. And if we give ourselves permission, it can give us time to reflect. If we can take a break from caring for others and focus on ourselves, we can spend the time to dream. We need to focus on the parts of our lives that are working and change the parts that aren't. We want to replicate those things that work well with small steps toward what is meaningful. Making a plan to move forward, even slowly, will make a huge difference in our quality of life. It allows people to live their dreams and to create a legacy for themselves and their families that they will be proud of.

When I work with women finishing cancer treatment, many feel lost. They feel stuck because they've put their life on hold for the last year with treatments, doctor appointments, tests, and scans. It's hard to know where to draw the line and say, "Okay, it's time to live again." We talk a lot about what their life has been for the last six to twelve months. We talk about the side effects, the things they have lost, the differences in their lives—good and bad. We need to embrace what we've endured to find the blessings and move forward.

I remember thinking, "Wow, wasn't it enough to have six surgeries that completely changed the landscape of my chest? Wasn't it enough that I put deadly chemicals into my body to make sure all the cancer cells are killed? And now I have to go into menopause at age forty!" It's hard to deal with at times, but as with any other life transition, we have to do it one step at a time. We won't always like the results of the transition, but we still must accept them to move forward. Some transitions we can move through very quickly. Others may take us years.

WRIGHT

Why is this message so important?

HENIFIN

We all go through periods of transition, and we all can get stuck or stumble along the way. Because of other circumstances in our lives, some transitions may take longer to embrace than others. We're all faced with conditions where we feel really out of control. Life hands us events we have no control over and the way to gain that control again is to work through the emotions and create a game plan. You are stronger than you think.

It's important for you to understand how valuable your life is and how many people you affect. Be open to making a difference and leaving this Earth better than it was when you arrived. I believe it is imperative to find out what God put you on this Earth to accomplish. You have a purpose; it's just tricky to find out how you fit in to the master plan.

Take time to think, to meditate, or to pray—use whatever way you choose to find a place of solitude where you can listen. We live in such a fast-paced world that most of us don't take the time to just think. We wonder why our creativity is not as active as it used to be. Part of the problem is merely not being still enough to hear. Our world is filled with noise and confusion. It's filled with noise from our cell phones, televisions, video games, and many more distracting devices. Take a "noise break" and just be still for a few minutes; give your mind a chance to reset and your creativity will increase again.

WRIGHT

How can you use your life transitions to improve your life?

HENIFIN

Focus on the positive, the dreams, and what really makes you unique as a person. We all have strengths and weaknesses, and we all use those strengths and weaknesses in different ways.

One thing to understand is that life transitions give us an opportunity to evaluate what's going right and what's not; this allows us to make adjustments in our journey.

One exercise I use to help others discover how to live their lives is to have them write their eulogy. Think about what you want people to say about you when you are gone. This exercise will let you imagine how to live your life to match that vision. What is it that you want to leave behind? What is your legacy? Discovering your gifts and putting them to use is a very powerful exercise. Even for those of us who are looking at our mortality, we can make a difference. It's important to realize we aren't dying tomorrow or next week. You may live another forty or fifty years; but when you do leave this Earth, what is it that you want to leave behind?

You can use life transitions to improve your life by being able to access what makes you happy. Ask yourself what brings you joy and find ways to replicate those feelings in all areas of your life. Sometimes your livelihood is something that you do for a paycheck, but it doesn't necessarily fulfill you. So you need to look at your core values and figure out what really satisfies and fulfills you as a person. Be grateful for what you have and who you have in your life. Focus on what you have, not what you lack.

I have always been labeled as "amiable" on the personality charts. But being in sales for many years, I was always trying to be more of a driver-type personality—more decisive, more aggressive or assertive. Looking around at the most successful salespeople, many were drivers and it seemed like the corporate environment was more conducive to the more assertive style. Every personality test I took repeated the outcome—I was still an amiable striving to be a driver.

After retiring from this environment, I was finally able to look closer at my core values and realized that being a driver didn't quite fit for me. I have finally embraced the fact that I am an amiable person and it works for me. It's funny how long it takes some of us to figure things out and accept what is.

WRIGHT

Why is passion important?

HENIFIN

Passion is what makes life worth living. It's what makes us different and what makes us happy. When I think of something that I'm passionate about, it's no longer work, but fun. It actually creates energy. It re-energizes me and it allows other people to do the same. You can work a twelve-hour day at something that you're passionate about and the time flies—it doesn't drain you. Passion allows you to use those gifts and talents in a way that works.

So discovering your passion is really important. It's imperative to practice your talents and learn to share those gifts with others. I've always had a pretty positive attitude about life. If you had asked me about my strengths a few years ago, I'm not sure I would have said anything about being positive. I took a class and read the book, *Now, Discover Your Strengths*, by Marcus Buckingham and Donald O. Clifton, and it turned my thinking around. My number one strength is positivity, so no wonder I'm able to look at the glass half full most of the time. This strength allows me to help women battling a life-threatening disease and give them hope.

Knowing your strengths and gifts allows you to find your passion, not your parent's passion or your teacher's or your boss's. What are you passionate about? An easy mistake is to embrace others' dreams and passions as your own.

I spoke with a lady who had worked in her family business for many years. She had been going through treatment for a very aggressive cancer that had gone to her liver. We were enjoying lunch in a quaint outdoorsy bistro, and I was telling her all about my life coaching and the new workshops I was starting. I asked her about her business and if it had been her dream.

She hung her head and admitted, "No, it was my husband's."

I couldn't help it—I asked, "So what is *your* dream?"

She straightened up and looked me right in the eye and said, "I don't know."

The reality was that this woman was looking very seriously at the last few years of her life and she wasn't living her dream—she was living someone else's. Don't make that mistake. Discover what your dream is and take steps to make it happen. Even if it's really huge, you might not make it but you will be much closer to it than you are right now.

Find your passion. Create goals around that passion. It will move you toward what's meaningful. Your life will be happier; it may not be perfect, but you will feel more fulfilled. Find what you're really passionate about and make a difference in your surroundings and your community.

WRIGHT

What is your passion?

HENIFIN

Breast Friends is a huge part of my life and my passion. Working with other women and helping them get through their traumatic experience of a cancer diagnosis and treatment is my passion. I love being their cheerleader, being their friend, and being there for them when they are having a tough day. Life coaching is also a part of this work; it allows me to connect with them at a deeper level. By using certain techniques, skills, and exercises, I can help women move past their cancer experience. I love being a part of the community of Breast Friends and offering support and friendship to the people who have been affected. I love just being there for them in whatever they might need.

What I have done with my passion is only a small example of what can be done when you are doing the right things for the right reasons. No matter what life transitions we go though, they are designed to give us the opportunity to really look at ourselves and make the needed adjustments to our path. None of us know how long we have on this Earth, but having a chance to look at your mortality and figure out what's really important in life is a gift in itself. Ask yourself, "What are my priorities?" "How do I want to leave this Earth?" "What legacy do I want to leave behind?" Allow yourself to dream. As a teacher, Luzy Z. Martin once asked me, "What would you do if you knew you could not fail?" Discover your passion and work toward making it a part of your daily life.

ABOUT THE AUTHOR

SHARON HENIFIN is the co-founder of Breast Friends, a national non-profit organization that helps women survive the trauma of cancer.

Sharon enjoys traveling, photography, reading, fishing, and camping with her husband and spending time with children, stepchildren, and grandchildren. Sharon would love to hear from you; her contact information is below.

SHARON HENIFIN

14325 SW Fanno Creek Loop

Tigard, OR 97224

503-349-3846

sharonhenifin@aol.com

www.thrivingbeyond.com

Breast Friends

www.breastfriends.com

mail@breastfriends.com

CHAPTER FOURTEEN

Healthy, Wealthy, and Wise:
Planning for The Encore Years®

An interview with . . .

ANDREA WHITE

DAVID E. WRIGHT (WRIGHT)

Today we are talking with Andrea White. She is a Master Certified Coach and the owner of Financial Conversations® and Transition Life Coaches, coaching and training companies that work with financial advisors, business owners, executives, families, and individuals. She is also co-owner of Whitewater Transitions, a group of certified coaches and consultants providing services to firms planning for or in the midst of a business purchase, transfer, or sale. Andrea earned the Master Certified Coach (MCC) designation through the International Coach Federation (ICF) and she also earned the designation of Certified Professional Co-Active Coach from the Coaches Training Institute. She holds a BA in Social Welfare, a master's in Business Administration, and she has a passion for making a difference in as many lives as possible.

Andrea, welcome to *GPS for Success: Goals and Proven Strategies.*

ANDREA WHITE (WHITE)

Thank you, David.

WRIGHT

So this book is about success and how to achieve it. Tell us about your topic, "The Encore Years®."

WHITE

Let's think about the term "encore." When an artist has completed a stirring and masterful performance, the audience demands an encore. What they are asking for is that the artist come back and do something wonderful, maybe something very different from what he or she had done in the main part of the performance or maybe something in character, but they know they want to hear more. They know the artist has more to offer.

The Encore Years is an appropriate title for a time when people reach a transition period in their careers, reflect on their life's work, and ask, "What's next for me?" For many, this may be a transition to retirement; for others it may be retooling for a new career or looking for a way to use experience and skills in a new, often more fulfilling way. Perhaps they have been laid off or sold a business. Maybe they are buying a business, or starting one. The Encore Years are not so much a chronological point, but more of a mindset. It has to do with that period in your life when you begin to ask what's next for me and how I can really use my experience, my skills, and my talents in a way that is both satisfying to me while making a difference in the world. Often this will happen when people are fifty to seventy-five years old, but it can happen at any point in life. It is characterized by the completion of any one phase of your life and looking forward to another. Like chapters in a book, this is where you close one phase and start on a new one.

Sociologically, the emergence of this concept has been fueled by a number of factors. As a society, we are living longer, we have access to better nutrition and healthcare, and hopefully we are making better lifestyle choices. Many of us are fortunate to live in relative comfort or abundance, which can encourage us to think more globally, and to have the resources to conceive and create more possibilities than ever before. Many people at this point in their lives have the freedom to go where they want to go and be the people they want to be. So creating a future we can really enjoy is what The Encore Years is all about.

WRIGHT

"Healthy, Wealthy, and Wise" is the title of this chapter. Isn't that placing a lot of emphasis on accumulation of money and material goods?

WHITE

I think we would all accept common definitions of what it means to be healthy and wise. Being healthy means doing the best you can to maintain your health and vitality. It means establishing and maintaining healthy behaviors around eating, exercise, and paying attention to mental health and wellness. Likewise, I am certain we would all like to leverage the knowledge and wisdom that many accrue with years on the planet.

When it comes to wealth, there is less agreement on what that means. I would suggest that it means having the financial resources to provide a comfortable lifestyle for you and those you love, while having healthy, fulfilling relationships with friends and family. There is also a component of gratitude and giving back that adds great richness to the lives of many people. Wealth is not just about money—it includes much more, and the "what" and the "how much" is up to each person to define for themselves. These con-siderations become increasingly important as people approach this transition period in their lives.

WRIGHT

So what is important about The Encore Years?

WHITE

Because we have accumulated experience and wisdom over time, in The Encore Years we have the opportunity to move from defining our lives as materially and socially successful to considering significance. The focus shifts from "how much?" to "what does it matter?" It is often said that at the end of their lives most people have more regrets about what they didn't do, than what they did do. So this is an opportunity to reflect, take some time, and move forward with a plan to add meaning to your life, to choose deliberately, and to add to your living body of work.

WRIGHT

So when is the right time to begin thinking about The Encore Years?

WHITE

That is a very good question and an important one. Ideally you would be planning your transition about five years ahead of your actual move. That way you can take steps to build a bridge from where you are to where you want to be. Like steppingstones, these plans would allow you to move degree by degree into what you are becoming. That being said, we don't always have the luxury of that time to plan. Most of us had that luxury as children and young adults—the time to consider what we wanted to be when we "grow up." The Encore Years is definitely another time in our lives when we may feel free to ask a similar question: "What do I want to have happen in the rest of my life?"

When we were in our twenties it might have been a logical linear decision. A person might say, "Well I'm good at science, and I want to make a lot of money helping others, so I'll be a doctor or a pharmacist." Or a person might say, "My mom is a CPA and I know that she'd love to turn the business over to me, so I'm going to become a CPA and take over her business." These are logical linear decisions. But later in life we have the ability and opportunity to choose either this linear logical approach, or access a totally different approach—one that involves not linearity or logic, but rather one that involves creative transformation. A person might say, "I've never been in the hospitality industry and I really love the idea of serving wonderful meals and working close to water, so I think I'm going to open a restaurant on the beach in San Diego." This may be something that you have never done, and maybe you don't know a lot about it, but you have an opportunity to create and transform.

So again, if you can start planning five years before the end of the current phase, that is when you are going to be in the best shape. This would be plenty of time to do some soul-searching to find out what really matters to you and what you really want to do. And sometimes we just have to do the best we can with the time we have.

> Try not to become a man of success but rather try to become a man of value.
> —Albert Einstein

Either way, it may be helpful to include work with a coach, special supportive friends, or a group of like-minded people in this process. They can see your life from a new perspective, help you think out of the box a little bit, and see in you gifts and talents and interests that you might not be able to see for yourself.

WRIGHT

So what do you think are the benefits of having a plan?

WHITE

First of all, there is great value in allowing yourself time to complete one phase of your life before boldly undertaking the next. So often we move from one thing to another without pausing to celebrate what was good about that previous phase, to recognize what might have been lost in the transition, and to contemplate what might be done to save what is good and to move powerfully into the next phase of your life.

> Always bear in mind that your own resolution to succeed is more important than any other one thing.
> —Abraham Lincoln

Second, with a plan, you can move more directly from the current situation to the desired future. Always bear in mind that you know where you are headed. Rather than wandering aimlessly, setting a goal and having a plan and speaking about your plan are important; this is what really breathes life into it.

WRIGHT

So with so many benefits, why doesn't everybody make a plan?

WHITE

This is another very good question. Our lives are dominated by maintenance of the ordinary—you need to change the oil in the car, mow the grass, get to the grocery store, and take the dog to the vet. So all of these activities are necessary for life, and they can become so time-consuming that many people will say, I just don't have time make a plan. The dominance of the ordinary pushes off taking time to plan the extraordinary.

Stephen Covey captures this idea when he talks about the "tyranny of the urgent" crowding out the important but not urgent activities of our lives. In other cases, people may be reluctant to ask for "more" because they feel it would make them appear ungrateful for what they do have, that they don't have anything else to contribute, they don't deserve more, or they have never allowed themselves to make a big plan or to ask for what they want. Some people might not make a plan because they don't know how to do it or they may be concerned about what others might think or say. I've heard more than one client say, "Oh my goodness, they'll think I've gone crazy. They might think I'm really off the deep end if I dream a big dream and/or make a plan that is totally out of the realm of what my friends and family might be thinking."

Counteracting this inertia, more and more we are finding role models of extraordinary people who have made major changes in their

> Courage is not the lack of fear. It is acting in spite of it.
> —Mark Twain

later years. Despite these models of lives full of meaning and satisfaction, some people may still say, "I don't have anybody in my life who's done that, so how would I know what to do?" It sounds simple but it is not easy. When we are in the former phase of our lives, we know who we are. A business card or an appellation, "Sydney's Mom" tells a lot about our identity. It tells our position and our status. When you retire or you make a transition from one phase of life to another, you set aside your title and your business cards, and with it people often feel they have lost their identity. Stripped of the old persona, creating a new identity means looking carefully at your wants and needs. It is all new and making a plan isn't something that comes naturally to everyone. It takes both courage and time.

WRIGHT

So you write of the seven-step process for making a plan. Would you discuss that with our readers?

WHITE

Certainly. The first two steps are where the rubber meets the road; they are the most important steps of the whole process. The first

> It is a terrible thing to see and have no vision.
> —Helen Keller

of the seven steps is to get in touch with your purpose, your vision, your passions, and your values. This is not work that everyone does easily or often. Helen Keller said, "It is a terrible thing to see and have no vision." Yet many people go through their lives unable or unwilling to create a vision of what's possible. Thankfully, for others it comes pretty easily. Regardless, everyone can follow this process to create a vision of what's next for him or her.

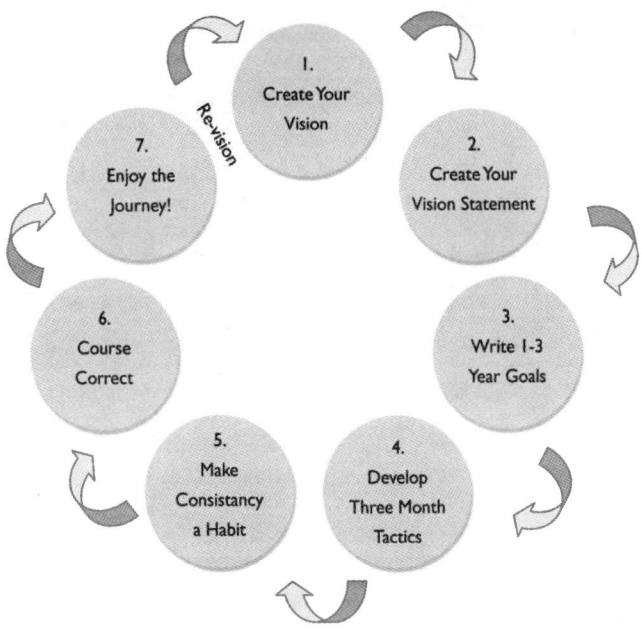

SEVEN STEPS TO PLANNING FOR THE ENCORE YEARS®
By Andrea White, Master Certified Coach

In creating a vision and getting in touch with your passion, you can take one of the two tracks we mentioned earlier. It could be a linear formation of your vision or a creative transformation.

A linear formation is a logical step-by-step process. For example, one might say, "I've been a CPA, I owned my CPA practice, so now I'm going to teach accounting and mentor CPAs." That would be a very logical, systematic, step-by-step approach and works for many. Contrastingly, you could go through a creative transformation such as, "I've been a CPA and I've owned my own practice. I should bring my expertise in running a practice to raise funds for and support micro businesses in Indonesia." Maybe you know nothing about Indonesia (yet) but this vision would be more out of the box.

This whole idea of getting in touch with your vision, passion, and values is critically important. You really have to think about revisioning what you are already doing, or going in a completely different direction. So again it might be a logical next step or it might be a new beginning altogether. This vision should be an image of the best future you could possibly imagine. You should be able to see the extraordinary life you would want to have. Since the mind likes images, a vision board with illustrations of what you want in your life would be very helpful. This is the first step of the seven-step process.

The second step in this process is to create a vision statement. We are back to words, and this part of the process begins by listing your assets. By assets I don't mean the house and the car and the boat, but rather the physical, personal, and professional assets that you bring to your life. For example: I'm dependable, I have expertise in communicating with people, in getting a job done, or I have financial resources or project management skills. Begin to think about your strengths, your knowledge, your skills, and your experiences.

If you have trouble doing this for yourself, ask three or four of your friends, "What are my assets? What are my strengths?" Put aside any embarrassment or discomfort you feel and hear what others say about you and your skills. Their perspective is often more accurate and helpful than your own. It is like cutting your own hair—most of us don't do it, and that is because we don't have the perspective to be able to see it from all sides. Your friends (or your coach, if you have one) can help you assess your skills and your interests, your experiences, and your strengths by being able to see you from the outside rather than from the inside. Crafting a vision statement from this exploration is what comes next.

So let me ask you, have you ever really considered what you really, really enjoy doing?

WRIGHT

Oh yes, at least I think so.

WHITE

I don't know your personal vision but I can say that often people aim too low. They might ask, "Should I do what I really enjoy or should I do what will earn the money I need?" This is the wrong question. A better question is, "How can I do what I really enjoy and earn the money I need?" So in creating a vision of what you want in the next phase of your life and what's important in your life, aim high and ask yourself, "What do I really, really like to do? What would I do if there were no constraints? If I could do anything I wanted, what would that be?" As long as you are not violating the rights of others, you have every right to have what you want.

Another way some people approach this is with a hypothetical situation. Ask yourself if twenty years from now a reporter were talking to you and writing an article about you, what would you most want that reporter to write? Or if someone were making a movie of your life, what story would you want them to tell? Would it have a happy ending or would it have a sad ending? Would it be very dramatic, would it be full of compassion or grief or drama? Just what would it be?

Finally, you might ask yourself, "If I knew that the next ten years were my last ten years, what would I want to accomplish and why?" This framework tends to bring the fuzzy future into focus a bit. Even if you

> If I am not for myself, then who will be for me? And if I am only for myself, then what am I? Any if not now, when?
> —Hillel

think you have twenty, thirty, or more years left in your life, which is an uncertain prediction at best, you can say, "I'm not going to worry about twenty or thirty years from now, I'm only going to worry about the next ten." From here you can create a vision statement of what you intend for the next period in your life.

A vision statement is not so much the statement of a destination as it is a statement of values and how you want to be in the world. It serves as a beacon calling us toward our best selves. It serves as a filter by which we know what to say "yes" to and what needs a "no." A vision statement that I appreciate is: "With grace and compassion, I serve others each day, enriching their lives with the gifts I freely give."

In his famous "I Have a Dream" speech, Martin Luther King, Jr. said, "I have a dream that one day this nation will rise up and live out the true meaning of its creed: 'We hold these truths to be self-evident: that all men are created equal.' I have a dream that one day on the red hills of Georgia the sons of former slaves and the sons of former slave owners will be able to sit down together at a table of brotherhood. I have a dream that one day even the state of Mississippi, a desert state, sweltering with the heat of injustice and oppression, will be transformed into an oasis of freedom and justice. I have a dream that my four children will one day live in a nation where they will not be judged by the color of their skin but by the content of their character."

The mission of the Barack H. Obama Foundation, which honors the father of the forty-fourth President of the United States, is "To provide people everywhere with resources to uplift their welfare and living standards in memory of Barack H. Obama: in the region of his birth, Kenya and beyond." Ask yourself, what is my vision? Is it big enough to last a lifetime?

So, for the first two steps, create the picture—the vision—and with it the words—the vision statement.

WRIGHT

What else should we know about these first two important steps?

WHITE

When you go about creating a vision statement, a couple of other things that are critically important are that you find a special place to work on your personal vision, both the image and the statement. There is something about where you are that influences how you think. There is great value in going to a new or different place than you do normally, and spending some time thinking about what is really important to you. It might be a neighborhood park, the side of a mountain, or at the beach. You might travel to a faraway place that has special significance for you or pick a special place in your own town. Any way that you do it, getting away can help you "see the way" more clearly. Getting to a different place—a quiet place in nature or whatever is refreshing for you—can really help you to clear your mind and to move forward creatively.

Again, in thinking about the vision statement, another format that you might try is this simple approach: "I am committed to being the best [fill in the blank] I can be—" and that might be the best writer, the best businessperson, the best parent, the best spouse, the best servant to the world, whatever it is. Then it continues, ". . . in order to do so, I will be [fill in the blank] and I will do [fill in the blank]." An example might be, "In order to be the best photographer that I can be, I will be open to opportunities to see with new eyes and to look at the world in new ways. I will practice my craft, put myself in situations where there are great pictures waiting to be taken, and make certain I take in generous feedback from other people about my work." So use pictures for the vision and words for the vision statement. Using both will help you create a clear and glorious picture of what you want to create.

Often our own vision can be shared or affected by others with whom we have a special relationship. As you seek ways to include a partner, spouse, a coach, a close friend, or a special family member, talk about your vision with them. Sometimes you will want to co-create a shared vision with people whom you would like to play starring roles in your particular future.

Finally, make your vision a part of who you are. Carry it with you in a picture or vision statement. Revisit it frequently. Learn

> No problem can withstand the assault of sustained thinking.
> —Voltaire

to think of it often. Just as no one need remind you to think of those you love, fall in love with your vision and allow it to come to mind continuously. In order to make your vision a reality you have to stay in touch with it. Even if it is not here today, and not showing up in a way that you want today, just staying in touch with it is critical to making it happen. As you live with it, feel free to revise it as you gain clarity and move ever closer to what you *really* want to do, and what you *really* want to happen.

WRIGHT

So what are the other steps of the seven-step process?

WHITE

Once you create your vision and vision statement (the two most important steps), steps three through seven are much more straightforward. Step three is to set one-, two-, or three-year goals that really get you into your vision. The time frame is up to you. Maybe you don't have a clue about how to get from here to your ultimate vision, but you probably have a sense of an individual step that could take you in that direction. So begin creating steppingstones, even if the journey seems very long. It is said that the longest journey begins with a single step and that is certainly the only way to begin. Most of us are good at setting goals, just make certain that in addition to being SMART (the acronym for Specific, Measurable, Achievable, Realistic, and Timely), they are also direct paths to achieving your vision. Focus!

The fourth step of the seven-step process, after you have created those one- to three-year goals, is to create the list of three-month tactics and strategies—exactly what are you going to do in order to make those goals happen?

One of the things that you are going to want to do is to talk about these goals and tactics, because when you speak about your goals, you are suddenly accountable to other people. If I tell you I'm going to work out three times this week it holds a much greater power for me than if I just tell myself the same thing. As you look at those goals for the one to three years, and create the monthly strategies for the next three months, think about how you might move toward them a step at a time. Each step should take you in the general direction of achieving your vision, even if it seems an indirect route at times.

The fifth step is creating a habit of consistency. We as human beings are simply a sum total of all the actions that we take. If we take steps consistently, even if they are small steps, we are going to move in the direction that we are headed; sooner or later we are going to get there. It is really important that you consistently visualize yourself achieving your goals. Certainly great athletes like Tiger Woods do this all the time. They visualize themselves making that long putt on the eighteenth to win the Masters. So if you don't really quite believe it, just act as if you believe it and see what happens! When we visualize, we access the subconscious mind that takes our thoughts at face value, without judgment, and acts on them. If we ask ourselves, "How could I be so stupid?" the subconscious mind starts building the answer for us. If we tell ourselves, "I am moving consistently toward my goals," the subconscious mind will act on that as well.

The next one, the sixth step in the seven-step process, is to "course correct" as needed. It is said that when a plane flies from Los Angeles to New York it is actually off course 96 percent of the time, whether due to wind or other conditions. It is either a little too high, a little low, it is going a little too slowly, a little too fast, or a little off heading. What a pilot does is to consistently adjust the altitude, direction, and speed, so that the plane can stay on course and reach its destination safely.

Likewise, when you are trying to achieve your goals, you are going to be off course sometimes, perhaps often. That is not a problem unless you view it as a problem. If you simply correct, and get back onto your path, you will arrive at your destination safely.

Then the final and pervasive step seven is to just enjoy the journey. Find ways to celebrate your success each day and each week. Celebrate successes that are both big and small because they are the fuel for your transition.

WRIGHT

I like the idea of enjoying the journey. So what can we expect in the transition?

WHITE

Any transition has the potential to be a bit of a roller coaster ride. You can expect that whenever you make changes in your life, you are going to have a sense of loss or grief for what you have given up or will have to give up. Many people are resistant to any change at all, so you can expect that there would be a natural pull to play it safe, to stay in our comfort zone, to do again what we have done in the past. But we all know that doing the same thing and expecting a different outcome is not really a reasonable approach. We have to be willing to face any uncertainty or fear that we have about doing something new. The bigger the dream, the scarier it probably is. In fact, some have talked about the terror barrier, which is that wall you run into when what you are going for is just too big and too scary. When you hit the terror barrier and bounce, you have to keep taking another run at it until you get through it and emerge on the other side.

Also, in transition don't be surprised if friends and family are perplexed at what you are doing. You are taking a new path, and as you do that, you will be changing—just when they had grown accustomed to the old you! They may rejoice and celebrate with you or you may find that they don't quite understand why you are doing what you are doing. So expect the unexpected in transition, and go with the joy and the excitement of going places that you haven't gone before.

WRIGHT

So this sounds like a big plan. Are there obstacles to creating a big plan and if so, what are their remedies?

WHITE

We address this issue frequently in our coaching when we ask people to really create their future rather than react to their present. Most frequently people express concern about earning "enough" money, however they might define that. A common theme is, "I'm not rich, I can't afford just to stop working and give away all my time. Besides, I'd like to rest for awhile." As we mentioned earlier, sometimes rephrasing the question makes all the difference. "How can you do more of what you want and make the money you need? So it is not an "either/or" situation, it is a "both/and" situation.

The concern we hear in dealing with Baby Boomers—part of the "sandwich generation"—is: "I just have too many responsibilities. I'm providing for a spouse [or a parent, a child or a grandchild, or some other family member], there is just no time for me." Again, asking a different question can be helpful. "How could you take care of yourself while taking care of others?"

Finally, we hear people say, "I don't have any experience in that or I don't have any skills or my experience and skills aren't really relevant." The better questions are: "What's the benefit of having no experience? Can I start with a beginner's mind? Can I ask people to help me? Can I come in with a clear point of view and do things that no one has ever done before?" When there doesn't seem to be a good answer, consider asking a different question.

People are often concerned about taking a risk or making a mistake. We respond to that with, "What's the worst that could happen and how bad is that?" If that is tolerable, then maybe you could just go ahead and work through the fear. Finally, if their thinking seems small or safe, ask, "What would you do if you knew you could not fail?" Often this gives them full permission to dream big and to undertake the next step in their life that can be so rewarding and help them move from success to significance.

WRIGHT

Sounds like a great challenge to me.

WHITE

In fact, that is perhaps how we should close, David. Any challenge begs the questions: "If not now, when? And if not you, who?" It calls for each of us to be all that we can be, to be deliberate, to be insightful, and to be creative in figuring out how we can have our body of work bring us satisfaction and make a difference in the world.

WRIGHT

Well, what a great conversation. I'm thinking about my Encore Years.

WHITE

Great! I hope this chapter allows many others to do the same.

WRIGHT

As a matter of fact, in the last five years I've given it a tremendous amount of thought. Now I've got some plans and some steps to follow, so I really appreciate all the information.

WHITE

You are welcome. This is not rocket science—it is a place where most of us should be spending some of our time. I'm hopeful it will be helpful to all our readers.

WRIGHT

Well, I really appreciate the time you have spent with me here, Andrea. This is a very, very important topic and I'm sure our readers are going to benefit from it.

Today we have been talking with Andrea White. She is a Master Certified Coach, and the owner of Financial Conversations, a coaching and training company that works with financial advisors, business owners, executives, families, and individuals. She is also co-owner of Whitewater Transitions, a group of certified coaches and consultants providing services to firms planning for, or in the midst of, a business purchase, transfer, or sale.

> Our deepest fear is not that we are inadequate. Our deepest fear is that we are powerful beyond measure. It is our light, not our darkness, that most frightens us. We ask ourselves, 'Who am I to be brilliant, gorgeous, talented, fabulous?' Actually, who are you not to be? You are a child of God. Your playing small does not serve the world. There is nothing enlightened about shrinking so that other people won't feel insecure around you. We were born to make manifest the glory of God that is within us. It's not just in some of us; it's in all of us. And when we let our own light shine, we unconsciously give other people permission to do the same. As we are liberated from our own fear, our presence automatically liberates others.
>
> —Marianne Williamson

ABOUT THE AUTHOR

ANDREA WHITE is a Master Certified Coach and the owner of Financial Conversations® and Transition Life Coaches, coaching and training companies that work with financial advisors, business owners, executives, families, and individuals. She is also co-owner of Whitewater Transitions, a group of certified coaches and consultants providing services to firms planning for or in the midst of a business purchase, transfer, or sale. Andrea earned the Master Certified Coach (MCC) designation through the International Coach Federation (ICF) and she also earned the designation of Certified Professional Co-Active Coach from the Coaches Training Institute. She holds a BA in Social Welfare, a master's in Business Administration, and she has a passion for making a difference in as many lives as possible. The Encore Years® is a registered trademark of Financial Conversations®/Business by Design.

ANDREA WHITE
**Financial Conversations®
and Transition Life Coaches®**
9008 South Maple Avenue
Tempe, AZ 85284-8112
480.777.8876
awhite@financialconversations.com
www.transitionlifecoaches.com
www.financialconversations.com

CHAPTER FIFTEEN
Geocaching Your Life: Get Out and Play

An interview with...
TROY BONAR

DAVID E. WRIGHT (WRIGHT)

Troy Bonar is one of the top speakers in the Safety, Security and Leadership Industry. He has worked with companies such as Conoco Philips, Crown Cork and Seal, Kinder Morgan, Toro, Chevron, Sunland Construction, the American Red Cross. He has also spoken for OSHA conferences and the National Safety Council along with many others. He is the creator of the innovative Safety Success Boot Camp.

Member of the ASSE, NASP, NFPA and also a member of the National Speakers Association, the Texas Speakers Bureau, World Speakers Bureau and American Speakers Bureau, and International Speakers Network

How did you become known as "the Samurai of Success"?

TROY BONAR (BONAR)

My journey in martial arts has been a wonderful experience and as I began to speak and write about success, my peers and students started calling me "the Samurai of Success." I guess it stuck and I began to tie ancient samurai principles into my teachings.

I am a true believer in learning as much as you can in life and applying success tips from others to your path. With martial arts systems, you take what works best for you and apply it to your health and your spiritual journey. This is the primary reason I have studied more than one martial art, including, Aikido, Bujitsu, Tae Kwon Do, Tang Soo Do, Kuk Sool, Hapkido,

Karate, Tai Chi, Iado, Kendo, and Judo. I have also studied acupressure and acupuncture.

I have been studying Martial arts since the age of twelve. Martial arts are just one facet of my life that has taught me many wonderful life lessons. But since this book is about GPS for success, I have chosen other great learning points to discuss. This correlation to geocaching and events I have experienced in my life will give you a different perspective of goals for proven success.

WRIGHT

What is "geocaching"?

BONAR

Geocaching is a worldwide game of hiding and seeking treasure. A geocacher can place a geocache or cache anywhere in the world, pinpoint its location using Global Positioning Satellite (GPS) technology, and then share the geocache's existence and location with the geocaching community online. Anyone with a GPS unit can then try to locate the geocache.

Geocaching adventures were introduced to me by one of my best friends, Paul Keehn, who is an independent filmmaker. Paul came to Texas to help me with the first of my many film projects. Paul had discovered geocaching and shared his adventures with me. I thought, "Wow, get out of the office, out of the house, go trekking out in the brush to find a treasure. It sounds, well, *fun!*" So when we needed to take a break from production, he explained geocaching to me and we went on a hunt to locate one. Talk about a correlation between our journey to success and looking for a cache! This is how geocaching is related to goals for proven success. We can refer to caches as "success points" that we are seeking along life's journey.

When applied to your life, this geocaching checklist will help get you to your successful destination. We will briefly go over each part of the checklist.

1. Identify your cache (success points/goals).
2. Make a plan.
3. Research your route. (Read other peoples logs).
4. Tell someone where you are going.
5. Be well equipped for the journey.
6. Use your waypoints to navigate from.
7. Pay attention to your surroundings (focus).
8. The closer you get, the more difficult it usually is (don't give up).
9. Log your success.
10. Share your experience with others.

IDENTIFY YOUR CACHE. (success points/goals)

You have to identify your cache or treasure. In geocaching they use a Web site with over 842,000 logged geocaches at the time of this publication.

There are just as many goals to achieve in life if not more. Your success points are limited only by your imagination. Just like your goals, you want to identify what you are aiming for. If you set out with no coordinates when seeking your cache, you have no destination; goal-setting is extremely important. Identify what you want and how far you are willing to go to get it.

WRIGHT

So geocaching is a treasure hunt?

BONAR

Life is a treasure hunt. We are constantly seeking the next treasure in life. When we settle for what we have, life becomes stagnant and dull. Treasures in life come in many forms. A treasure or cache that we seek could be a job or assignment, an award, having a child or starting a family, finding a partner, or a trip you have wanted to take. It could be as simple as meeting someone you have admired, or being able to spend time with people you care about. All of these things can be a cache that you can find along life's journey.

WRIGHT

What about a "multi-cache" (offset cache)? What is that?

BONAR

In the geocaching community, this is one of several cache types. A multi-cache ("multiple") involves two or more locations, the final location being a physical container. There are many variations, but most multi-caches will provide a hint about how to find the second cache, and the second cache has hints to the third, and so on.

When applied to our path to success, this is truly the example of the adventure of life. We use the goals for proven success along the way to reach our big prize or success destinations. It has been said before that "Success leaves clues." Following those clues on your trek will lead to the goal or prize. If you don't follow the clues left by others, you may stumble upon your destination but it may take longer to get there or you may run into serious obstacles along the way that could have been avoided by following the clues left by others.

MAKE A PLAN.

I remember when I first heard about goal-setting, I was involved in a network marketing system. The best things I took away from the business were goal-setting skills and the book/reading list.

Setting goals and making a plan for success were key things that helped my business grow. Even though I decided to transition into a different area in my life, it would never have been possible if I had not learned so much during my involvement with success-oriented people. I actually have reached many of the goals I set while in network marketing. It is so true that if you make a plan to reach your goals and put that energy and thought out there into the universe, many things will eventually come around when you take action.

RESEARCH YOUR ROUTE. READ OTHER PEOPLES LOGS.
(Listen to those who have pioneered the way.)

When we apply the practice of checking the logs of others with our lives, we can learn from others who have gone before saving us time, money, and unnecessary struggles.

In geocaching, people leave tips on the Web site for caches that have been successful. There are so many great tips out there from people who have gone before. Ninety percent of what we learn has been passed on or experienced by someone before we learn it; the other 10 percent is our experiences in life. Use that 90 percent out there by investing in yourself with books and audio programs like this. When you do, you are already taking the steps to success.

In a similar way I continue to train with other masters and martial artists. In the leadership and business industry, I listen to and read other people's books because, as they say, "Iron sharpens Iron." When you train, associate with, and learn from sharper people, it helps you move from your waypoints to your destination. A good partner, mentor, or coach helps you grow beyond your current skills and knowledge base, allowing you to have the tools and knowledge necessary to reach your full potential. In the workplace, a good supervisor or boss motivates you to become better at your profession. A good teacher pushes you to bring out your best. Parents express their expectations for children to meet. We can all become better with coaching or mentoring.

I have had some great mentors in my life, from the first person I worked for (a man I respected greatly, a Mr. Dawson Way) to my martial arts teachers who pushed me when I first began and created an atmosphere full of challenges to increase my skill set so I would be able to handle the struggles on my road to success.

When I taught martial arts full-time, I struggled for a few years trying to run a school on my own, but then I listened to others who had gone before. I learned marketing and business strategies that helped to grow the school. The interpersonal skills I had learned from the books and tapes and the seminars I had attended helped me develop a bond with my students. We ended up with world championships three years in a row prior to my transition to another path in life.

This is just one of the success points our school had. More than the trophies and awards, when you have students come to you years later to say, "Thank you for making a positive impact in my life," those moments are the real treasures. When an employee takes the initiative, when a child tells the truth, or a teenager makes a healthy choice—these are the success points in life that we search for. What did we do to help make them happen? We had goals for them and helped them achieve those goals.

You need to look at the difficulty level of your cache so that you are prepared. Are you trekking across fields? Will you have rivers to cross or mountains to climb? Knowing the difficulty of your goal will help you put in the right amount of effort and action needed. Finding out from other successful people how they made the journey is key to a successful cache. These points are usually logged by geocachers who have gone before. Did they climb the mountain, and what path did they take? Where there struggles or obstacles in the path? Did they learn anything along the way?

TELL SOMEONE WHERE YOU ARE GOING.

For safety, let someone know where you are going. Before you go out for a cache, you want to let people know where you are going. This is also true for your goals in life—you need to let people know where you are heading. Some people will want to come along, or they will check back with you to see if you arrived at your destination. For the safety of your goals it is best to tell people. Speaking about your goals to others allows them to show support and assist you in getting where you are going.

Bring friends and family with you; sharing the experience can be very rewarding. People want to be around successful people. Friends and family can share in your success once they understand that it is an adventure; some will want to come along and some will not. Take the ones who want to come along on your journey with you. When people hear of your success or hear from those who went with you how much fun and interesting it was, they may get the bug to get out and go for it.

When my friend told me about geocaching, I thought he was a little nuts. Then he came back after some successful caches and told me about his adventure. He even showed me some of the treasures he had found. I was stoked—I wanted to go with him the next chance I had. When others see your success points in life they will be motivated to come along or try to reach some success points of their own. So for the safety of your success, let people know where you are going.

BE WELL EQUIPPED FOR THE JOURNEY.

The tools you use when geocaching are usually a handheld GPS. This modern technology is great, but you also need to take along a compass and a map.

In all we do, we need to use the most current tools to get where we are going, but we cannot forget the basics. The basics of success are very important. The biggest of these is goal-setting. Along with goal-setting there are resources from others including guide books, maps of previous plans, audio commentary, and so forth.

I mentioned previously that I had been exposed to a reading list when I was involved with network marketing. I read every book available on it, and I think it was one of the biggest influences on my life. I was not a reader in school, as a matter of fact, I was an average student. I was always told that I was not reaching my potential. To be honest, I was bored out of my mind. When my teachers found out that I was going to author a book or two, they probably had a seizure. I was a last-minute book report kid. I would read the book the day before and stay up all night writing the report. I think while in school I only read about twelve books, and only because I had to.

I know there are many students out there who are in the same boat. If I could give them one tip that will help them tremendously it is to read as much as possible. The more books on communication, leadership, and development you read, the better equipped you will be in life.

I remember that some of my co-authors, were on that reading list. I can recall reading their books and applying their messages to my journey and my business. I was actually listening to an audio book by one of my co authors when I was contacted to collaborate in this book project.

USE YOUR WAYPOINTS TO NAVIGATE FROM.

In geocaching, a waypoint is a point along the path that you use as a reference or a guide to your destination. I believe waypoints to your success can be achievements or events—both positive and negative. The key is turning that negative around and using it as motivation to reach new success points.

When I stopped teaching martial arts full-time, it was one of the biggest *waypoints* in my life. I believe that everything happens for a reason. I think my transition to developing my own learning system, instead of teaching with the association that I had grown up with, was just a waypoint in my life. I had always thought that I would be teaching the same thing all the way to my grave, but in hindsight, I was cutting myself short and settling for the status quo. I believe now, that the changes I made in my life helped set me on a path to greater things. I believe I was destined to expand my sphere of influence and go on a journey down a whole new pathway.

I remember another of the waypoints in my life; it was a tough decision considering my career. Many of you may face career changes throughout your lifetime, sometimes it is unexpected. I made the choice to resign from a position for ethical reasons when working for a small company. It was a rough time. I went from a great income to working 3 jobs just to pay the bills. I wish I had known then what I know now, because I would have been better prepared. This waypoint in my life forced me to make some decisions.

> "When it is dark enough, you can see the stars."
> —Charles Austin Beard

I have found that during every low point in my life, I was able to come out of it better and stronger. I actually have tripled my original income since then, and the blessings keep pouring in with every new challenge that I am faced with. I truly believe that the path to success will have its hard times, but we can truly turn those tough times around. John F. Kennedy once said, "We do these things . . . not because they are easy . . . but we do them because they are hard."

What you do with that struggle or hard thing in your life is important. Getting past the hurt, betrayal, exclusion, sadness, loss, violation, aggression, all of these things do not have to hold you back. When you can live beyond the events that stop you in our tracks you can move on with knowledge and understanding, and you are stronger from the experience. It is a root you stumble over on your trek through life's forest. You may fall and break a bone, but you can heal and carry on to your destination. On a rainy day, you may still feel the scarring from your injuries in the past. You know it is there, but those old injuries don't have to stop you.

There are many examples on the path to success that could be waypoints for you—anything from conceiving a child to getting a promotion, even losing a job.

In terms of our journey to success, I like to think that a waypoint is any significant event or accomplishment in our life that will require a new direction of travel. The waypoint is not a destination per se, it is where we travel from on our continuous journey.

Maybe a waypoint for you is when you graduated from school. You have accomplished graduation, now where do you go from there? Continue education, service, start working? Maybe you have lost your job. This can be a life-changing event. What changes can you make in your life or changes that you are forced to make in your life? Now may be the time for you to set out for that cache you have always wanted to get.

In times of hardship, we often learn to be more resourceful and better stewards of what we have. This prepares us for more treasures in life, but only if we re-plot a journey on our map, prepare for the trip, get out there, and play the game. Is success guaranteed? Definitely not, but if we don't plan our trip or identify our next cache, then there will be no success.

PAY ATTENTION TO YOUR SURROUNDINGS. (focus)

One of the hazards associated with geocaching is that people can be distracted and not keep focused on their planned route. When you get distracted you could easily be injured, become turned around, or lost. You could end up taking the wrong trail and delay your destination or wear yourself out trying to get to your cache.

When you are out there on your journey to find your own personal cache, there are many distractions. Don't let the little things draw your attention away from the cache and success points of your life. Follow your plan, keep on your route using your map, guide, and the tips that others have left behind.

Some of the many things that help you stay focused is to review your plan on a regular basis, check your progress, and remind yourself of the prize or destination.

There are many ways to do this that have been discussed throughout the past by great goal-setting icons. You can use dream boards with pictures of what you are trying to accomplish, goal-setting boards or reminders posted on your refrigerator, in your car, screen savers on your PC, laptop, or phone. Goals could be printed on your desk calendar, dry erase boards, or personal stationery. Your success points could be posted on your social networking sites. There are many ways to remind yourself of your destination. Stay focused, and you will have a successful cache adventure.

> "One who follows the wind will eventually fall off a cliff!"
> —Troy A. Bonar

ENVIRONMENTAL TIP!

Practice "Cache In Trash Out." When you go on this journey, you can do something good by helping to get rid of the trash along the way. As you journey along, don't leave any garbage for people to find. Help make the environment and road to success more enjoyable for others. Don't hurt the people or world around you on your way to success. Leave the path to success better than the way you found it.

THE CLOSER YOU GET, THE MORE DIFFICULT IT USUALLY IS. DON'T GIVE UP.

Remember that distances can be deceiving. Understand the difference between distances as the crow flies (a direct line) versus true distance of travel. A geocache can take longer to find depending on trails, rivers, and other obstacles.

Don't get discouraged when you don't arrive at your destination right away. A successful life takes time and doesn't always work out exactly as we plan, but it is amazing the wonderful things that happen along the path.

> "Turn your face to the sun and the shadows fall behind you."
> —Maori Proverb

We may discover beauty where we would never have looked. We may spend quality time with people we have been taking for granted or would never have met. We may discover new treasures along the path to our cache, but none of this can happen if we don't "Get out and Play."

The people who really focus on their cache are the ones who overcome the obstacles and find what they are looking for. Caches are not always obvious or easy to locate, even with a plan, guide, or other tips. This is a treasure hunt for success and those X's in the sand sometimes disappear because of wind and rain. So when you get to your destination you may have to dig a little to find what you came there for.

LOG YOUR SUCCESS

On your journey to success, you want to leave your mark. When you reach your goals, make a positive impression on those around you. Make your mark on the world but don't stop there, move on to the next cache—the next goal.

We have all heard the phrase "success leaves clues." We don't want to hoard success, we want to allow others to achieve greatness also. In geocaching you either put the prize back for someone else to discover or you replace it with something of equal or greater value. In our lives such as home or work, how many of us are making it better? Are we giving to others equally—are we adding value?

SHARE YOUR EXPERIENCE WITH OTHERS.

By sharing your experience you will help others to succeed. This doesn't necessarily mean bragging about your accomplishment—you are showing others that it is possible. Sharing your experiences keeps the reality of success. The reality is that if you identify your objective, tell people about your destination, give yourself the tools and knowledge to get there, and listen to the tips about the journey from others, you will be able to reach your geocaches of life.

Ultimately it comes down to the battle cry of geocachers around the globe: *"Get Out and Play!"*

One thing I have found when teaching martial arts was that every person who became a student had a goal in mind. There were many people I would talk with who would say, "I always wanted to do that." I would reply, "What's keeping you?" Many of them took action because they knew me and they respected my passion for the arts.

I took a position with a business consulting and training company and found that coaching and mentoring people and helping them reach their business goals was fun and interesting. I continued into the consulting and leadership development field with my own corporation. I did not do so because I was tired of working for someone else, I did it because I was getting stagnant where I was. There were other economic benefits also. I knew there were others out there who could do the easy things I was doing and I wanted more of a challenge. I also wanted to get more out of my time.

I have been training people for years. I had an opportunity to attend a speaking boot camp by Jonathan Sprinkles. That action made a huge change in my life, setting new success points into action. I realized there were so many more opportunities associated with what I was currently doing. I could become better at what I was doing with my profession and life. I decided to take some steps at that boot camp and set some new personal goals.

One of those goals was to speak at a major event, and within a few months I was booked at a large business conference. My next goal was to become one of the best in my industry; a few months later I was named one of the top five safety trainers in the World. I also had the goal to write a book. Not only was I able to participate in this book, but through goal-setting I was able to have over eight books in the publishing process.

I accomplished all of this because I have taken action.

When I told people I was going to be a speaker, I started something by attending Jonathan's boot camp. When I told people I was going to write a book, I got started and contacted publishers, setting things in motion.

Life is not finished with me yet. I have experienced so much in my short time on Earth, but I look at my friends who are in their golden years and think of how much more life there is to live. I also talk with people who have a terminal illness who are accomplishing wonderful things.

So we ask ourselves, "What is next?" "What is my next treasure hunt?"

I have a list of caches still out there for me to find. There are many more things to accomplish in life, no matter your age or abilities. Just remember that you have to get out and play the game!

Playing the game is where the fun is! No one wants to be left at the sidelines. No one wants to be on the team but never get to shoot for the goal. Being a part of life is where the joy is; winning is just a bonus.

One of my favorite songs comes from the movie "Camp." The soundtrack has many powerful songs, including one that really says a lot. It is titled "Century Plant" and was written by Victoria Williams.

Outside my house is a cactus plant
they call the century tree
Only once in a hundred years
it flowers gracefully
and you never know when it will bloom

Chorus:
Hey, do you wanna come out
and play the game?
It's never too late.

Clementine Hunter was fifty-four
before she picked up the paint
Old Uncle Taylor was eighty-one
when he rode his bike
across the plains of China
And the sun was shining on that day
just like today.

Chorus:
Do you wanna come out
and play the game?
It's never too late
Hey, do you wanna come out

and play the game?
It's never too late

Didn't know how to tell her
for all the (over) thirty years
he kept locked up inside himself
and no one saw the tears
and then she went away
and he woke up that day.

now he brings roses to his sweetheart
she lives most anywhere
he sees someone suffering
he knows that despair
he offers them a rose
and some quiet prose
'bout dancin' in a shimmering ballroom
'cause you never know when
it will bloom

Chorus:
Hey, do you wanna come out
and play the game?
It's never too late.

These lyrics ring true; that is why this song is so powerful. It talks about the fact that you never know when you will bloom—age is not restrictive—you don't have to be in any specific phase of your life when you step out and accomplish something great.

I had a student come to me when she was sixty-three. She wanted to work on stretching and mobility. Nine years later she is now mobile, thirty pounds lighter, younger in appearance, and she is a second degree black belt. She got out and played the game.

I know young people who are accomplishing more before they graduate high school than many accomplish in a lifetime. Take action by following the geocaching checklist.

Let's review our checklist to geocaching your life:

1. Identify your cache (success points/goals).
2. Make a plan.
3. Research your route (read other people's logs).
4. Tell someone where you are going.
5. Be well equipped for the journey.
6. Use your waypoints to navigate from.
7. Pay attention to your surroundings (focus).
8. The closer you get, the more difficult it usually is (don't give up).
9. Log your success.
10. Share your experience with others.

The key is getting out and playing the game, grab your gear, plan to find your next cache—it's treasure-hunting time for all who want to take the journey. There are millions of opportunities, or "life's caches" to be found. Happy hunting!

ABOUT THE AUTHOR

TROY A. BONAR, nicknamed "The Samurai of Success" by his peers, is a leading authority on safety, security, and leadership with over fifteen years of business experience. Troy combines his life experiences with ancient warriors' wisdom to assist business and individuals in achieving success in the modern world. Troy Bonar has spoken to groups such as Chevron, Exxon, BP, Wendy's, the USAF, and OSHA. Troy serves on the advisory board of the American Red Cross, is a member of the NSA, the World Speakers Association, and was recently named one of the "Top 5 Safety Trainers in the World." Troy's books, seminars, and keynote speeches are humorous, real, and "life-challenging."

TROY BONAR

President, Safety Personnel Services, Inc.

P.O. Box 6333

Abilene, TX 79608

888-677-3726

Samuariofsuccess.com

TroyBonar@live.com

CHAPTER SIXTEEN
The Versatility Factor for Interpersonal Success

An interview with...
DAVID GILMAN

DAVID WRIGHT (WRIGHT)

Today we are talking with David Gilman. David is a Learning and Development professional. He has been in the field directly since college and now has over 25 years experience. He is a former training manager at Solomon Brothers, Prudential, and GE.

David, welcome to *GPS for Success*.

David, your firm's name is Gilman Performance Systems or GPS for short—very appropriate for this *GPS for Success* book. How and when did you start your firm?

DAVID GILMAN (GILMAN)

In the mid 1980s, I worked internally as a trainer for a firm that was acquired and our department was disbanded. I started consulting on a part-time basis while I worked as a training manager for other firms. In the early 1990s, I developed a sufficient client base to devote myself to a full-time consulting business. The business grew quickly and I added five staff members in addition to our consulting team.

WRIGHT

Given that your firm does sales, leadership, and 360 degree feedback development for both small and global firms, how did you choose this one topic for *GPS for Success*?

GILMAN

In thinking about the early years of my career, I realized that the foundation of my work was deeply influenced by some simple principles. One principle can be applied in almost any situation, personal or professional.

In any interaction—whether one-on-one, in a group meeting, making a presentation, or leaving a voice message or sending e-mail—people try to influence each other in one of two ways: they either state their views directly or they ask questions indirectly.

People who exhibit Direct behaviors speak louder, are faster-paced, have higher energy, use concrete/definitive words, make statements, and ask fewer questions.

In comparison, people who exhibit Indirect behaviors speak in a softer manner, spend more time thinking about what they are going to say, and use tentative words/phrases such as "possibly," "I think," "we may want to—," "maybe we can—."

Therefore, if a person is more Direct or Indirect in his or her communication or influence style, this affects how he or she comes across to other people: in other words, how this person achieves a result, makes a recommendation or a request, disagrees with somebody, and reacts under stress.

COMMUNICATION APPROACH

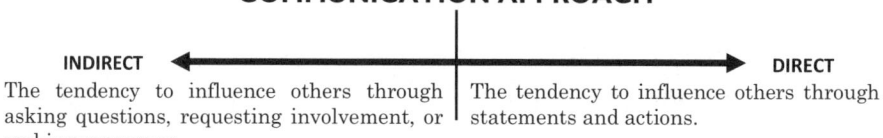

INDIRECT
The tendency to influence others through asking questions, requesting involvement, or seeking consensus.

DIRECT
The tendency to influence others through statements and actions.

WRIGHT

So, isn't being Direct better?

GILMAN

It would be easy to say "it depends," so let's look at this from potential positives and negatives of Direct and Indirect behaviors. I have asked well over five thousand people in positions of authority—from presidents/partners to the non-exempt ranks—about the pluses and minuses of both approaches and have summarized the results below:

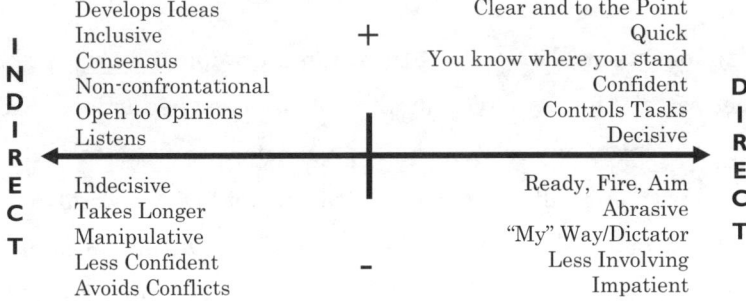

**POSSIBLE POSITIVES AND NEGATIVES
OF EACH COMMUNICATION APPROACH**

As you can see, there is no one correct way to be. Interpersonal success is not about just being Direct or Indirect—real success is dependent upon your ability to be Versatile.

WRIGHT

What do you mean by being Versatile?

GILMAN

A simple definition of Versatility is one's ability to move back and forth on the continuum of Direct and Indirect depending on the situation. If you are dealing with a person who is more Direct, it is appropriate to move yourself toward this person's direct style. You do not have to match their directness. Your objective is to maintain productive communication. The key for productive communication is for the other person not to feel the "negatives" listed on the previous chart.

For example, in the graphic on the next page, we see Ralph's bandwidth or range of Versatility to be fairly narrow. No matter what the situation, Ralph's pretty much Ralph. Sally's ability to move back and forth on the Versatility continuum is much wider. Just based on this, Sally demonstrates greater Versatility than Ralph.

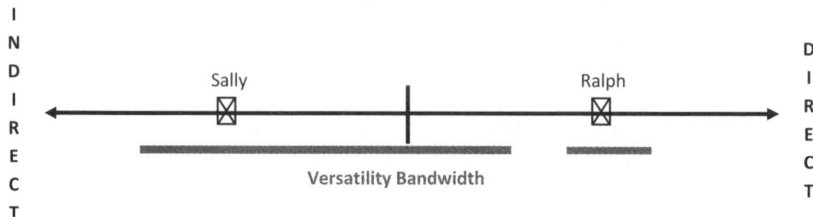

We can only control our side of the communication and perhaps influence the other party's thinking. We cannot control his or her actions. Each of us own fifty percent of any relationship—personal or professional. What do we want to do with our half? Be more versatile or not? Do we want to deal with issues to win or build a sustainable relationship? Or, do we minimize the issue, avoid dealing with it, sulk, play the victim, or blame others?

The lack of Versatility is seen easily on television situation comedies. For example, *Everybody Loves Raymond* has the mother character, Marie, who is very Direct and her son, Ray, who displays a more Indirect style. Neither displays versatile behavior, which is part of the comedy. Another example of this lack of Versatility is seen in the classic sitcom *All in the Family*, with Edith (Indirect) and Archie (Direct). Later in the chapter I provide specific details on increasing your Versatility. See the Appendix 1 on Strategies to Improve Interpersonal Effectiveness and also Appendix 3, Increasing Versatility Summary.

WRIGHT

Is "Direct" and "Indirect" similar to Introvert and Extrovert used in the popular MBTI/Myers Briggs?

GILMAN

Actually, the MBTI scales measure energy source, information gathering, decision-making functions, and how we prefer to organize ourselves. Both types of communication approaches (Direct and Indirect) can be present in all of these functions, but they do not directly correlate to any of them. The bigger difference between Direct/Indirect and MBTI is the Direct/Indirect approach measures observable behaviors (what you actually do or say), whereas the MBTI measures preferences (what you like or prefer or what you don't like). MBTI does not measure what you actually do; it is often difficult to "guess" someone's MBTI type. Direct/Indirect is based on behaviors, allowing you to draw conclusions and apply strategies to improve relationships immediately.

WRIGHT

How can you tell if a person is more Direct or Indirect and what is the potential effect of being one way or the other?

GILMAN

The Direct style person is usually louder, faster-paced, and more definitive in his or her wording. Opinion is stated as fact and comes across in a stronger way. A Direct person would say, "We need to do that by the third quarter." However, this statement may be this person's opinion only. His or her directness does not leave much room for discussion, especially if the person is in a position of leadership. Co-workers may not push back or challenge him or her and the opinion is treated as fact, perhaps to the detriment of the decision. A potential discussion about options is lost and the outcome, based only upon this person's opinion, may not yield the best results.

By contrast, the Indirect, soft-spoken person probably uses lengthy explanations and at times goes into a level of detail that can cause people to tune out. Needless to say, this doesn't make for a conversation that comes to a precise conclusion. This can be a problem if action needs to be taken quickly.

However, Indirect people are often seen as more diplomatic because they think things through. They are considered to be better listeners since their "pacing" allows for more mental processing time. Direct people may come across as more confident because of their definitive word choice and fast pace. However, Indirect people will collect data and make decisions based on facts versus opinions and they make their decisions by involving others.

Being aware of both the strengths and potential weaknesses of these communication styles is very important.

STYLE IDENTIFICATION

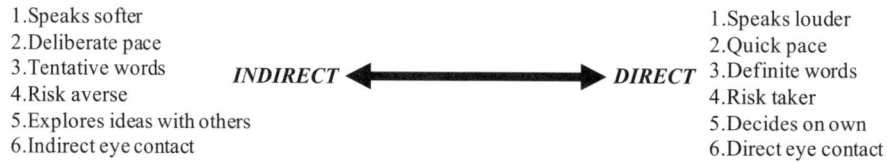

1.Speaks softer
2.Deliberate pace
3.Tentative words
4.Risk averse
5.Explores ideas with others
6.Indirect eye contact

INDIRECT ⟷ *DIRECT*

1.Speaks louder
2.Quick pace
3.Definite words
4.Risk taker
5.Decides on own
6.Direct eye contact

WRIGHT

How accurately do people see themselves and their Versatility?

GILMAN

We developed a survey on Communication style that goes beyond the Direct/Indirect model discussed here. We incorporate the individual's self-perception as well as others' perceptions of him or her. From these comparisons we know that about one-quarter of people do *not* see themselves as others see them. Because the survey dimensions are based on observable behaviors, others' perceptions are seen as more accurate than self-perceptions.

Our survey also measures Versatility—the degree to which others see the individual as easy to be with and attempting to persuade, listen, resolve conflict, and be diplomatic.

Again, these indicators of Versatility are often seen very differently by one's self compared to other peoples' perspectives. It is interesting that those who are Indirect tend to see themselves as more persuasive than others see them. Those who are more Direct see themselves as better listeners and more diplomatic than others see them.

WRIGHT

How important is Versatility?

GILMAN

How people position their reasons in order to persuade others is a powerful determination of their success in getting ideas across. This is an example of Versatility. In making a request or recommendation or even in saying "no," putting a concise reason upfront helps Indirect people to be seen as more confident and Direct people to be seen as more thoughtful since they have given the rationale behind the request: *"Because of ABC, I 'need' or 'recommend' or 'am not able to—' "*

You might think more Direct people are more successful. Being confident and decisive are natural traits that you often find in leaders. Leaders with Direct communication styles often come across to other people as inspiring. However, leaders with Indirect communication styles can be just as successful as Direct leaders. Indirect leaders ask for input from several people, gain their commitment by involving them in data gathering, and then make the decision. However, some Indirect leaders ask for too many opinions, get paralyzed with weighing too many different views, and are seen by others as being indecisive.

Versatile Indirect leaders can be very powerful in getting the needed results in situations that call for using influence on a global level. They are also successful in organizations that are matrix/cross functional or team based.

In our personal lives, do opposites attract or detract and lead to divorce? Opposites can be very content with their differences. They can build on each other's strengths and respect the other individual's style and what he/she brings to the relationship. Such successful relationships usually involve self-aware people who are quite versatile and understand the other person's style. They move toward each other for success.

The concept of Emotional Intelligence has been very popular for the last ten years. Indirectness and Directness are discussed in many of the books. Self-awareness and social interaction are viewed to be signs of emotional intelligence. The concept of Direct-Indirect communication *for the situation* is also a fundamental part of emotional intelligence.

We have provided more than five thousand 360 degree feedback surveys completed by bosses, work peers, and/or direct reports. As a result, we can accurately predict if the person is more Direct or Indirect through the results of his or her survey. A person's strengths or weaknesses can be due largely to his or her Direct/Indirect style when delegating, coaching, managing change, or trying to influence others. This is critical for predictable reactions under stress, and how one handles stress is very much a part of emotional intelligence.

WRIGHT

What do you mean by "predictable reactions under stress"?

GILMAN

Under stressful situations, Direct individuals tend to react by attacking or with enforcing behaviors and they make comments using a very strong tone of voice. In the attack mode, they don't deal with the actual task or problem. Instead they use sarcasm or they get mad on a personal level (e.g., "How could you have done that"). Or they try to enforce with a demanding, strong tone of voice, verbally pushing to get something done. They are looking for immediate action and don't want a discussion (e.g., "That had better be done by tomorrow morning").

Under stressful situations, Indirect individuals tend to avoid or not deal with the situation. When they should be responding to another person, or an email, or stating critical information at a business meeting, they disappear. They may also tend to comply or give in, even when they disagree. What could have been a productive discussion loses a potentially valuable view point.

Is an Indirect person avoiding a more Direct person because of the force and push-back nature of the Direct person's style? The famous question that we should ask ourselves is this: "Do we control our emotions or do our emotions control us?"

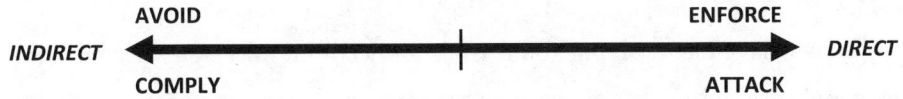

WRIGHT

Can one be Direct at home and Indirect at work or vice versa?

GILMAN

About one-fourth of the thousands of people who have been through our training programs answer this question with a resounding Yes. When we dig deeper about why this occurs, we are not surprised to find differences between the work and home environments. For example, when I worked on Wall Street I commuted with a friend who was Indirect, low key, and calm. However, when she went through the revolving doors of One New York Plaza, her energy level went up and I also noted a more direct, business-like manner, which she used to meet the frenzy of the demanding work environment.

WRIGHT

What do you suggest people do to increase Versatility?

GILMAN

First, be self-aware and watch out for the perceived negatives that we talked about in the beginning of our conversation. For example, a person with an Indirect communication style can be tuned out of conversations with Direct people because he or she is perceived as indecisive. Again, at the end of the chapter, there are suggestions to help increase Versatility.

However, for an in-depth communication style web-based survey, readers can go to our website www.gpsadvantage.com and click on the "Versatility Factor" link. This web survey goes beyond the Direct/Indirect model discussed in this chapter and will further help people increase their Versatility as well as their knowledge of how other people perceive them.

WRIGHT

It seems simple yet challenging at the same time.

GILMAN

What we have been talking about is not only communication style but also how people are "wired." These are the tendencies we are born with, our DNA, our genetic predispositions mixed with habits that we develop or behaviors learned over the years that have been reinforced.

Conscious effort in learning new behaviors has been shown to help people increase their Versatility. It can be as simple as those who are more Direct can try to focus on listening and make more of an effort to ask the opinions of others. Indirect individuals can try to deal with uncomfortable situations and state their opinions. Even these efforts in changing one's mindset and behavior can yield dramatic and positive results both personally and professionally.

Awareness "in the moment" is critical. Becoming more versatile will result in more effective communication which leads to better results for the individual, their firm, their family, and their other relationships.

THREE EXAMPLES OF DIRECT-INDIRECT INTERACTIONS:

MARRIAGE:

A couple is shopping at a toy store. The wife leaves the husband in the aisle that has plastic basketball hoops that are extendable. He pulls three models down and reads the side panels to compare them. The wife comes by with three other unrelated items in her cart and as she passes by says, "Just pick one basketball hoop." He puts one back and leaves two on the ground while he continues to compare. She comes by again and without a word just puts one in the cart and keeps going.

Is this grounds for divorce, or do they respect each other? Does he narrow down the options while she makes the final decision? Is there respect for his initial analysis and her decisiveness? Do they respect the strengths of each other?

WORK:

Does the Direct manager who delegates quickly to an Indirect individual cause an issue unknowingly? The limited fast-paced explanation may leave the Indirect person needing more detail/information. Or the manager asks "Any questions?" as he/she reaches for the Blackberry, which the Indirect worker interprets as "This meeting is over." The Indirect worker hesitates to go back to his/her manager for clarity since the manager is viewed as impatient in the eyes of the Indirect worker, causing the work to be delayed or perhaps completed with errors.

The manager forms an opinion of the worker and the worker forms an opinion of the manager, thereby reinforcing negative judgmental views by both parties in an on-going cycle.

CULTURE:

A global firm sends an Associate from the New York area to run a meeting in Europe. He is more Direct, fast-paced, and action-oriented and tends to use statements rather than open-ended questions. He is quickly labeled a "New Yorker" or even worse as an "Arrogant American." Do any of the European attendees have enough Versatility to give him some feedback? Or do they politely avoid it but the word gets back to New York not to send him anymore?

Remember, we all own fifty percent of any relationship; how do you want to handle your half?

WRIGHT

What do you recommend as a next step for our readers?

GILMAN

First, the readers should think about whether they are more Direct or Indirect. Next is their level of Versatility.

Appendix 1 has examples of Direct and Indirect behaviors with strategies to help increase Versatility. Appendix 2, The Direct/Indirect Communication Style Inventory, will help readers determine their own and, more importantly, other people's communication styles so that they can consciously work to increase their Versatility. Following this is Appendix 3, which describes what actions to take or avoid when the other person's style is either Direct or Indirect.

I would like to close this chapter with the following "equation":

Interpersonal Success = *Increasing one's Versatility*
for better Relationships both personally and professionally

Appendix 1
Strategies to Improve Interpersonal Effectiveness through Versatility

Direct Behavior	Strategy
• swift reaction	→ develop plans with target dates
• direct actions	→ involve others
• opinionated	→ let people know what you think, but be open to their views → ask others for their opinion before giving yours
• impatience	→ give people the time they need unless it affects timelines
• impulsive action	→ accept input from others, check facts first, count to ten
• overwhelming energy	→ tone down, do not overpower, work out

Indirect Behavior	Strategy
• unhurried reaction	→ be more decisive, work in a faster timeframe, be less concerned with and spend less time over "what ifs"
• avoid change	→ take initiative to start change, focus on the positives
• avoid conflict	→ speak up when you disagree, concisely give your reason
• lower confidence level	→ know your facts, use statements with a tone of authority
• cautiousness	→ don't overanalyze, review limited number of variables/options—decide

Appendix 2
The Direct/Indirect
Communication Style Inventory

Check one statement in each of the eleven pairs that describes your behavior regardless of the situation. What would others say if they completed this on you?

INDIRECT	DIRECT	
☐		1. Uses tentative wording **or**
	☐	Uses definite wording
☐		2. Takes fewer chances; more risk adverse **or**
	☐	Takes more chances; more of a risk-taker
☐		3. Gestures and body movement calmer **or**
	☐	Gestures and body movement faster
☐		4. Needs to assert more **or**
	☐	Needs to listen more
☐		5. Deliberate, thinking through pace **or**
	☐	Quicker, says what is on his or her mind pace
☐		6. Thinks through decisions cautiously **or**
	☐	Decides on one's own
☐		7. Explores others' views **or**
	☐	States own views
☐		8. Pushes for others to decide **or**
	☐	Pushes less for others to decide
☐		9. Speaks softer **or**
	☐	Speaks louder
☐		10. Expresses ideas/views more tentatively **or**
	☐	Expresses ideas/views more strongly
☐		11. Leans back/more casual when talking **or**
	☐	Leans forward/engaged when talking
		TOTALS
INDIRECT	**DIRECT**	

Of the eleven choices, how many Indirect versus Direct behaviors do you exhibit?

Appendix 3
Increasing Versatility Summary:
Actions to Take or Avoid

If a Person's Style Is Indirect	
Actions to Take	**Actions to Avoid**
• provide deadlines	• over-assertiveness
• be patient, but persistent	• giving deadlines that could be perceived as unrealistic
• prepare the person in advance	• stating strong opinions and not providing facts
• give time to clarify, to think through	• rushing the decision process
• minimize conflict	• using your "positional power" instead of discussing alternatives
• involve him/her, ask for the person's opinion	
• listen attentively	• being rapid, fast-paced
• present your view without overpowering	• making controlling statements ("you need to—")
• ask "How—" questions	• putting the person in a public spotlight ("Bob, we didn't hear from you.")
• minimize risk, provide assurances	
• use even pace	
• be supportive	

If a Person's Style Is Direct	
Actions to Take	**Actions to Avoid**
• explain *what* first	• showing hesitancy
• be specific	• making ambiguous statements
• stick to business	• being slow-paced
• be concise	• wasting time
• give the person options for making the decision	• making the decision for the person
• be time conscious and efficient	• showing little confidence
• be open/flexible	• pushing facts/details
• support the person's needs	• being too conversational, never getting to the issue
• be fast-paced	• being indecisive
• provide structure	• placing too much emphasis on procedure/process
• quickly provide the person with your time when asked	

ABOUT THE AUTHOR

DAVID GILMAN is celebrating more than twenty-five years as a training and organizational effectiveness professional. His broad range of accomplishments include development of more than one hundred training programs, more than fifty competency models, and more than thirty feedback instruments in organizational performance improvement, leadership, and professional staff skills training, and sales/business development.

David has facilitated over three hundred offsite meetings/team effectiveness sessions for company presidents and their staffs through intact department and project teams.

Prior to establishing GPS, David was a manager in the training departments of Salomon Brothers, Prudential Relocation, and GE. He also held design and delivery training positions with the SCM Corporation and the NYC Transit Authority.

David has served as the President of the Westchester Chapter of the American Society for Training and Development and holds an MBA in Management and Organizational Behavior and a BA in Business and Industrial/Organizational Psychology.

David is very proud of GPS's *more than one hundred and fifty repeat clients*— a true indicator of client service and customer loyalty.

DAVID M. GILMAN

President and Principal Consultant

GILMAN PERFORMANCE SYSTEMS, INC.
PO Box 565, 499 Federal Road
Brookfield, CT 06804-0565
203-740-9767 (p)
203-775-6817 (f)

dgilman@gpsadvantage.com
www.gpsadvantage.com
www.yourbestmeeting.com

DIRECTORY

GEORGE THORNE
545 B Avenue
Coronado, CA 92118
619-866-8023
www.onevoiceforgrowth.com

SCOTT SCHWEFEL
www.scottschwefel.com

CHRISTINE HAMILTON
SALES POWER SOLUTIONS
5510 Butte View Court
Rocklin, CA 95765
(877) 630-5525
CHamilton5525@aol.com
www.ChristineHamilton.com

DR. STEPHEN R. COVEY

www.stephencovey.com

BART QUEEN

P.O. Box 80335

Raleigh NC 27623

866-609-2333

www.SpeakAmerica.com

www.UltimatePowerSpeak.com

GLENNA GRIFFIN

P.O. Box 80335

Raleigh NC 27623

866-609-2333

www.SpeakAmerica.com

www.UltimatePowerSpeak.com

www.ChristineHamilton.com

KATHRYN JORDAN
8217 Sawgrass Way
Radford, Virginia 24141
kathy.jordan@thesuccessassociates.com
www.thesuccessassociates.com

JULWEL KENNEY
Maywood, NJ 07607
866-511-4743
julwelkenney@jkpartners.org
www.julwelkenney.org

LES BROWN
Les Brown Enterprises
P.O. Box 27380
Detroit, Michigan 48227
800-733-4226
speak@lesbrown.com
www.lesbrown.com

SCOTT SCHILLING

4020 N. MacArthur Boulevard, Suite 122-183
Irving, TX 75038
972.659.8941
scott@ScottSchilling.com
www.ScottSchilling.com

JUDY MACKENZIE

West Vancouver, Canada
judy@tevoconsulting.ca
www.tevoconsulting.ca

JOHN GRAY

www.askmarsvenus.com

SHARON HENIFIN

14325 SW Fanno Creek Loop

Tigard, OR 97224

503-349-3846

sharonhenifin@aol.com

www.thrivingbeyond.com

Breast Friends

www.breastfriends.com

mail@breastfriends.com

ANDREA WHITE

Financial Conversations®
and Transition Life Coaches®

9008 South Maple Avenue

Tempe, AZ 85284-8112

480.777.8876

awhite@financialconversations.com

www.transitionlifecoaches.com

www.financialconversations.com

TROY BONAR

President, Safety Personnel Services, Inc.

P.O. Box 6333

Abilene, TX 79608

888-677-3726

Samuariofsuccess.com

TroyBonar@live.com

DAVID M. GILMAN
President and Principal Consultant

GILMAN PERFORMANCE SYSTEMS, INC.
PO Box 565, 499 Federal Road
Brookfield, CT 06804-0565
203-740-9767 (p)
203-775-6817 (f)

dgilman@gpsadvantage.com
www.gpsadvantage.com
www.yourbestmeeting.com